D U K E · U N I V E R S I T Y · P U B L I C A T I O N S

THE SPANISH GUILD MERCHANT

Title page of an account book of the Consulado of Barcelona, 1582.

THE SPANISH GUILD
MERCHANT

A History of the Consulado, 1250-1700

By ROBERT SIDNEY SMITH

Assistant Professor of Economics, Duke University
Sometime Amherst Memorial Fellow

19  40

DUKE UNIVERSITY PRESS
DURHAM, NORTH CAROLINA

PRINTED IN THE UNITED STATES OF AMERICA BY
THE SEEMAN PRINTERY, INC., DURHAM, N. C.

1198275

D. P. G.

Et praesidium et dulce decus meum

PREFACE

Although the history of the Spanish guild merchant spans nearly six full centuries, several considerations have prompted me to offer this study of the Consulado based principally upon the records of the first four hundred years. In the first place, the idioms and paleography of documents from the earlier period presented problems, as well as a certain fascination, which gravitated my attention to the oldest source material during the first stages of research. Since the entire work needed to be grounded in a careful exploration of origins and fundamental purposes of guild organization, familiarity with the period of infancy and early development was acquired more rapidly than a full understanding of the period of institutional maturity and decline. Furthermore, in order to confine the publication plan to a practical limit, it seemed desirable not to enter upon the Consulado's history in the eighteenth and nineteenth centuries.

The close of the seventeenth century is a logical breaking point in the history of Spanish guilds. The Consulado was considerably modified after the accession of Philip V, and the coming of the Bourbon monarchy really signalized the end of an epoch in the institution's history. Chapter VII limns some of the developments of the last two centuries, and the Bibliography suggests some of the sources for the study of guild history in this period; but a thorough examination of the later Consulado has not yet been undertaken.

Precedents exist for reporting the dead weight in pounds and ounces of the notes accumulated in the preparation of an historical monograph. In this respect I prefer to remain unconventional. I recognize, however, that the following pages betray a constant struggle between the desire to achieve reasonable economy in space and the urge to make known a myriad of interesting and irrelevant facts exhumed from the archives of Spanish guilds. It has been my intention, perhaps too often honored in the breach, to refrain from narrating such incidents as the following: In March, 1572, the Barcelona guild voted to pay Martí Comes, a laborer, the sum of £10 "on account of the injury and nausea inflicted upon him when the flag fell from the guild-hall onto his head." I trust that even the footnotes have not been overburdened with Comes cases.

Ten years ago Professor Earl J. Hamilton awakened my interest in some neglected topics of Spanish economic history, and subsequently it was my good fortune, during one of the many years he has spent in search of price material, to visit numerous archives and university centers in his company. In paleographic skill, linguistic ability, and all that makes a patient, if sometimes insistent, investigator *persona grata* in a strange land, Dr. Hamilton has afforded me an example of excellence which I deem a priceless experience. Since the completion of the archival work, his constant encouragement and painstaking criticisms have been invaluable incentives.

Without the intelligent and sympathetic co-operation of the staffs of many archives, delays in the search for material would have been increased and my mistakes multiplied. I am especially grateful to Don Miguel Bordonau y Más, formerly Chief of the Division of Manuscripts in the Archivo Histórico Nacional, who combines to a rare degree the highest intellectual ability with the generosity and friendliness characteristic of most Spaniards. Don Ferran Valls i Taverner, Chief of the Archivo General de la Corona de Aragón; two members of his staff, Padre Francisco Miquel y Rosell and Don Jesús Ernesto Martínez Ferrando; and Don Jordi Rubió Balaguer of the Institute of Catalan Studies extended me innumerable courtesies during several prolonged visits in Barcelona. (While I write this, news comes that the famous Institut d'Estudis Catalans has been rechristened Biblioteca Provincial de Barcelona.) I am sincerely grateful also to Padre Antoni Pons Pastor of Majorca, Don Juan Pons y Marqués of the Archivo Regional de Mallorca, Don Feliu Durán i Canyameres of the Archivo de la Audiencia Territorial de Barcelona, Don Carlos Moya Riaño of the Municipal Archives, Cádiz, Don Rafael Picardo y O'Leary of the Biblioteca Provincial de Cádiz, Don Juan Tamayo y Francisco of the Archivo General de Indias, Don Teófilo Guiard y Larrauri of the Municipal Archives, Bilbao, and M. Henri Robin, Director of the Departmental Archives, Perpignan. All of these, and others whom I cannot name, have contributed materially to whatever success I may have had in working with the records of Spanish history.

An Amherst Memorial Fellowship enabled me to work in Spain from the summer of 1930 to the spring of 1932. On numerous occasions, Professor Laurence B. Packard, formerly Chairman of the Amherst Memorial Fellowship Committee, has given me precept and example for the wise use of time in research and historical study.

A grant-in-aid from the Social Science Research Council made it possible to return to Spain in the summer of 1936. For obvious reasons, the season was inauspicious, although prior to the ides of July I was able to gather some new data for the present and other historical studies. For generous financial assistance in the publication of this volume I am indebted to the Research Council of Duke University and to the Trustees of Amherst College.

Substantial portions of Chapters I and IV have been published as articles in *The Juridical Review* (Edinburgh) and *Politica* (London). To the editors of these journals I am obliged for permission to reprint.

R. S. S.

June, 1940.

CONTENTS

ABBREVIATIONS

AAH   Archivo General Central de Alcalá de Henares.

AC   Archivo Consular (Bilbao and Burgos).

ACA   Archivo General de la Corona de Aragón, Barcelona.

AGI   Archivo General de Indias, Seville.

AGS   Archivo General de Simancas.

AHM   Archivo Histórico Regional de Mallorca.

AHN   Archivo Histórico Nacional, Madrid.

AM   Archivo Municipal

BAB   Biblioteca del Ateneu Barcelonés.

BM   British Museum.

BPC   Biblioteca y Museo Provincial de Cádiz.

BSAL   *Boletín de la Sociedad Arqueológica Luliana.*

Capmany, *Memorias*   *Memorias históricas sobre la marina, comercio y artes de la antigua ciudad de Barcelona.*

Dietari   *Dietari del antich consell Barceloni.* See Bibliography.

IEC   Institut d'Estudis Catalans, Barcelona.

R. de I. *Recopilación de leyes de los reynos de las Indias.*

THE SPANISH GUILD MERCHANT

CHAPTER I

ECONOMIC AND POLITICAL FOUNDATIONS

I

Before the end of the thirteenth century the Consulado de Mar appeared in eastern Spain as an institution for facilitating the settlement of commercial disputes and for promoting and protecting the trading interests of Aragonese merchants at home and abroad. Although not indigenous to any of the lands which formed the united Aragonese kingdoms, or Crown of Aragon,[1] the Consulado was easily adapted to the economic and political structure of the early municipalities in eastern Spain. Eight towns in Aragon, Catalonia, Majorca, Roussillon, and Valencia possessed the consular establishment before 1450. Soon after the union of Aragon and Castile the Catholic Kings transplanted the organization to Castilian soil, where it flourished for more than three centuries. The present chapter combines a chronological record of individual Consulados in Spain and Spanish America with an inquiry into the origins and purposes of the institution in the medieval and early modern periods.

Except occasionally in the formative stage, the Consulado was always a court. Originally a maritime tribunal, or sea consulate,[2] early in its development the consular court acquired jurisdiction in litigious matters of commerce and trade distinct from maritime intercourse. Typically, the Consulado was also a guild. In the beginning the guild was an association of

[1] Political alignments changed several times during the thirteenth, fourteenth, and fifteenth centuries; but, generally, the Corona de Aragón may be understood to mean not only the Kingdom of Aragon, but also Catalonia, Cerdagne, Roussillon, and the Kingdoms of Majorca and Valencia.

[2] *Consulatus maris*, or *consolat de mar*, to distinguish it from municipal councils, which were frequently called consulates. The municipality of Perpignan, created in 1196, was "le premier exemple d'establissement du consulat, non seulement pour le Roussillon mais même pour le Catalogne" (B. Alart, *Privilèges et titres relatifs aux franchises, institutions et propriétés communales de Roussillon et de Cerdagne*, Perpignan, 1874, p. 6).

[3]

merchant-shippers, masters, and shipowners; but the evolution of the sea consulate as a commercial court paralleled the transformation of the maritime association into a comprehensive guild merchant, a corporation which finally embraced large landowners and industrialists.

This guild-court was essentially the product of the social environment of the late Middle Ages. Merchant guilds were common in ancient times; and commercial courts were an element of the Greek, if not of the Roman, judicial system.[3] But the existence of a direct link between Graeco-Roman institutions and the medieval sea consulate is doubtful.[4] In general, the rise of the Consulado followed in the wake of expanding trade in the western Mediterranean, and its organization is first encountered in the towns which were most prominent in maritime commerce. The institution arose in the Italian city-states, notably Pisa and Genoa, about the end of the twelfth century. Moving northward and westward, it took root in Provence and Languedoc; and, in the course of the thirteenth and fourteenth centuries, emerged in several towns along the Aragonese coast from Perpignan to Valencia. Contemporaneously, the Consulado flourished in several island cities of the western Mediterranean.

Doubtless the consular guild is generically related to the *frairies*, *charités*, *hansas*, and *gildes* characteristic of the age in which the merchants traveled overland in armed bands or took ship with their goods to traffic in foreign ports;[5] but the Consulado acquired its particular forms in the period dominated by the "sedentary merchant."[6] The records of the Spanish guild commence with the formal organization of resident merchants

[3] W. A. Sturges, "Commercial Courts," *Encyclopaedia of the Social Sciences* (New York, 1931), IV, 533-535.

[4] Although the *collegium mercatorum* mentioned by Livy (*Ab urbe condita*, lib. ii, cap. 27) has been pointed out as a prototype of the Consulado.

[5] H. Pirenne, *Economic and Social History of Medieval Europe* (London, 1936), pp. 94-96. As a court, the Consulado was clearly related to other "consulates" of the Middle Ages, especially to the consulates, both temporary and permanent, established in foreign ports, and to the consulates on board merchant ships, usually instituted for the duration of a voyage (L. Blanchard, "Du consul de mer et du consul sur mer," *Bibliothèque de l'École des Chartes*, XVIII, 427-438; W. A. Bewes, *The Romance of the Law Merchant*, London, 1923, p. 85).

[6] N. S. B. Gras, "The Rise of Big Business," *Journal of Economic and Business History*, IV (1932), 382-408.

and shipowners in a seaport or river town. Without aspiring to supplant municipal government, the guild formed an important part of town economy. Not only in its infancy but throughout a long life, charity, piety, and patriotism, as in other guilds, motivated the work of the Consulado; but the predominant and most permanent objective of this mercantile association was the protection and advancement of the economic status of the merchant class. Recognizing the power of this class and not oblivious to the government's fiscal interest in the accumulation of mercantile wealth, both the sovereign and the municipality endowed the guild with valuable privileges and powers. Representing primarily interests in maritime trade, the early Consulado centered its attention on the protection of property rights in ships and cargoes. Not the least significant of the guild's objectives was the defense of shipping from piracy and reprisal; and it becomes evident, as one reads the records of the institution, that the Consulado met a specific need created by the inability of public authority per se to deliver commerce from these medieval, and modern, scourges of the sea.

The court of the consuls owed its origin to the alleged inadequacy of ordinary courts and civil procedure to deal speedily, competently, and economically with litigation over maritime and mercantile affairs. The "pressure of circumstances" which created the *jus mercatorum*[7] also brought forth the customary law of the sea; and when it was found impractical to apply these codes in the existing law courts, special tribunals arose to satisfy the demand for a judicial procedure suitable for merchants. The phenomenon was common to many parts of Europe. In the late Middle Ages many English seaports had marine courts, "sitting from tide to tide and administering the law maritime to merchants and mariners," in which cases were argued before the mayor and burgesses and a jury of mariners and merchants.[8] In a similar fashion the English court of piepowder applied the international law merchant in the complaints of both native and

---

[7] Pirenne, *op. cit.*, p. 53.

[8] *Select Pleas in the Court of Admiralty*, ed. for the Selden Society by R. G. Marsden (London, 1894), I, xiii, xlix.

foreign merchants;[9] and on the Continent numerous fair and market courts grew up in response to needs comparable to those which gave birth to the Consulado in Spain. The consular court may be regarded as one of the many legal institutions brought forth by the economic renaissance of the late medieval period.

Innumerable records furnish evidence that a fundamental motive of the Spanish Consulado was to secure the expeditious, economical, and equitable adjudication of disputes concerning maritime and mercantile contracts. An early privilege (1325) granted to the councilors of Majorca reveals their determination to circumvent the legalism and obstructions encountered in the ordinary courts through the institution of the Consulado.[10] The sea consulate of Barcelona was established "in order to do away with the expenses of lawsuits and the strife of judicial proceedings among merchants and navigators."[11] Pointing to the procedure of the consular court in Perpignan as a model for the sea-consuls of Montpellier, the king declared that the trammels of ordinary justices had reduced many merchants to poverty.[12] Urging the inauguration of a consular tribunal in Marseilles, the merchants asserted that the inability of foreign traders to secure fair treatment at moderate cost in the ordinary courts of the city was a cause of reprisals.[13]

Pleading for consular privileges, the merchants of Burgos represented that in ordinary courts mercantile cases were "never terminated," because lawyers found ways to prolong litigation,

[9] C. Gross, "The Court of Piepowder," *The Quarterly Journal of Economics,* XX (1906), 231-249.

[10] AHM, *Rosselló vell,* f. 243: "Notum facimus universis, quod ex parte fidelium nostrorum juratorum et proborum hominum Maioricarum est coram nobis propositum supplicando quod cum plerumque questiones et contrastus inter mercatores, patronos, marinarios et alios moveantur et suscitentur . . . dignaremur pro utilitate communi regni et civitatis Maioricarum et *ut tolleretur amfractus et judiciorum ordinariorum strepitus* super huius modi questionibus et contrastibus providere de remedio opportuno. . . ."   [11] Capmany, *Memorias,* IV, 158.

[12] A. Germain, *Histoire du commerce de Montpellier* (Montpellier, 1861), II, 385-387.

[13] Archives Départementales des Bouches-du-Rhône, *reg.* 686*. E. Génevois (*Histoire critique de la jurisdiction consulaire,* Paris and Nantes, 1886, p. 2) believed that "Le développement des affaires commerciales et la difficulté de faire juger les contestations des négociants par les jurisdictions de droit commun, telles ont été, à un moment déterminé . . . les causes principales de la création des tribunaux consulaires."

no matter how unjust the claim. The resulting "great loss and injury to business" caused merchants to lose confidence in each other and in their agents.[14] Similarly, the petitions for the organization of the Consulado in Seville complained of the plethora of suits among merchants trading with America and of "the long delays experienced in their settlement, with grave injury and loss to merchants."[15] Elimination of the obstructions to mercantile justice, it was claimed, would provide a means of increasing royal revenues, since business would expand.

The impetus for the establishment of an exceptional commercial jurisdiction was well supported by learned opinion. As a means of promoting trade, Xenophon proposed rewards for the judges of the commerce court, "to be given to such as should decide points of controversy with the greatest justice and expedition, so that persons who wished to sail might not be detained."[16] Writing on the merchant guilds of Italy and France, Bodin observed that the affairs of merchants were of such a peculiar nature ("je ne scay quoy de particulier") that commercial disputes could be settled wisely only by merchant-judges.[17] In Catalan law one finds the principle that mercantile causes are *de natura* summary and that a summary procedure necessitates special judges like the consuls of the sea.[18] Since

[14] *Ordenanzas del Consulado de Burgos de 1538*, pp. 154-157.

[15] *R. de I.*, lib. ix., tit. vi, ley 1.

[16] "On the Means of Improving the Revenues of the State of Athens," in A. E. Monroe, *Early Economic Thought* (Cambridge, Mass., 1924), p. 36. Capmany (*Memorias*, I, 153) thought that Xenophon would have found this proposal unnecessary, if he had been familiar with the expeditious procedure of the consular tribunal.

[17] J. Bodin, *Les six livres de la république* (Paris, 1580), lib. iii, cap. 7. Straccha asserted that "In curia mercatorum aequitatem praecipue spectandam et ex bono et aequo causas dirimendas esse et de apicibus iuris disputare minime congruere" (B. Straccha, *Tractatvs de mercatvra sev mercatore*, Cologne, 1595, p. 470). In an Aragonese privilege of 1303, a special mercantile procedure is justified, "ut mercatores occasione ipsarum contencionum non opporteat diutius litigare nec expensas aut labores immoderatos plus debito sustinere" (ACA, *registro* 210, f. 77).

[18] *Constitvtions y altres drets de Cathalvnya*, I, 235-236. Two illustrations of the imperative nature of such actions may be cited. An Italian writer was convinced that disputes over the wages of seamen had to be settled instanter (C. Targa, *Reflexiones sobre los contratos marítimos*, Madrid, 1753, p. 314), doubtless because of the mariner's inability to support himself unless paid soon after the completion of a voyage. In 1336 the king of Aragon had occasion to decry the injuries suffered by shipowners and mariners who lost the opportunity to take advantage of favorable weather when delayed by prolonged litigation (Capmany, *Memorias*, IV, 94).

the consular court derived its authority from the sovereign, a significant motive for the creation of the consular jurisdiction may be found in the king's desire to favor the merchant class, as a result of which business profits might be enlarged and the sources of revenue improved.[19]

II

For the major portion of the period under study, the term "Consulado" signifies the dual organization of the merchant guild and guild-court. The convergence of the mercantile corporation and the consular court did not occur simultaneously in all places; nor did the process of evolution follow a uniform pattern. In some instances the office of sea-consul antedates the establishment of the court and guild. As a result of the division of labor among members of the municipal council, or commune, certain officials acquired extraordinary duties with respect to commerce and navigation. Thus, at the beginning of the thirteenth century, the sea-consuls of Pisa "made their appearance as an influential body, to whose essential functions pertained the protection of the interests of legitimate trade."[20] Likewise in Genoa, the earliest consuls of the sea were "merely public functionaries."[21] In Montpellier, the municipal councilors, preoccupied with "the government and general affairs of the town," contrived to lighten their work by establishing the sea consulate as a subordinate executive office. The sea-consuls (consuls de mer) superintended the highways and canals which gave the town access to the sea and administered other matters affecting

---

[19] An intimation of this conclusion is found in seventeenth-century writings: "The motives and causes of the establishment of the said two tribunals are. . . . In the first place, because the mercantile arts ought to have the maximum protection and encouragement, whence the state and the royal fisc may reap great material benefits" (A. Bosch, Svmmari . . . dels titols de honor de Cathalunya, p. 455). The Grand Master of Malta thought that the erection of the Consulado, "before which the complaints and controversies of all maritime business can be settled and decided with a saving of money and time," was essential to the augmentation and preservation of commerce (J. M. Pardessus, Collection de lois maritimes, VI, 325). Solórzano (Política indiana, lib. vi, cap. xiv, par. 3, 22) developed similar points of view.

[20] A. Schaube, "Das Konsulat des Meeres in Pisa," Schmollers Staats- und Socialwissenschaftliche Forschungen, VIII, Heft 2 (Leipzig, 1888), 8.

[21] A. Schaube, "Das Konsulat des Meeres in Genua," Zeitschrift für das gesamte Handelsrecht, XXXII (Stuttgart, 1886), 490.

the conveniences of navigation and trade.[22] The first specific mention of consuls of the sea in Barcelona concerns two municipal officers elected by the city council, but the records do not indicate the nature of their duties.[23] Earlier, a kind of consulate may have existed in Barcelona by virtue of the letters missive of James I (1257), which instructed a council of prudhommes, or notables, of the strand *(probi homines ripariae)* to draft ordinances for the government of the port.[24] The council was justified by the expressed need of regulations governing maritime matters, the lack of which was held responsible for "grave perils and serious losses" both on land and at sea. The maritime statutes prepared by the council, or consulate, were promulgated in 1258.[25] Although the council of the strand constituted a policing agency under the statutes of 1258, the meager records of its subsequent activity do not show conclusively that the council was the predecessor of the sea consulate chartered in 1347.[26]

[22] C. d'Aigrefeuille, *Histoire de la ville de Montpellier* (Montpellier, 1875-82), II, 395. From the "Establimen de la election de cossols de mer," reproduced in Germain, *op. cit.*, I, 239, it appears that the office existed prior to 1258.

[23] In Jan., 1301, the sea-consuls swore "bene et legaliter se habere in ipso consulatu, non inspecto honore, amore vel timore alicuius" (AM, Barcelona, *Libro de deliberaciones y bandos de 1300 a 1301*, f. 12). The election of consuls appears to have taken place semiannually until 1326 (*Libro de deliberaciones y bandos, 1326 fineix 1327*, f. 1), after which the *Deliberaciones* are silent concerning *consules maris*. In 1315 the sea-consuls audited the accounts of the Catalan consul in Seville (*Libre de deliberacions, 1314-1315*, f. 29), but further details of their work are unavailable. In the bankruptcy laws promulgated in 1432 the statement was made that the Consulado of Barcelona did not exist in 1283, nor in 1304 (Capmany, *Memorias*, IV, 221).

[24] "Carta *consulatus* ripariae Barchinone" is the caption of the chancery copy of this document (ACA, reg. 9, f. 7).

[25] Capmany, *Memorias*, II, 23-30 (Latin text); A. Capmany, *Código de las Costumbres Marítimas de Barcelona*, Appendix, pp. 15-21 (Spanish); R. C. Cave and H. H. Coulson, *A Source Book for Medieval Economic History* (Milwaukee, 1936), pp. 160-168 (English). In the latter work, "Council of the honest water-men of Barcelona" is a curious translation.

[26] Scraps of data suggest that the "Consulate," or seacoast council, of 1257 may have functioned during the last half of the century. A privilege granted "to all the merchants of Barcelona" in 1279 provided for the election of two merchants, "qui procurent, administrent, & faciant omnia quae necessaria viderint ad communem utilitatem ipsorum . . . super mercationibus suis bene & fideliter" (Capmany, *Memorias*, II, 367); and the same year two merchants, "assignati per . . . Regen Aragonum super eo quod mercaturae fiant & tractentur in Barchinona bene & legaliter," designated procurators to complain to royal justices that unfair duties were levied on the shipping of Barcelona in Narbonne and Tortosa (*ibid.*, II, 401-402). It is possible

The Consulado as a department of municipal government was rarely, if ever, the definitive form of the institution. In thirteenth-century Pisa the sea-consuls were recognized as direct representatives of the *ordo maris,* a maritime-mercantile guild; and, "without being functionaries of the state, they exercised with the agreement and consent of the state . . . a special surveillance over all that touched their interests in maritime commerce."[27] Furthermore, as judges, the consuls governed the *curia ordinis maris,* or guild-court of Pisa. In Aragon, the primary sources of information concerning the early constitution of the Consulado are privileges, or royal charters, specifically relating to the establishment of the guild-court, or consular tribunal.

III

In 1283 the city of Valencia received the first of the consular privileges granted by the kings of Aragon.[28] In the following century the crown made similar grants to other towns in the far-flung Corona de Aragón, establishing the Consulado in Majorca (1343),[29] Barcelona (1347),[30] Tortosa (1363),[31] Gerona (1385)[32] and Perpignan (1388).[33] The sea consulate of San Felíu de Guíxols was founded in 1443.[34] Probably sim-

---

that in 1282 the "Consulate" represented Barcelona in a dispute concerning duties in the port of Blanes (*ibid.,* II, 38-39).

[27] L. de Valroger, "Étude sur l'institution des consuls de la mer au moyen-âge," *Nouvelle revue historique de droit français et étranger,* XV (Paris, 1891), 52.

[28] The charter is reproduced in Appendix I. The concession to the city of Valencia was exclusive within the kingdom of Valencia (AM, Valencia, *Llibre del Consolat de Mar,* Appendix, Doc. 4).

[29] AHM, *Libre de Sant Pere,* f. 74. It is doubtful that the consular charter granted by the authority of James II in 1325 (AHM, *Rosselló nou,* f. 297) became effective.

[30] Capmany, *Memorias,* II, 124-125.

[31] ACA, reg. 971, f. 6.

[32] ACA, reg. 1690, f. 142. This copy is more accurate than the text edited by G. M. de Brocá (*Revista Jurídica de Cataluña,* XXII, 573-574) from the Municipal Archives of Gerona.

[33] *Llibre de privilegis de consulat de Perpinya,* pp. 31-33. Here a merchant guild (*congregatio mercatorum*), without judicial powers, had been sanctioned in 1276 (A. Ripoll, *De magistratus Logiae Maris,* p. 4).

[34] I have edited the charter from a parchment found in the Municipal Archives of San Felíu (*Revista Jurídica de Cataluña,* XXXIX, 130-132).

ilar tribunals existed in Saragossa[35] and Calatayud,[36] although a dearth of documents precludes an adequate study of their formation and activity. In spite of the occasional mention of the sea consulate of Tarragona, no archival records of such an institution have come to light.[37] It is probable that the Consulados of Messina and Trapani, if not other sea consulates in Sardinia and Sicily, owed their establishment to privileges of Aragonese kings;[38] and the Consulado of Malta, founded in 1697, was an offshoot of the Aragonese institution.[39]

In the Middle Ages the economic and institutional development of Languedoc and Provence was similar in many respects to that of Catalonia. Roussillon, whose chief city was Perpignan, continued nominally under Aragonese rule into the modern period. In Marseilles, as well as in Montpellier, the first sea-consuls were apparently public officials without judicial powers.[40] However, it seems likely that the first consular tribunals antedated the privileges of 1463[41] and 1466,[42] the earliest which have been found to authorize the guild-court in Montpellier and Marseilles, respectively. After the seventeenth century, the evolution of commercial courts and merchant guilds

[35] Ignacio de Asso, *Historia de la economía política de Aragón*, pp. 366-368. Asso believed that the Consulado functioned as early as 1304.

[36] ACA, reg. 210, f. 77. This privilege of Sept., 1313, confirmed the right of the merchants to elect two *prepositi* as judges of minor disputes over contracts; but no accounts have been found of the subsequent activity of a Consulado in Calatayud.

[37] R. S. Smith, "El Consulado de Mar en Tortosa y en Tarragona," *Revista Jurídica de Cataluña*, XXXX, 26-29.

[38] L. Genuardi, *Il libro dei capitoli della Corte del Consolato di mare di Messina* (Palermo, 1924). For comparative purposes, occasional references will be made to the Consulado in the Italian possessions of Aragon, but no archival data have been secured for the study of the institution in Sardinia, Sicily, or Naples.

[39] F. Valls i Taverner, "El Consolat de Perellos," *La Paraula Cristiana*, X (Barcelona, 1929), 137-139.

[40] L. Blancard, *op. cit.*

[41] Germain, *op. cit.*, II, 385-387. This privilege permitted the sea-consuls of Montpellier to do "tout ansy et en la mesme forme et manière que font et ont accoustumé faire au Consulat de mer de la ville de Perpignan." At this date the Consulado of Perpignan possessed most of the attributes of the institution in Barcelona.

[42] L. Magnan, *Histoire des juges consuls et du tribunal de commerce de Marseille* (Marseille, 1906): a privilege confirming "la jurisdiction des marchands de la ville de Marseille." As early as 1420 magistrates of the city were required to settle commercial cases in accordance with the opinion of three "merchant-assessors" (Archives Départementales des Bouches-du-Rhône, reg. 686*).

in Marseilles, Montpellier, and Perpignan deviated widely from the development of the Spanish Consulado.[43]

On the Iberian peninsula the Consulado was an Aragonese or Catalan institution until the close of the fifteenth century. The importance and longevity of individual establishments varied directly with the commercial significance of the towns in which they were located. The Consulado of Gerona had little importance in the sixteenth century;[44] and the records of the Consulates of Tortosa and San Felíu—extremely meager for all epochs—do not extend beyond the early eighteenth century. Asso concluded that the Consulado of Saragossa expired before 1678;[45] and subsequent agitation for its revival was fruitless.[46]

The political reconstruction following the accession of the Bourbon monarchy did not radically alter the juridical framework of the Consulado in Barcelona and Majorca,[47] although

[43] In 1549 the *bourse commune des marchands*, a mercantile association with limited judicial power, was set up at Toulouse (Archives Départementales de l'Hérault, reg. B. 80). A similar *bourse* created in Marseilles in 1599 has been referred to as "la première modalité de la Chambre de Commerce" (J. Fournier, *La Chambre de Commerce de Marseille*, Marseille, 1920, p. 2). In spite of the opposition of the Parlement de Toulouse, the privileges of the sea-consuls in Montpellier were confirmed as late as 1611; but the office was finally suppressed in 1691 and the functions of the consuls absorbed by the *bourse*, as in Marseilles (Archives Départementales de l'Herault, regs. B. 91 and B. 192; d'Aigrefeuille, *Histoire de la ville de Montpellier*, II, 401-402).

Opposition to the dissolution of the consular establishment was more lasting in Perpignan, where the Consulado flourished at least until the middle of the eighteenth century (Archives Départementales des Pyrénées-Orientales, regs. C. 1534, C. 1542, and C. 1543).

[44] In 1585 it was difficult to find a person willing to accept the office of consul. In spite of the resultant "gran dany de dita Ciutat, y detriment dels commerçants," no proof has been found that the Consulado survived this period (*Constitvtions y altres drets de Cathalvnya*, I, 131). Gerona lies inland, and the natural center of its commercial activity was the near-by port of San Felíu de Guíxols (R. S. Smith, "Documentos del Consulado de Mar en Gerona y en San Felíu de Guíxols," *Revista Jurídica de Cataluña*, XXXIX, 128-132).   [45] *Op. cit.*, pp. 368, 392-393.

[46] C. Herranz y Laín, *Estudio crítico sobre los economistas aragoneses* (Zaragoza, 1885), pp. 26-27. I am unable to find, in Saragossa or elsewhere, the anonymous "Memorial a la Diputación del Reino de Aragón, suplicando la formación y establecimiento de un Consulado y Casa de Contratación en la ciudad de Zaragoza," cited by M. Colmeiro, *Biblioteca de los economistas españoles de los siglos xvi, xvii y xviii* (Madrid, 1880), p. 33.

[47] The continuation of the Majorcan Consulado was approved by Philip V in the decree of Nov. 28, 1715 (*Novísima recopilación de las leyes de España*, lib. v, tit. x, ley 1), and a similar decree, Jan. 16, 1716, salvaged the Consulado of Barcelona from the sweeping reforms of the "Nueva Planta" for Catalonia (*ibid.*, lib. v, tit. ix, ley 1). None of the early acts of the Bourbon king expressly mention the Valenciar

the guild organization lost some of its prerogatives. After several decades of waning influence or inactivity, which correspond with a period of commercial and industrial stagnation, agitation among the merchant class led to the revival of the guild-court system in Barcelona, Palma, and Valencia.[48] (The city of Majorca became Palma in 1715.) But the formation of the Tres Cuerpos de Comercio in Barcelona (1758)[49] and Valencia (1762)[50] and the erection of a new Consulado in Palma (1800)[51] did not modify drastically the institutional forms which had prevailed since the fourteenth century. One of the Three Commercial Corporations was the court of the consuls; the Comunidad de Comerciantes was a comprehensive guild merchant; and the Junta Particular de Comercio, a permanent executive committee of the guild.

The reorganization of the Valencian Consulado made way for the establishment of a consular deputation in the port of Alicante. For more than a century the merchants of this town had protested against the delay and expense involved in carrying their cases to the Valencian court; and their resentment diminished only slightly after the inauguration of the deputation, which was a court of first instance only. Alicante finally secured an independent Consulado in 1785.[52]

IV

The introduction of the Consulado into Castile resulted from the repeated recommendations extolling the advantages

---

Consulado. According to a memorial composed about 1761, this Consulado "dexo de continuar" soon after the opening of the century (British Museum, Egerton MS 513, f. 172-177).

[48] For the background of this development, consult E. Larruga's MS, *Historia de la Real y General Junta de Comercio, Moneda, y Minas*, I, 478-479, 540, 804, 890-922.

[49] *Reales cédulas de erección, y ordenanzas de los Tres Cuerpos de Comercio de el Principado de Cathaluña, que residen en la ciudad de Barcelona* (Barcelona, 1763).

[50] *Reales cédulas de erección y ordenanzas de los Tres Cuerpos de Comercio, que residen en la ciudad y reyno de Valencia* (Madrid, 1777).

[51] *Real cédula de S. M. y Señores del Consejo por la qual se establece un Consulado de Mar y Tierra, en la ciudad de Palma y su puerto* (Madrid, 1800).

[52] *Real cédula . . . para la erección de un Consulado Marítimo y Terrestre comprehensivo de esta ciudad de Alicante y pueblos del Obispado de Orihuela* (Madrid, 1785). On the antecedents, see AM, Alicante, *armario* 5, lib. 67, f. 288; Larruga, *op. cit.*, I, 924-988, 1116-1172.

the merchant class had derived from this institution in Aragon. In Burgos and Bilbao, where merchant guilds antedated the Consulado by half a century or more, the alleged advantages of the Aragonese Consulado focused on the judicial attributes of the consuls; and the privileges creating the Consulados of Burgos (1494)[53] and Bilbao (1511)[54] were primarily designed to complete the guild organization by giving it a judicial arm. Numerous petitions from merchants engaged in trade with America bore fruit, after many years' delay, in the erection of the Consulado, or Universidad de los Cargadores a las Indias, of Seville in 1543.[55] The transfer of the work of the Seville guild to Cádiz (1717), necessitated by the removal of the House of Trade to the Atlantic port, left only a consular deputation in the former city; but in 1784 a new Consulado was established in Seville.[56]

Although a pragmatic of 1632 authorized the organization of the Consulado in towns which had "a sufficient number of merchants,"[57] only one city qualified during the seventeenth century. After a long delay, attributed to the opposition of the merchants of Burgos, the fifteenth-century Cofradía de Mercaderes y Mareantes of San Sebastián obtained consular privileges

[53] *Cédula* of July 21, in *Ordenanzas del Consulado de Burgos de 1538*, pp. 153-162.

[54] *Cédula* of June 22, in T. Guiard y Larrauri, *Historia del Consulado y Casa de Contratación de Bilbao*, I, 563-571.

[55] *Cédula* of Aug. 23, in *Ordenanzas para el prior y cónsules de la Universidad de los Mercaderes de la ciudad de Sevilla*, f. 69-72. As early as 1525, the king ordered that "attention should be given to the supplication of the merchant-traders of Seville that they be given authority to elect, among their own number, a prior and consuls, in the same manner as is done in Burgos" (A. Herrera, *Historia general de los hechos de los Castellanos en las Islas y Tierra Firme del Mar Oceano*, Madrid, 1726, dec. iii, lib. vii, cap. 1). The *cédula* of Aug. 23, 1543, is said to have been granted "on the basis of a memorandum presented by Ciprian de Charitate, in the name of merchants of all nationalities residing in the city of Seville, showing the great advantages for the increase and preservation of commerce which arose from the establishment of a Consulado, as was seen from experience in . . . Burgos, Barcelona, and Valencia" (Academia de la Historia, *Colección de Muñoz*, XXXIV, No. 2, f. 4).

Cibrian de Caritate, probably the individual mentioned above, was a slave trader who in 1542 purchased for 10,000 ducats licenses to export two thousand slaves to Hispaniola (AGS, *Contadurías generales*, leg. 3,052).

[56] *Real cédula . . . para la erección de un Consulado Marítimo y Terrestre comprehensivo de esta ciudad de Sevilla y pueblos de su arzobispado* (Sevilla, 1784).

[57] *Novísima recopilación*, lib. ix, tit. ii, ley 4.

in 1682.[58] The Consulado of Madrid was projected in 1632, but its organization was not consummated until 1827.[59]

Meanwhile, Charles III had approved the proposal to establish Consulados in the Spanish ports "habilitated" for trade with America under the laws of 1778.[60] Subsequently, the crown chartered the Consulado Marítimo y Terrestre in Corunna (1785),[61] Málaga (1785),[62] Santander (1785),[63] San Cristóbal de Tenerife (1786),[64] San Lúcar de Barrameda (1806),[65] Granada (1817),[66] and Vigo (1820).[67] Proposals to erect the Consulado in Almería, Badajoz, El Ferrol, Gijón, Mahón, Pamplona, Reus, and Soria were unsuccessful.[68]

[58] Archivo Provincial de Guipúzcoa, *Sección* 2, *negociado* 22, leg. 43; *Euskal-Erria: Revista Bascongada*, XIV (San Sebastían, 1886), 92-93.

[59] *Reglamento provisional del Real Consulado de Madrid, aprobado en 30 de diciembre de 1827* (Madrid, 1828). Concerning the failure to erect the guild in the preceding centuries, see AAH, *Fomento*, leg. 975, and E. Larruga, *Memorias políticas y económicas*, IV, 271-272.

[60] *Reglamento y aranceles reales para el comercio libre de España a Indias de 12. de Octubre de 1778* (Madrid, 1778), pp. 63-64.

[61] *Real cédula . . . para la erección de un Consulado Marítimo y Terrestre, comprehensivo de la ciudad de la Coruña, su puerto, el de Vigo, y todos los puertos y pueblos del arzobispado de Santiago* (Madrid, 1785).

[62] *Real cédula . . . para la erección de un Consulado . . . de Málaga y pueblos de su obispado* (Málaga, 1785).

[63] *Real cédula . . . para la erección del Consulado de Mar y Tierra . . . de Santander* (Madrid, 1786).

[64] *Real cédula . . . para la erección de un Consulado . . . de San Christoval de la Laguna de Tenerife, su puerto y demás Islas Canarias y pueblos de su obispado* (Madrid, 1787).

[65] *Reales ordenanzas del Consulado de San Lúcar de Barrameda y su provincia* (Madrid, 1806).

[66] AAH, *Fomento*, leg. 974. Although this *legajo* contains a MS copy of the "Ordenanzas del Real Consulado Marítimo y Terrestre de la ciudad y provincia de Granada," the ordinances were apparently never published.

[67] AAH, *Fomento*, leg. 969. Vigo withdrew from the jurisdiction of the Consulado of Corunna, but the ordinances of the Vigo institution appear not to have been printed.

[68] Ordinances drawn up for Almería shortly after 1778 did not become effective (AAH, *Fomento*, leg. 974); and the drafting of statutes for a Consulado in Badajoz was abandoned in 1829 (*ibid.*, leg. 858). In 1803 the crown promised to approve ordinances for El Ferrol, but there is no evidence that the promise was fulfilled (*ibid.*, leg. 973). The petition of Mahón was denied in 1811 (*ibid.*, leg. 983). As early as 1776 the merchants of Pamplona tried unsuccessfully to form a Consulado in Navarre (Archivo de Navarra, Pamplona, "Informe del Tribunal [de la Cámara de Comptos] sobre la solicitud de los comerciantes de Pamplona que pretenden poner Consulado"). The request of the town of Reus was turned down in 1810 (AAH, *Fomento*, leg. 996). The merchants of Soria drafted ordinances in 1777. In rejecting them, the crown pointed out that the prospective income of the Consulado scarcely reached

V

Toward the end of the sixteenth century Philip II sanctioned the erection in Mexico and Lima of Consulados "on the pattern of those of Seville and Burgos," in view of "the great advantage and convenience" secured from the institution in Spain.[69] These were the only early Consulados in the New World, and the Spanish government was slow to establish the guild-court in the American ports opened to trade in 1778. Finally, royal orders from Madrid founded the Consulados of Caracas and Guatemala in 1793; Buenos Aires and Havana in 1794; and Cartagena, Chile (successor to the old Lima guild), Guadalajara, and Vera Cruz in 1795. The organization of the Consulado of Manila was confirmed in 1828.

The Consulados of Burgos and Bilbao, all the Consulados established or reorganized in the eighteenth century, and the few institutions created after 1800 functioned continuously until 1829. In the latter year, which marked the promulgation of Spain's first commercial code, uniform Tribunales de Comercio replaced the consular court throughout the country, and all judicial functions of the guild organization were transferred to the new courts.[70] With the revision of the Código de Comercio in 1868 special commerce courts were definitively abolished,[71] although as late as 1934 the merchants of Valencia achieved a partial revival of the ancient court of the consuls.[72] As the Junta

---

7,000 reals a year, "a sum which indicates the insignificant commerce of this capital" (E. Larruga, *Memorias políticas y económicas*, XXI, 194-198).

[69] *R. de I.*, lib. ix, tit. xlvi, ley 1. The Consulado of Lima was organized in 1613, "en la forma que le hay en . . . Sevilla, Burgos, y Mexico" (*Ordenanzas del Real Tribunal del Consulado . . . de Lima*, Lima, 1820). E. Ruíz Guiñazú, in *La magistratura indiana* (Buenos Aires, 1916), p. 131, states that the Consulado of Mexico was erected during the viceregency of Lorenzo Suárez de Mendoza (1580-1583); but the enabling *cédula* of June 15, 1592, is the earliest document found in the *Ordenanzas del Consulado de la Universidad de los Mercaderes de esta Nueva España* (Mexico, 1772).

[70] Some of the American Consulados existed until late in the century. The Consulado of Buenos Aires was not suppressed until 1862 (Ruíz Guiñazú, *op. cit.*, p. 322).

[71] "Due to abuses they were abolished in 1868, and this form of exceptional jurisdiction passed to the civil or ordinary courts, where it remains today" (L. B. Register, "Spanish Courts," *Yale Law Journal*, XXVII, 1917-18, 777).

[72] The inauguration of the new Consulado was a notable civic occasion. According to the Madrid *A B C* (Dec. 26, 1934), "El acto de la jura de los primeros cónsules

de Comercio, the guild flourished in a greatly modified form until the middle of the nineteenth century, finally winding up its historical career as the chamber of commerce.

---

del Consulado de la Lonja de Valencia ha revestido una solemnidad y austeridad impresionante; se ha verificado hoy, primer día de Navidad, tal y como tenía lugar en el siglo xiii y siguientes, en el histórico salón del Consulado de la Lonja valenciana." An interesting question is the possible adaptability of such an institution to the Spanish corporative state of 1940.

CHAPTER II

THE COURT OF THE CONSULS

In the organization of the consular court, practice varied widely. The brief charter of the sea consulate of Valencia[1] pro-vided for two judges, "who shall be elected each year at Christ-mas time by the prudhommes of the sea *(probi homines maris)*." Although one might assume that the *probi homines maris* were representatives of a mariners' and navigators' association,[2] the existence of a thirteenth-century guild in Valencia is debatable. It seems more likely that the prudhommes were "select men," possibly a committee of the most influential navigators and ship-owners designated by the municipality to organize the court.

Though the Consulado was established to "settle the terms of contracts and disputes between seafaring men and merchants," the organization of the original court specifically excluded all except men in maritime pursuits *(homens de la art de la mar)*. No motives were advanced for the failure to include merchants; but in 1358, declaring that pestilence and war had so decimated the ranks of the *homens de la art de la mar* that they were unable to carry on the work of the consular tribunal, the king placed a merchant in one of the consulships.[3]

Details concerning election procedure are available in the privileges of 1418 and 1420.[4] The two consuls were chosen in separate elections. The retiring merchant-consul and his mer-

---

[1] Reproduced in Appendix I.

[2] The first chapter of the procedural code of Valencia (see below, p. 22) reads: "Cascun any, la vespra de la festa de Nadal de nostre Senyor, los pròmens navegants, patrons e mariners, o partida de aquells, apleguen conseyll en la sglésia de sancta Teccla . . . e aquí per elecció, e no per rodolins [lot], tots en una concordants, o la major partida, elegexen dos bons hòmens del art de la mar en cònsols." Travers Twiss (*Black Book of the Admiralty*, Appendix, Pt. IV, p. 451) thought this passage proved the existence of a Valencian "Guild of Mariners"; but the *art de la mar* may refer only to occupation or profession of the men authorized to elect the sea-consuls.

[3] *Aureum opus*, f. 126; AM, Valencia, *Llibre del Consolat de Mar*, Appendix, Doc. 17, "Carta paccional feta entre los mercaders e mariners de Valencia sobre la iuredictio e exercici del Consolat" (1362). [4] *Aureum opus*, f. 181-182.

chant-associates in the Consulado prepared a panel of eight names from which the merchant-consul for the ensuing year was drawn by lot. The other consul with his associates and predecessors in office nominated four individuals, one of whom was drawn by lot to be the consul of the maritime classes (i.e., *"marinarii, navigantes, ductores, patronique navigiorum quorumlicet"*). In 1493 the *probi homines maris* lost their right to select a consul; thereafter, one of the consuls was a merchant and the other was drawn from a panel of burgesses eligible for a certain municipal judgeship.[5]

The consuls possessed only original jurisdiction. Appellate jurisdiction belonged at first to a judge of appeals appointed by the crown in 1284;[6] later, the appellate judges were elected in the same manner as the consuls.[7]

The consular charters of Barcelona, Majorca, Perpignan, Tortosa, and San Felíu authorized the direct election of consuls and appellate judges by the municipality.[8] In Barcelona the deliberative assembly known as the Council of One Hundred selected the consular judges. At the beginning of the fifteenth century the Council established the rule of choosing one consul from the class *(estament)* of burgesses *(ciutadans)* and the other from the merchant class. The appellate judge was invariably a member of the mercantile *estament*.[9] When the city adopted the practice of choosing municipal officials by lot (1498), qualified merchants and burgesses were enrolled on the lists from which the respective consular offices were filled.[10]

[5] ACA, reg. 3647, f. 148-153: royal privileges confirmed in 1604.

[6] *Aureum opus*, f. 162-163.

[7] F. Valls i Taverner, *Consolat de Mar*, II, 38-39. In 1360 a merchant and a navigator alternated in the appellate judgeship (*Aureum opus*, f. 126), but two judges of appeals, one from each class, were provided for in 1362 (ACA, reg. 1181, f. 109) and 1420 (*Aureum opus*, f. 181-182). After 1493 the judge of appeals was always a merchant (ACA, reg. 3650, f. 177).

[8] Although the charter of Gerona empowered the merchants to elect two *consules mercatorum* and a judge of appeals, no data concerning election procedure have been found.

[9] AM, Barcelona, *Llibre de consells, ordinacions i lletres missives, 1399-1412*; Ripoll, *op. cit.*, pp. 7-9.

[10] *Dietari*, II, 190-192; *Rúbriques de Bruniquer*, I, 101. The list of consuls from 1446 to 1714 (Capmany, *Memorias*, Appendix, II, 42-49) shows that the "first" consul was frequently a nobleman *(caballero)* or a physician.

Information on the organization of other consular courts in Aragon is scarce. According to the privilege granted in 1449, the two consulships of Majorca were held by a merchant and a shipowner, respectively; while a merchant and a shipowner alternated in the office of judge of appeals.[11] After 1401, both the consuls and the judge of appeals in Tortosa were merchants, chosen by the electors of the other officials of the city.[12] The court in San Felíu had only one consul, who was elected by the municipal council.

In contrast to the usual practice in Aragon, the consular judges in Bilbao, Burgos, San Sebastián, and Seville were guild officials, over whose selection the municipal government had no direct control. In Burgos, the general assembly of the guild chose seven electors, who in turn chose the prior[13] and two consuls by plurality vote.[14] In Bilbao, every guildsman eligible to vote nominated two persons for *fiel* and four for *diputados*.[15] The *fiel* was drawn by lot from the two nominees for *fiel* receiving the largest number of votes, and the two *diputados* were drawn from the four nominees who received the largest number of votes for this office.[16] The appellate judge in Burgos and in Bilbao was the *corregidor* of the city, a crown official.[17] The organization of the San Sebastián Consulado was similar to the structure of the Bilbao institution.

Merchants *(cargadores)* engaged in the American trade, who constituted the guild of Seville, met in general assembly to choose by direct ballot the thirty electors of the prior and con-

[11] *Privilegis del Collegi de la Mercadería*, f. 9.

[12] ACA, reg. 2196, f. 23. As in Barcelona, the two sea-consuls of Perpignan were a *consul de mer burges* and a *consul de mer mercader* (Archives Départementales des Pyrénées-Orientales, reg. C 1543).

[13] Typically, in Castile, the prior was the titular head of the guild and one of the three judges of the consular court.

[14] Ordinances of 1538, cap. 4. Chance and majority rule were curiously combined in most guild elections. In the assembly of the Burgos guild each merchant wrote his own name on a slip of paper. The slips were shuffled and one name was drawn. The merchant thus chosen drew twenty-one names from the ballot box, and from the twenty-one names the seven electors were drawn by lot.

[15] Later, the consular judges were a prior and two consuls, as in Burgos.

[16] Ordinances of 1560, caps. 6-7. The minutes of the election of 1600 are reproduced in Appendix II.

[17] *Novísima recopilación de las leyes de España*, lib. ix, tit. ii, ley 1; Ordinances of Burgos, 1538, cap. 2.

suls. The judge of appeals was one of the *jueces oficiales* of the House of Trade.[18]

II

According to the charter of the Valencian Consulado, the consuls must possess "a knowledge of the practice or custom of the sea." Other records describe them as "experienced men endowed with ability and worthiness"[19] and as "the most able, the most competent, and the most experienced" individuals of the merchant class.[20] Wealth carried considerable weight as a qualification.[21] Since the chief interest of the consuls doubtless lay in the success of their own business ventures, they may have lacked the incentive of professional pride in the success of the court.[22] Yet, there is no evidence that their judicial duties, extending over a year or two, acted as an appreciable deterrent to their wealth-getting pursuits. For various reasons, including the legitimate requirements of their own business, the consuls had the right to designate surrogate judges to occupy the consular bench.[23]

III

The consuls of Valencia were pledged to settle disputes "according to the use or custom of the sea . . . briefly, summarily,

[18] Ordinances of 1556, caps. 1-4. In 1588 the consul's term of office was increased to two years, one consul being elected each year (*R. de I.*, lib. ix, tit. vi, ley 9).

[19] Ordinances of Bilbao, 1560, cap. 1.

[20] Charter of the Consulado of Gerona (1385).

[21] Veitia Linage (*Norte de la contratación de las Indias occidentales,* lib. i, cap. xvii, par. 21) objected to exclusion from the consulship of underwriters of maritime insurance, since a large number of wealthy individuals were found in this business and "se busquen siempre las de mas caudal" for prior and consuls. As a matter of fact, Veitia Linage admitted that insurers were sometimes elected, although the law barring tax farmers seems to have been observed (Ordinances of the Consulado of Seville, 1556, cap. 5; *R. de I.*, lib. ix, tit. vi, ley 16).

[22] Not infrequently the ordinances established a heavy fine for the individual who declined an office to which he had been elected, and the payment of the fine did not exempt him from discharging the duties of that office. See, for example, the Ordinances of Seville, 1556, cap. 8.

[23] Ordinances of Seville, 1556, cap. 10; *R. de I.*, lib. ix, tit. vi, leyes 40-41; Ordinances of Bilbao, 1560, cap. 12.

Although the consuls of Barcelona could not leave the city without the permission of the councilors (IEC, B^a 192), it is doubtful that they were unreasonably detained by the business of the court. The Ordinances of Burgos explicitly recognized that the consuls might have occasion to be absent for the inspection of their wool washing-pits outside the city.

and forthwith, without the noise or formality of a judgment, *sola facti veritate attenta*, that is to say, looking solely to the truth of the facts."[24] Under oath they promised that they would "correctly and honestly deport themselves in their office" and would "do justice alike to the rich as to the poor, and to the poor as to the rich, observing always their fealty and loyalty to our lord and king."[25] It was frequently stated that the consuls were equal in status to royal judges, and often they received safe-conducts, exempting them from arrest and certain civil actions.

In addition to the oath and the character of the consuls, the ability of the Consulado to achieve the equitable settlement of disputes depended upon its rules of procedure. The earliest procedural law was drawn up in Valencia, probably early in the fourteenth century.[26] The so-called "Judicial Order of Valencia"[27] was observed in the consular tribunals of Barcelona, Majorca, and Perpignan, as well as in similar courts in Aragon, Castile, France, and Italy.[28] Supplementary procedural law developed in Barcelona during the fifteenth century,[29] and additional rules of procedure are found in the royal orders and

[24] Twiss, *op. cit.*, IV, 489. In the early English admiralty courts judgments were given "summarie et de plano sine strepitu et figura judicii . . . sola facti veritate inspecta" (Marsden, ed., *Select Pleas in the Court of Admiralty*, I, lvi).

[25] Twiss, *op. cit.*, IV, 453; AM, Valencia, *Manual de consells y establiments, 1327-1331*, f. 88. The oath used in the Consulado of Barcelona is in IEC, B^a 192, frontispiece; that of Bilbao, in T. Guiard y Larrauri, *Historia del Consulado de Bilbao*, I, 221-222.

[26] Unless revised upon the acquisition of new privileges, the compilation of procedural rules does not antedate the decree of Nov., 1336, specifically mentioned in chap. xxxvi of the code. It is certain that a copy of the Valencian rules of procedure was forwarded to the Consulado of Majorca in 1343 (IEC, B^a 192, f. 7).

[27] John E. Hall made the first English translation: "The Judicial Order of Proceedings before the Consular Court," *American Law Journal*, II, 385-391, and III, 1-13. Travers Twiss published an English version (1876) in *The Black Book of the Admiralty*, Appendix, Pt. IV, 450-495. The best Catalan text is that of F. Valls i Taverner, *Consolat de Mar*, II, 37-61.

[28] In the original Catalan, or translated into French, Italian, Spanish or some other language, the "Judicial Order" is found in nearly every impression of "The Book of the Sea Consulate," or *Llibre del Consolat de Mar*.

[29] The texts of two MS copies of the "Orde Judiciari dels Consols de la Mar de Barcelona" have been published in the *Revista Jurídica de Cataluña*, XXIII, 233-258, and XXV, 289-307; also, in Valls, *op. cit.*, II, 63-99.

ordinances of the Consulados of Bilbao, Burgos, and Seville. The essential features of the Valencian code persisted beyond the end of the seventeenth century and had some influence on the adjective law of later commercial codes.

The court of the consuls was in session regularly on certain days of the week, or as business required.[30] Since the purpose of the Consulado was to obviate litigation, as well as to avoid protracted proceedings, upon the submission of either a written or a verbal complaint the consuls usually attempted to effect a settlement out of court.[31] Failing in this, they commenced hearings. If the plaintiff entered the plea in writing, the consuls sent a copy of the complaint to the defendant, who was required to answer within a designated time.[32] The defendant might either set forth the reasons for his defense or institute a cross-action. Delays were granted for furnishing proof of allegations and for producing witnesses.[33]

Having concluded the taking of evidence and the examination of witnesses, the consuls retired to consult with their assessors *(promens* or *adjuntos)*; that is, the two or three merchants or mariners whom they were bound to summon to hear every case before the Consulado. The consuls handed down the decisions or decrees of the court. In the Consulados of Aragon the decision had to conform with the opinion of the assessors.[34]

[30] Monday, Wednesday, and Friday mornings in Seville, unless circumstances required afternoon sessions also (Ordinances of 1556, cap. 9). In Valencia it was permissible to hold court during Christmas holidays, Holy Week, and even at night (AM, Valencia, *Llibre del Consolat de Mar*, Appendix, Doc. 29).

[31] Ordinances of Seville, 1556, caps. 12-13. In Bilbao the consuls would not entertain a plea in writing until they had failed to adjust differences through compromise (Ordinances of 1560, cap. 72).

[32] The *Liber decem dierum et citacionum Consulatus Logiae Maris Barchinone, 1697-1715* (IEC, B^a 200) illustrates this phase of the procedure.

[33] "Judicial Order of Valencia" (hereinafter cited as JOV), caps. 8-9; "Judicial Order of Barcelona" (hereafter, JOB), caps. 12-13. The consuls frequently ordered the taking of depositions in other Consulados or in courts outside their jurisdiction (IEC, B^a 198, *Literarum, 1562-1582*, and B^a-196, *Littere compulsorie ad recipiendum testes*).

[34] JOV, cap. 10; Ripoll, *op. cit.*, pp. 122-155. Thus, according to Pardessus (*Collection de lois maritimes*, V, 237), "les consuls étaient simplement instructeurs du procès; lorsque la procédure était terminée, ils allaient, si la cause concernait la

In the Castilian consular courts the majority vote of the prior, consuls, and assessors determined the decision.[35]

When dissatisfied with the consuls' decision, an aggrieved party might appeal within ten days. In the petition for review the appellant set forth the nullities or injustices by reason of which he considered himself wronged; but no new evidence was accepted in appellate proceedings.[36] The judge of appeals consulted with assessors (but not those who had taken part in the first instance) and issued a decree which, in the Aragonese Consulados, was definitive, whether it revoked, amended, or affirmed the original decision.[37]

In verbal proceedings the parties stated their respective claims before the consuls and their assessors. The court reached a decision in private consultation but promulgated the decree without delays for proof or other formalities.[38] Both the consuls and the merchants selected as assessors might be challenged *propter affectum* and surrogate consuls and assessors admitted to the cause.[39]

The police powers of the consuls were sufficient to insure the proper functioning of the court and the execution of their de-

---

navigation, trouver les prud'hommes de mer; à qui ils faisaient rapport des faits et de moyens respectifs, et qui décidaient la question." An English parallel in the High Court of Admiralty is noted by Twiss, *op. cit.*, IV, 465, n. 1.

[35] Decisions handed down by the consuls and judge of appeals in Majorca and the citation of a typical case in the Consulado of Barcelona are reproduced in Appendix III.

[36] JOV, caps. 11-14; Ripoll, *op. cit.*, 153-164. The rule on new evidence was adopted in 1336, after it was realized that the alternative procedure delayed and increased the cost of appeals (AM, Valencia, *Llibre del Consolat de Mar*, Appendix, Doc. 9). No plea having been entered within thirty days after giving notice of appeal, the suit was considered abandoned.

[37] JOV, cap. 15. Apparently, until 1331 a second appeal was permissible in Valencia (Capmany, *Memorias*, IV, 93-94). In Bilbao, Burgos, and Seville appeals might be taken from appellate decisions which revoked the decisions of the consuls (charter of the Consulado of Burgos, 1494; *R. de I.*, lib. ix, tit. vi, leyes 42-43).

[38] JOV, caps. 17-18; JOB, cap. 10. Note especially that, "For the wages of a mariner, which he claims from the master, it is not requisite to make the claim in writing" (JOV, cap. 28). Cf. also Ripoll, *op. cit.*, pp. 73-87.

[39] JOV, caps. 39-40. According to Hevia Bolaños (*Curia Filípica*, lib. ii, cap. xv, par. 8), it was necessary to prove the motive for the challenge (*recusación*). Various rules obtained for selecting alternates and for limiting the number of challenges (Ordinances of Bilbao, 1560, caps. 21 and 75; Ordinances of Seville, 1556, cap. 11; *R. de I.*, lib. ix, tit. vi, ley 38).

cisions. Several circumstances, such as a reasonable suspicion that the defendant might depart from their jurisdiction, permitted the consuls to arrest the defendant and to demand bond to cover the costs of court or the amount of the claim entered by the plaintiff.[40] A party receiving judgment secured an order requiring the condemned party to pay within ten days or to disclose "moveable goods, clear and unencumbered, upon which the said sentences may be executed." Otherwise, the consuls might "take possession of the moveables . . . designated by the other party."[41] Property seized to satisfy judgment was sold at public auction, but payment was not made until the party gave bond to return the money in case "any one should appear who has a prior claim or a better right to the said proceeds than himself."[42] In the absence of apparent means to liquidate an obligation, the consuls might order the imprisonment of the debtor. They believed that such a person "ought to remain forever in prison and in irons, until he has satisfied his sentence of condemnation."[43]

As a rule, a litigant in the court of the consuls might avail himself of the services of lawyers, although attorneys could not appear in court nor prepare documents to be presented therein.[44] Even in the case of minors and absentee litigants it was felt that the designation of someone other than a lawyer as procurator constituted the soundest practice.[45]

[40] Orders of arrest and for furnishing bond *(seguretat de juy)* are found in the *Liber comunis de provisionibus curie Consulatus Maris Barchinone, 1622-29* (IEC, Bª 199). Municipal ordinances seem to have been necessary to curb abuses of the *seguretat de juy* (Capmany, *Memorias*, IV, 245; IEC, Bª 192, f. 95-96 and 114; Ripoll, *op. cit.*, pp. 59-73).

[41] JOV, cap. 23. See also ACA, reg. 1121, f. 83; Capmany, *Memorias*, II, 133-134; and orders in the MS *Littere citatorie et mandati decem dierum* (IEC, Bª 196).

[42] JOV, caps. 24-26; IEC, Bª 198, *Liber securitatum juditii, empararum et aliorum, 1698-1714.*

[43] JOV, cap. 30. So, too, in Majorca: ACA, reg. 1121, f. 83.

[44] *Ordinacions, y svmari dels privilegis, consuetuts, y bons usos del Regne de Mallorca*, p. 68; Ordinances of Bilbao, 1560, cap. 72; Ordinances of Seville, 1556, caps. 12-13.

[45] IEC, Bª 191, F. 170, "Ordinatio que juristes ni causidichs no poden entrevenir en los juys de Consolat," amending chap. xv of the "Judicial Order of Barcelona." In 1478 the consuls requested that "al Juy dels Consols per absents, malalts, viudes puxen entrevenir causídichs"; but the city councilors refused permission (*Rúbriques de Bruniquer*, IV, 9). See also ACA, reg. 3647, f. 148-153, on the exclusion of lawyers from the Valencian Consulado.

IV

According to the Valencian procedural code,[46] "The consuls determine all questions which concern freight, damage to cargoes laden on board ships, mariners' wages, partnerships in shipbuilding, sales of ships, jettison, commissions entrusted to masters or to mariners, debts contracted by the master who has borrowed money for the wants or necessities of his vessels, promises made by a master to a merchant, or by a merchant to a master, goods found on the open sea or on the beach, the fitting out of ships, galleys, or other vessels, and generally all other contracts which are set forth in the Customs of the Sea."

Since the early consulate was predominantly a maritime court, its jurisdiction extended nominally to matters affecting the ownership or management of seagoing vessels and the ownership and custody of goods transported overseas. Commencing with the letters missive to the Consulado of Perpignan in 1393,[47] a series of royal acts widened the jurisdiction of the consular court so as to comprehend nearly every type of commercial cause, whether related to maritime trade or not. Thus, in Barcelona after 1401 the consuls took cognizance "not only of all maritime causes, questions, and disputes, as they customarily have done, but also of all mercantile questions, suits, controversies, contracts, and civil disputes . . . arising from whatsoever companies, loans, contracts, or mercantile acts . . . and of whatsoever matters arising from primarily mercantile disputes."[48] All the Castilian Consulados were originally chartered as commercial courts, and their jurisdiction was comprehensive of all matters of commerce and exchange. In Seville the consuls were competent in all litigious matters arising from the purchases and sales, exchange dealings, insurance, company agree-

---

[46] JOV, cap. 22. The jurisdiction of the Valencian consuls is set forth in greater detail in a document reproduced in Appendix IV.

[47] *Llibre de privilegis de consulat de Perpinya*, pp. 66-71; ACA, reg. 1911, f. 70. The municipal corporation requested this extension of the sea-consuls' jurisdiction, which was first granted for five years and then made perpetual.

[48] Capmany, *Memorias*, II, 192-194. Almost identical privileges were issued to Majorca (AHM, *Libre de Sant Pere*, f. 77) and Tortosa (ACA, reg. 2196, f. 23) in 1401 and to Valencia in 1493 (ACA, reg. 3647, f. 148-153).

ments, charterage, accounts, and factorage of merchants engaged in trade with America.[49]

Pari passu with the development of substantive commercial law the jurisdiction of the Consulado increased beyond the specific limits of its early privileges. Thus, the development of statutory regulations for bills of exchange and banking, insurance and sea-loans, and bankruptcy prescribed certain contractual relationships, the observance of which the consuls were required to enforce.[50]

In determining the jurisdiction of the Consulado, it was essential to consider both the subject matter of the controversy and the personalities of the parties litigant. The Barcelona procedural law declared that "the consuls do not have jurisdiction in the causes of drapers which concern retail sales, nor of shoemakers with respect to cobbling, nor of other individuals in matters of personal use or use in one's craft (*offici*) of goods previously purchased in a mercantile sense (*mercantivolment*)."[51] In Majorca all contracts of *merchants*, including purchases for personal use as well as for resale, were considered mercantile and subject to the jurisdiction of the consuls.[52] In a country in which the laws of personal status (*fueros*) created rigid social stratification, it is not surprising that the person rather than the subject of litigation frequently determined the authority of the consular judges. Hevia Bolaños maintained that "although a non-merchant, in a mercantile case, can bring suit in the Consulado against a merchant, a merchant cannot bring an action in the Consulado against a non-merchant, even in a mercantile dispute . . . for the plaintiff must follow the *fuero* of the defendant."[53] By and large, the Consulado was a

[49] R. de I., lib. ix, tit. vi, ley 22.

[50] Since the guild considerably influenced the formation of these statutes, detailed references to them will be made in later chapters.

[51] JOB, cap. 3. See also Ripoll, *op. cit.*, pp. 37-57.

[52] AHM, *Libre de Sant Pere*, f. 103. However, it was later declared that the sale of wood to carpenters, of pigments to dyers, and of iron to smiths could not occasion actions cognizable by the consuls, unless the case arose from the first sale of imported goods (ACA, reg. 3644, f. 37). In Perpignan, a case involving "a certain quantity of wine purchased commercially (*mercantiliter*) by . . . a merchant from . . . a muleteer" came under the consuls' jurisdiction (*Llibre de privilegis de consvlat de Perpinya*, pp. 101-104).   [53] *Op. cit.*, lib. ii, cap. xv, par. 23.

court for the members of the merchant guild, and other courts
were employed by shopkeepers, craftsmen, and individuals possessing privileges and immunities foreign to the merchant
class.[54]

The Valencian charter enjoined the consuls to decide maritime controversies "according to the custom of the sea, just as is
customarily done in Barcelona." Although all reasonable doubt
has not been removed from the issue, it is extremely likely that
"the custom of the sea" is to be found within *The Consulate of
the Sea*, or *Llibre del Consolat de Mar*, a monumental code of
maritime custom probably first known as "The Maritime Customs of Barcelona."[55] Additional references to this customary
law, one of which specifies the *"written* customs of the sea,"
are contained in the procedural law of Valencia.[56] In the early
sea consulate equity *(sola facti veritate attenta)* obviously pre-
supposed adherence to whatever custom, both written and un-
written, had been accepted as the bases for rendering justice in
maritime claims. Upon the occasion of alleged departures from
the precepts of the *Consolat de Mar*, the sea-consuls in Perpignan were advised by the crown to refrain from deciding
cases on the basis of "Roman or of common law."[57] Thus, in
addition to the *Consolat de Mar*, privileges and royal orders
issued to the Consulados, statutes and municipal ordinances, and
general ordinances drawn up by the Consulados and approved
by the king, determined the substance of maritime and commercial jurisprudence in Spain until the adoption of the first commercial code in 1829.

[54] In a dispute between the bailiff *(batlle)* and the Consulado of Valencia, a
ruling was made that "si questio o contrast sera entre Jeheu e Jeheu o Moro e Moro,
los quals son del for ordinari del dit Batlle sobre los dits naufraigs [shipwrecks] e
altres cosas pertanyents als dits Consols, quel *demanador* pusque elegir qualsevulla"
(IEC, B*a* 192, f. 15-18).

[55] Hence the title of a recent edition of this famous book: *Les Costums Maritimes
de Barcelona, universalment conegudes per Llibre del Consolat de Mar* (Barcelona,
1914). References to the historical criticism of this code will be found in my articles,
"Recent Criticism of 'The Consulate of the Sea,'" *The Hispanic American Historical
Review,* XIV (1934), 359-363, and "The *Llibre del Consolat de Mar:* A Bibliography,"
Law Library Journal, XXXIII (Nov., 1940).

[56] JOV, caps. 22, 30, 31, 41.

[57] *Llibre de privilegis de consolat de Perpinya,* pp. 120-121.

V

According to dependable authorities, the jurisdiction of the Consulado (both original and appellate) was exclusive (*privativa*).[58] Under the procedural law of Valencia the consuls took cognizance of an exception to their jurisdiction claimed by the defendant. If they found that they were competent under the laws defining their jurisdiction, they compelled the defendant to plead in their court.[59] Numerous decrees enjoined other courts from interfering with the prosecution of cases before the consuls and required such courts to refuse all pleas entered in contravention of the Consulado's exclusive jurisdiction.[60]

Jurisdictional disputes arose persistently throughout the long life of the institution, and an examination of nearly a hundred questions of jurisdiction supports the conclusion that the conflict of jurisdiction was one of the major deficiencies of exceptional commercial courts. Frequent were the disputes between the Consulado and the bailiff's court, a tribunal which took cognizance of matters affecting the interests of the crown. Injunctions issued by the bailiff forced the Consulado to consult the king in order to determine whether the consuls had exceeded their authority. On many occasions, according to opinions handed down by the king's justices, the bailiff had interfered illegally with the procedure of the consular court.[61]

[58] Hevia Bolaños, *op. cit.*, lib. ii, cap. xv, par. 29; Veitia Linage, *op. cit.*, lib. i, cap. xvii, par. 27; Juan de Solórzano Pereyra, *Política indiana*, lib. vi, cap. xiv, par. 27.

[59] JOV, cap. 16. "And if they find . . . that the matter does not appertain to them, they shall remit the parties to their proper judge."

[60] AC, Bilbao, *Reg. 1 de Executorias*, No. 6, "Executoria real, declarando tocar y pertenezer al Tribunal del Consulado . . . el conocimiento de la causa principiada ante el señor Corregidor . . . sobre la restitución y entrega de la mitad de un navio" (1546).

[61] In 1354 the bailiff of Barcelona enjoined the consuls from executing a sentence which would have returned a stolen sail to its owners. The governor-general of Aragon found that the consuls possessed authority to enforce this decision (Capmany, *Memorias*, II, 133-134). The competence of the Consulado of Valencia was denied in a matter respecting goods shipped on a vessel commandeered by the bailiff for "certain secret business of the crown" (Archivo General del Reino de Valencia, *Bailía General, Letres è privilegis*, lib. i, f. 66). In another controversy it was established that the bailiff took cognizance of actions arising from shipwreck, in respect to property of undetermined ownership (*bens vacants*) (Arxíu de la Batllía General de Cathalunya, *Procesos*, 1701, No. 1, *letra* E). Similar disputes are dealt with in the following

The conflict of jurisdiction between the Consulado and courts of admiralty may be understood in the light of the development of naval defense as a permanent branch of government. Many disputes, such as questions of competence in the causes of seamen on armed vessels, represented the Consulado's assertion of rights appropriate to the epoch in which the freedom of the sea depended largely upon the initiative of private associations like the guild merchant. When the royal navy became a reality, the jurisdiction granted to admiralty courts sometimes comprehended matters formerly dealt with by commercial courts. In 1395 the crown ruled that actions arising from commerce in armed vessels pertained to the jurisdiction of the consuls, except in the case of ships armed by the king or directly employed in his service.[62] The competence of an admiralty court was denied in cases involving ships armed by "many individuals" of Barcelona.[63]

Masters of the mint residing in Barcelona, Perpignan, and Valencia enjoyed certain judicial prerogatives which led them to challenge the jurisdiction of the Consulado in suits arising from the commercial transactions of mint officials and employees. In most cases the crown was extremely careful to preserve the judicial powers of the mint organization.[64]

In spite of the unusually potent privileges of the clergy, the Consulado several times successfully defended its jurisdiction in litigation arising from the business ventures of priests.[65]

---

printed papers (copies in AM, Barcelona): *Por el Magistrado de la Lonja . . . contra los Dotores . . . del Consejo de su Magestad en el de la Baylia General de Cathaluña* (Barcelona, 1679); *Regia sentencia lata in S. S. R. Aragonum Concilio . . . contra Consules et alios oficiales Logiae Maris Barcinonae* (Barcelona, 1680).

[62] AHM, *Libre de Sant Pere*, f. 76-77. Similar cases are found in ACA, reg. 2267, f. 68 and IEC, B^a 192, f. 83-86.

[63] ACA, reg. 2944, f. 3-7 (1444); Capmany, *Memorias*, II, 252-257.

[64] Numerous jurisdictional disputes, referred to royal ministers for determination, are found in: *Llibre de privilegis de consvlat de Perpinya*, pp. 97-100, 105-106; *Aureum opus*, f. 171-172; ACA, reg. 2130, f. 111; reg. 2276, f. 56; reg. 2234, f. 35; Archives Départementales de Pyrénées-Orientales, reg. B. 254, f. 92. The dates are from 1400 to 1600.

[65] IEC, B^a 191, f. 91-92; B^a 192, f. 110, 113, 131-132. A commercial transaction of a clergyman must involve buying and selling "pro lucro captando," according to Ripoll (*op. cit.*, pp. 50-51).

The relations between the Consulado and higher courts were a frequent source of confusion in commercial litigation. By evocation *(evocación)* or a process analagous to certiorari, higher tribunals repeatedly ordered the consuls to send up to them cases in which proceedings had already begun in the Consulado. The Supreme Court, or Audiencia, of Catalonia and of Majorca had authority to issue writs for this purpose on the grounds of the defendant's poverty, widowhood, or infancy. Upon proof of one of these conditions, the higher tribunal ordered a *restitutio in integrum*, or the nullification of the proceedings in the Consulado pending the determination of the litigants' judicial rights. The consuls frequently alleged, not without justification in many instances, that litigants conveyed property to widows, indigents, and minors in order to evade the Consulado's jurisdiction and "to immortalize the mercantile and maritime causes and controversies, which it is proper to settle with swift justice."[66] After 1481 any conveyance of property to widows, minors, and indigent persons within one year prior to petitioning for the withdrawal of a case from the jurisdiction of the Consulado constituted grounds for denying the plea.[67]

Contrary to the procedure established for the consular court, appeals from interlocutory and even definitive decisions of the consuls were often carried to the Audiencia or to a provincial governor, instead of to the judge of appeals of the Consulado. After prolonged disputes, which were said to have threatened the "total ruination" of the consular jurisdiction in Perpignan, the crown established the following rules: (1) mercantile suits involving £50 or less could not be removed from the original jurisdiction of the Consulado on any ground; (2) decisions involving £100 or less should be executed by the consuls, under proper bonds, in spite of any writ or restraining order issued by

[66] IEC, B*a* 192, f. 42-46; AM, Barcelona, *Letres closes, 1435-36,* f. 80-81; Capmany, *Memorias,* IV, 209-213. Similarly, early in the sixteenth century the Burgos Consulado complained that trade was hampered by the fact that the widows of merchants, and minors, carried their complaints to the Real Audiencia in Valladolid (Ordinances of Burgos, 1538, in the preamble).

[67] IEC, B*a* 192, f. 116-119; *Constitvtions y altres drets de Cathalvnya,* I, 199-201; *Ordinacions y svmari dels privilegis . . . del Regne de Mallorca,* f. 181-186.

a higher court or crown official.[68] In countless cases the proceedings were returned to the Consulado when it was ascertained that the steps taken by the defendant to secure the evocation or appellate hearing by a higher court were contrary to the prerogatives of the consular judges.[69] Doubtless in more than one instance disputes over jurisdiction arose because the consular judges had "an exaggerated notion of their prerogatives."[70]

VI

Reasonable doubt may exist as to the economy of proceedings in the Consulado. In addition to documentary and notarial fees, the practice of the court required the payment by each party to a suit of a fixed percentage of the amount of the disputed claim.[71] In Valencia this *salari* was, as the word suggests, directly the remuneration of the consuls. In other Consulados, notably Barcelona and Majorca, the consuls received a fixed stipend from the city, and the emoluments of the court went into the city treasury.[72] The prior and consuls in Burgos, who were salaried officials of the guild, were forbidden to demand fees from the litigants.[73]

The other costs of court are not given in the procedural code of Valencia, but a complete schedule of fees for summons *(missatges)* and writs *(scriptures)* forms a part of the "Judicial Order of Barcelona."[74] About the only thing omitted is the cost of drawing one's breath in the presence of the consuls. In 1440, "in order to end the abuses introduced in the court of the

[68] *Llibre de privilegis de consvlat de Perpinya,* pp. 41-54 (1616-18); pp. 55-62 (1647).

[69] ACA, reg. 1426, f. 86 (1368); reg. 1430, f. 79 (1371); reg. 1440, f. 59 (1379); reg. 1446, f. 112 (1384); AHM, *Libre de Sant Pere,* f. 161 (1459), f. 74-75 (1379), f. 76 (1380); AHM, *Rosselló vell,* f. 346 (1368), f. 344-345 (1345), f. 352 (1402). [70] Guiard, *op. cit.,* I, 544 n.

[71] In Valencia, Barcelona, and Perpignan, "three pennies in the pound from either party" (i.e., 1.25 per cent) in original and appellate cases (JOV, cap. 37-39; JOB, cap. 10).

[72] In Majorca the *salari* was increased from one to three pence in the pound, in 1345, because of the great discrepancy between the income of the court and the remuneration of the consuls and judge of appeals (AHM, *Libre de Sant Pere,* f. 74).

[73] Ordinances of 1538, cap. 7.

[74] JOB, cap. 17-18. See also the "Tatxes dels salaris del notari i escriva del Consolat," in the Appendix of the *Llibre de privilegis de consvlat de Perpinya.*

sea consulate, by reason of the exaction of certain immoderate fees for documents," the city of Barcelona ordered a horizontal reduction in the schedule of notarial charges.[75]

In the early Consulado each litigant paid his own costs in the first instance; and in appeals the appellant who lost his case paid the costs incurred by the respondent.[76] Since the court frequently compelled the payment of notes and bills of exchange in which the borrower promised to meet the obligation without expense to the lender, the consuls received authority in the fifteenth century to assess the condemned party with all the costs of court.[77] Bearing in mind that the consular judges could demand bond for the payment of costs, prior to the commencement of hearings, it would appear that the expense of taking a case before the consuls was sufficiently great at least to preclude frivolous actions. Unfortunately, data for comparing it with the probable costs of prosecuting a case in an ordinary court are not available.[78]

[75] AM, Barcelona, *Privilegiorum et aliorum diversorum instrumentorum: liber secundus*, f. 27. Notaries protested, and certain upward revisions occurred in 1443 (AM, Barcelona, *Registre de deliberacions*, 1442-1446, f. 33-35).

[76] JOV, cap. 19-20. In the case reproduced in Appendix III (B) no costs were imposed in the first instance; in the appeal the plaintiff was assessed all the costs for having "mal appellat."

[77] Capmany, *Memorias*, IV, 257; *Llibre de privilegis de consvlat de Perpinya*, Appendix.

[78] In the Consulado of Cagliari (Sardinia) costs were deemed excessive, because the consuls collected not only fees and "salaries" which were comparable to the costs of ordinary courts but required litigants to give the assessors "three, four, and six lumps of sugar." In 1633 the salaries were fixed and the assessors prohibited from taking "sugar, pepper, or anything else" (F. de Vico, *Leyes y pragmáticas reales del Reyno de Sardeña*, Cagliari, 1714, lib. ii, tit. xlviii, cap. 3).

CHAPTER III

THE GUILD AND THE MERCHANT CLASS

I

Data concerning Spanish mercantile associations prior to the fourteenth century are negligible. Records dealing with the structure of municipal government furnish information on the position of the merchant class in the municipality during a period in which the existence of a formal guild organization is doubtful. Continually bargaining with the crown for particular rights and constitutional guarantees, the towns of Aragon achieved an extraordinary degree of autonomy during the thirteenth century. Although it is improbable that the medieval city was really a democratic body politic, the prevailing system of "functional" representation did give effective expression to the varied and conflicting interests of several economic and social groups.

The outlines of this development in Barcelona are fairly clear. The ordinance-making power was vested in the Council of One Hundred (Consell de Cent Jurats), while the executive authority rested largely in the hands of four or five councilors *(consellers)*. The earliest councilors were noblemen and privileged burgesses *(ciutadans honrats)*; but in 1257, the last year in which the crown exercised the right to select the councilors, James I named a merchant, an apothecary, and a tailor as *consellers*.[1]

For many years the Council of One Hundred was predominantly a body of *ciutadans*. Gradually, the merchants and other occupational groups won the right of representation. After 1388, twenty-four electors nominated by the Council of One Hundred chose the *consellers*. With eight appointees each, the merchants and burgesses named two thirds of the electors, the

[1] Capmany, *Memorias*, II, Appendix, pp. 67-68.

[34]

other third being chosen by the craftsmen (*menestrals*) and tradespeople (*artistes*).[2] In the fifteenth century the merchants joined forces with the *menestrals* and *artistes* in the so-called uprising of "the men of straw" (*homens de la busca*) and successfully withstood the opposition of the burgesses to a drastic reorganization of the city government.[3] After 1455 the mercantile class, or *estament*, always elected one of the councilors and one fourth of the Council of One Hundred. Considered as merchants were "merchants engaged in trade (*mercaders mercadeiants*), cloth merchants, owners (or masters) of ships and galleys, provided they are not burgesses, tax-farmers, or retailers of woolen textiles and silk goods."[4]   1198275

Municipal institutions experienced a similar development in other parts of the Corona de Aragón. James I created the government of the "city and realm of Majorca" in 1240. The municipal council of six consuls (later called *jurats*) was a self-perpetuating body until 1382, after which the *jurats* were chosen by lot. From the beginning the council customarily comprised one nobleman, two burgesses, two merchants, and an artisan.[5] Until the abolition of the council form of government in 1715, the merchant class enjoyed the right to elect one third of the councilors.

The estates (*mas*) in Gerona, Perpignan, and Valencia were three in number, merchants forming the largest constituent of

---

[2] *Rúbriques de Bruniquer*, I, 84. The *menestrals* included tailors, silversmiths, and shoemakers; while notaries, barbers, shopkeepers, and apothecaries were numbered among the *artistes*. Lawyers and physicians belonged to the *ciutadan* class.

[3] "En lany 1451 . . . tingué principi lo debat, y discordia grandíssima quey hague sobre lo regiment de la Ciutat dels Mercaders, Artistes, y Menestrals de una, y Ciutadans de altre . . . y fou ab tanta passió, que als Ciutadans los deyan per sobre nom la Gavella de la Biga, y als altros la Busca, y axi deyen la questió de la Biga, y de la Busca . . . ço es Biga als Ciutadans per ser homens hazendats, y poderosos, y que podian sustentar qualsevol pès com a Bigas, y Jasseras grossas, y los altres que es lo Poble, cada hu dells en particular, es com una Busca, que un petit vent, o ayre la trastorna, y acaba" (*Rúbriques de Bruniquer*, I, 91-92). Further details of this social revolution are found in J. Coroleu, *Los Dietarios de la Generalidad de Cataluña* (Barcelona, 1889), pp. 29-41.

[4] AM, Barcelona, *Libre Bermell*, lib. iii, f. 188-194. At this time the total membership of the Council, despite its name, was 128, comprising an equal number of *ciutadans*, *mercaders*, *menestrals*, and *artistes*. Increased to 144 members in 1493, the Council of One Hundred remained at this size until 1714.

[5] A. Capmaner y Fuertes, *Cronicón mayoricense*, pp. 10, 74.

the so-called "middle estate" *(ma mitjana)*. In Perpignan each class elected one third of the membership of the general municipal council, and the merchant class chose two of the five executive consuls.[6] Although representation in the municipality of Valencia was by parishes, doubtless the merchants as well as members of the craft guilds of each parish elected some of the *jurats* and members of the general council.[7]

Until the end of the fourteenth century the Consulado in Aragon functioned primarily as a court, directly responsible to the municipality (except possibly in Valencia) and indirectly responsive to the demands of the merchant class—at least to the extent that the merchants were able to influence certain spheres of municipal government. In most cases, the formal organization of the merchants in a guild was not contemporaneous with the formation of the consular court. In 1394, under the terms of a royal privilege secured by the city, the sea-consuls of Barcelona were instructed to convoke an assembly of all the merchants and in this meeting to elect a council "for the direction of mercantile affairs."[8] This mercantile guild-council was a permanent organization with a membership normally limited to twenty merchant-councilors, not including the consuls of the sea who were usually members ex officio. The council of twenty elected the two conservators of trade *(defenedors de la mercadería)*, whose duties were: "looking after, preserving, and defending everywhere the aforesaid mercantile profession, both from letters of marque or licenses for reprisals granted or to be granted to whatsoever individuals, foreigners or denizens, from searches, or taxes, tolls, reprisals, and from all other impositions or duties and exactions, imposed or to be imposed upon all merchants who are subjects of ours, both within and without our dominions, for whatsoever reason or cause." The council determined the measures necessary to "preserve" and "defend" trade, and its orders were executed by the *defenedors*. The deliberations of the councils of

[6] A. Bosch, *Svmari . . . dels titols de honor de Cathalunya*, pp. 421, 428; P. Vidal, *Histoire de la ville de Perpignan*, p. 77.

[7] L. Tramoyeres Blasco (*Instituciones gremiales: su origen y organización en Valencia*, pp. 316, 322-323) discusses craft guilds but is silent regarding the organization of merchants.   [8] Capmany, *Memorias*, II, 186-188.

twenty, where available, furnish the most detailed information on guild life and of the fears and aspirations of the merchant class.[9] Substantially identical privileges for the organization of the guild-council and the appointment of *defenedors* were issued to the Consulados of Perpignan (1394),[10] Tortosa (1449),[11] and Valencia (1493).[12]

Although James the Conqueror, in 1246, ceded a plot of land in Majorca for the erection of a merchants' exchange *(lonja)*,[13] the building was not constructed until the fifteenth century, and no data relating to a merchant guild prior to 1409 have been unearthed. Having promised to furnish four galleys for one of the crown's Sardinian expeditions, the impecunious municipality made several concessions to the merchants in exchange for assistance in floating a loan. Among other things, the *jurats* promised to urge upon the king that "an approved guild" in Majorca would redound to the honor and profit of the commonwealth. The sovereign readily consented to the formation of the guild (Collegi de la Mercadería), the establishment of the council of twenty, and the election of conservators of trade.[14]

Asso's sketchy description of the Consulado of Saragossa was based upon documents subsequently destroyed.[15] Apparently,

[9] In 1796 the archives of Barcelona possessed twenty-eight volumes of *Deliberacions* of the council, but now only a handful remain (IEC, B^a 30).

[10] ACA, reg. 4322, f. 121; *Llibre de privilegis de Consulat de Perpinya*, pp. 62-66. Here the council had a membership limited to fifteen.

[11] AM, Tortosa, an uncatalogued parchment; ACA, reg. 3152, f. 9, and reg. 3381, f. 14. No records have been found to link the Consulado of Tortosa with the *confratria nautarum*, which possessed a charter as early as 1456 (*Colección de documentos inéditos del Archivo General de la Corona de Aragón*, VIII, 482-489).

[12] ACA, reg. 3647, f. 148-153. In 1303 James II permitted "all the merchants of the city of Valencia" to form a *confratria*, but this guild seems to have existed only for charitable and pious works (ACA, reg. 201, f. 68). The two *jurati mercatorum*, drawn from the panel of nominees for the consulship (after 1418), may have exercised some of the functions of *defenedors* until 1493 (*Aureum opus*, f. 181-182).

[13] Campaner, *op. cit.*, p. 11; BSAL, I, 1.

[14] *Privilegis del Collegi de la Mercadería*, f. 2-4.

[15] According to officials of the municipal archives of Saragossa, most of the medieval records were burned soon after Asso wrote his *Historia de la economía política de Aragón* (Zaragoza, 1798). Other archives of the Aragonese capital appear to be equally barren for this subject.

the earliest extant document is the confirmation of the privileges of the merchant guild, or Confratria Sancte Marie Mercatorum, founded some time before 1264.[16] After 1292 a committee of two merchants, designated by this merchant guild, and two owners of irrigated land *(arraicos)* supervised the construction and operation of the sluices and irrigation ditches along the river Ebro, in order to prevent interference with navigation.[17] Not later than 1391, according to Asso,[18] the guild acquired privileges which permitted it to name three mayordomos as judges of mercantile causes. A fifteenth-century document refers to the judicial authority of the mayordomos as based upon "ancient usage,"[19] but the charter of the consular court and records of guild history doubtless have not survived.

II

Formally speaking, the guild of Majorca was the Collegi de la Mercadería. In Barcelona, Gerona, and Perpignan the Matricula dels Mercaders was synonymous with the merchant guild.

In Barcelona considerable formality attended the matriculation of merchants. After 1479 no one was legally a member of the *estament mercantivol*—a condition essential to qualifying for consular offices and municipal employments customarily held by merchants—until he had been habilitated by the mercantile section of the Council of One Hundred.[20] The affirmative vote of two thirds of this body was necessary for the approval of each petition. The petitioner had to prove that he was an active merchant, a native of Catalonia, and a Christian by birth. After 1599 only the sons, grandsons, and nephews of Catalans, who

[16] *Colección de documentos inéditos del Archivo General de la Corona de Aragón,* VI, 422-426. The guild was formed "ad sepelliendum defunctos confratres . . . et etiam super aliis negociis dicte confratrie," but it acquired other functions in time (AM, Zaragoza, *Libro de los corredores, 1446,* f. 1).

[17] ACA, reg. 116, f. 63-64; reg. 159, f. 205; reg. 180, f. 34; reg. 3152, f. 55; reg. 3363, f. 11.

[18] *Op. cit.,* p. 367.   [19] ACA, reg. 3134, f. 146 (1441).

[20] Although on various occasions the crown promised to refrain from the practice, a number of "merchants" acquired their status by royal fiat (E. Moliné y Brasés, *Les Costums Maritimes de Barcelona,* pp. 346-347). Such merchants were specifically debarred from matriculation in 1683, in return for a subsidy to the exchequer (Capmany, *Memorias,* IV, 316-320).

had resided in Barcelona for four years or more, were considered for matriculation.[21] As early as 1563 the guild council of twenty, in a secret session, began to examine all applications for admission; and names were submitted to the Council of One Hundred only if approved by fourteen members of the guild council.[22]

This practice of habilitation continued throughout the sixteenth and seventeenth centuries. As in 1598, when all of the twenty-two applications were rejected,[23] the matriculation committee often failed to admit merchants who considered themselves eligible. It is undeniable that the merchant class sought to take advantage of a restricted guild membership. Numerous changes in the procedure of admission were adopted during the sixteenth century, at the end of which the council of twenty reported that the "excessive number" of applications constituted an "abuse."[24] Yet in 1702, faced with a declining membership, attributed to the preference of wealthy merchants for the privileges of other classes but probably due to the decadence of commerce, the guild requested the crown to concede to matriculated merchants all the honors and prerogatives of the *ciutadan* class.[25]

Merchants eligible for membership in the Collegi of Majorca were all native merchants who paid the guild duty on

[21] IEC, B*a* 189, *Libre de la matricula dels mercaders*, f. 1; Capmany, *Memorias*, IV, 325.

[22] This practice was adopted, "attesos los grans abusos . . . se han fets per raho de dit memorial posant en aquel diverses persones que no convenen por lo benefici ni honor del stament mercantivol" (IEC, B*a* 200, *Deliberacions, 1563-1568*). In the council of twenty (so it was stated in 1702), "se haga diligente exámen y averiguación de la limpieza de sangre, vida, costumbres, trato y otras circunstancias" (Capmany, *Memorias*, IV, 341). By virtue of an ordinance adopted in 1594, the council was required to give preference to individuals married to the daughters of matriculated merchants *(ibid.)*. [23] *Dietari*, VII, 100.

[24] Capmany, *Memorias*, IV, 313-316. In 1480 two merchants were admitted to the Matricula. No further sessions of the committee were held until 1533, when ten merchants were accepted. From 1533 to 1574, records for thirty-two years are available. No petitions were granted in eight years, and 196 merchants were admitted in the other twenty-four years. Records also exist for a period of forty-eight years between 1652 and 1707. In thirteen of these years no petitions were granted, and ninety-one habilitations occurred in thirty-six years (IEC, B*a* 147, *Expedientes*).

In 1660 the matriculation fee was £50 (IEC, B*a* 170).

[25] Capmany, *Memorias*, IV, 344-345.

merchandise imported and exported from the island.[26] The membership rolls are not available for any period. Although *ciutadans* were expressly excluded from the guild in 1447, two years later the Collegi found its matricula so curtailed that it secured permission to admit *ciutadans* who were actively engaged in business. The *ciutadan-mercader* was also admitted to the council of twenty and the office of conservator of trade.[27]

Drawing by lot *(insaculació)* for members of the council of twenty and for the *defenedors* in Majorca was inaugurated in 1454, following the adopting of this electoral practice in the offices of the municipal government. The names of members of the guild nominated by the *defenedors* and approved by the mercantile section of the municipal council were inscribed on appropriate rolls. Ten councilors and one *defenedor* were drawn each year.[28]

In Barcelona this system of drawing lots for municipal and consular offices commenced at the end of the fifteenth century.[29] Separate ballot urns were prepared for members of the council of twenty, *defenedors,* minor officials of the guild and several municipal offices reserved for matriculated merchants. The consuls, councilors of the council of twenty, and conservators of trade prepared the permanent lists of eligible persons, and on "election" day a young boy was employed to draw the required number of names from each ballot box *(bossa).*[30]

---

[26] *Privilegis del Collegi de la Mercadería,* f. 4.

[27] *Privilegis del Collegi de la Mercadería,* f. 8, 15, 18-20; ACA, reg. 3435, f. 101. The pretension of the guild of notaries to have notaries admitted to the offices of the Consulado and Collegi was denied in 1460 (ACA, reg. 1425, f. 3; reg. 3424, f. 51-52, 58).

[28] *Privilegis del Collegi de la Mercadería,* f. 15-16, 24; AHM, *Llibre extra-ordinari del Real Collegi de la Mercadería, 1694-1707;* P. A. Sancho, "Régimen interior del Colegio de la Mercadería," BSAL, II, 85-86.

[29] The "new" royal privilege on *insaculació* for the municipality was effective for the first time in 1498 *(Rúbriques de Bruniquer,* I, 101-102).

[30] IEC, B*a* 192, f. 103-105; B*a* 253, *Llibre intitulat de anima dels insiculats.* The *bossa primera de vells* (the older merchants) contained thirty-eight names and furnished twelve members of the council of twenty. The *bossa segon de jovens* (the younger merchants) held ninety-two names, from which came eight members of the council. One *defenedor* was drawn from each *bossa.* Similar *bossas* held the matricula for other offices. For a revised statute on membership in the council of twenty and other offices, see Appendix II.

The Matricula of Perpignan was established in 1449.[31] To secure matriculation, which qualified an individual for offices of the Consulado and certain municipal posts, a merchant must prove that he was actively engaged in trade and secure the approval of (1) all the incumbent members of the city council and (2) the majority of those who had previously occupied the seats of merchant-councilors in the municipal government. In 1499 the drawing of lots for various offices superseded direct elections. Similar methods of matriculation and of selecting the officers of the Consulado existed in Gerona and Tortosa, but little information concerning the practices is at hand.[32]

III

The Universidad de los Mercaderes which became the Consulado of Burgos in 1494 may have been organized in the fourteenth century. The fact that Castilian merchants trading in Flanders possessed a guild as early as 1336 has been accepted as evidence of a contemporaneous mercantile association in Burgos, the capital of Castile.[33] Unmistakable references to the Universidad and to its prior and consuls before 1443 have not been found.[34]

The few available records do not discuss the guild organization prior to 1494, and regulations governing the election of officers of the Consulado appeared for the first time in the Ordinances of 1538. In addition to the prior and consuls, who were judges of the guild court, the guild had an administrative council of nine *diputados:* the prior and consuls retiring from office

[31] Archives Départementales des Pyrénées-Orientales, reg. C. 1542-1543.

[32] ACA, *Indice alfabético y traslado de las bulas, privilegios . . . del General de Cataluña,* II, f. 308 (a reference to matriculated merchants in Gerona); AM, Tortosa, *Libre de les provisions fetes en los consells de la ciutat* (a reference to balloting by lot for consuls and judge of appeals, in 1439).

[33] E. García de Quevedo, *Ordenanzas del Consulado de Burgos de 1538,* pp. 23-26. Pascual Madoz (*Diccionario geográfico-estadístico-histórico de España,* Madrid, 1849, IV, 586) asserted that the merchants of Burgos formed a *corporación* in the middle of the fourteenth century, but the source of this information is not given. In 1785, and again in 1806, the Consulado claimed that the guild existed in 1379 (García de Quevedo, *op. cit.,* pp. 30-31).

[34] García de Quevedo, *op. cit.,* p. 34; *Indice de documentos referentes a la historia vasca,* p. 11.

and six merchants of their selection. Meetings of the council, as well as general assemblies of the guild, were held at the discretion of the prior and consuls.[35] The Ordinances of 1572 state that members of the guild were "residents of Burgos who gained their livelihood through trade and commerce."[36] No additional qualifications are expressed, nor are there records of the matriculation of merchants, as in Aragon.

According to Guiard,[37] the merchant guild of Bilbao, governed by a *fiel* and *diputados*, originated in the fourteenth century; but documentary evidence of its existence prior to 1489 has not been adduced. Until its own general ordinances were approved in 1560, the Consulado of Bilbao adhered to the regulations governing the Burgos guild.

Under the Ordinances of 1560, all the captains, masters of ships, merchants, and traders residing in Bilbao formed the assembly of the guild.[38] By ballot and lot the guildsmen chose the consular judges and an administrative council of four, the latter being drawn from the nominees for the office of consul. As in Burgos, the prior and consuls convoked meetings of the guild council and general assemblies of the merchants as circumstances demanded.[39] In the early years of the seventeenth century, stormy sessions of the Consulado arose from the attempts —sometimes unsuccessful—to prevent foreign merchants and native retail traders and shopkeepers from participating in the guild assembly.[40]

The preamble of the ordinances of the San Sebastián Consulado states that the Cofradía de Mercaderes y Mareantes was

[35] Ordinances of 1538, caps. 4, 12, 15, 21.
[36] Ordinances of 1572, cap. 35.
[37] T. Guiard y Larrauri, *Historia del Consulado de Bilbao*, I, lxxxii. *Fieles de los mercaderes* are mentioned in a capitulation of 1435 (*ibid.*, I, lxii). J. Finot (*Étude historique sur les relations commerciales entre la Flandre et l'Espagne au moyen âge*, p. 61) found no express mention of merchants from Bilbao and San Sebastián trading in Flanders until the end of the fourteenth century, and "ce n'est qu'en 1494, bien après les autres nations de la péninsule ibérique, qu'ils eurent leur hôtel ou maison consulaire à Bruges."
[38] Ordinances of 1560, caps. 3-6. Excluded from the guild were "Maestres de Naos postiços [absentee? or honorary?] y Factores, y Tratantes que vivieren con otros, y no tenga casa, y vivienda sobre sí" (*ibid.*, cap. 8). Notaries, procurators, and craftsmen (*oficiales mecánicos*) were specifically debarred (*ibid.*, cap. 17).
[39] Ordinances of 1560, caps. 18-20.   [40] Guiard, *op. cit.*, I, 536-538.

erected in 1463. No archival data on the history of this establishment have been found. Nevertheless, it is possible that the institution was a consular court and merchant guild from 1489 to 1682, though lacking the name of Consulado.[41] All merchants *(negociantes* and *comerciantes)*, shipowners, captains, and masters were eligible for membership in the guild. Furthermore, the prior and consuls had authority to compel individuals possessing the requisite qualifications to affiliate and to accept offices to which they might be elected.[42]

No records of the organization of merchants in Seville prior to 1543 have been found.[43] The membership of the guild chartered in 1543 was limited to merchants engaged in trade with America—importers and exporters at wholesale and silver merchants. Only residents of Seville, married or widowed, at least twenty-five years of age were accepted.[44] The administrative council of the guild comprised five *diputados* elected in the same manner as the consuls. The retiring prior and consul also served for one year as counselors *(consejeros)* of the guild and court.[45]

IV

The salaries paid to guild heads should furnish some evidence of the relative importance of their work. The municipality paid the consuls of Majorca £50 a year after 1600, and the

[41] By the privileges of 1489, "se dió a su mayordomo jurisdicción para conocer de plano y sin figura de juicio . . . en los casos y cosas que por razon del oficio de marear naciesen entre ellos. Las mismas establecieron otras disposiciones para el govierno del muelle, cobranza de los derechos impuestos para su conservación . . . todo lo cual era un principio de consulado" (P. de Gorosabel, *Diccionario histórico-geográfico-descriptivo . . . de Guipúzcoa*, Tolosa, 1862, p. 452).

[42] Ordinances of 1766, cap. 2, citing chapters of the Ordinances of 1682.

[43] Ordinances approved in the fourteenth century describe the jurisdiction of *alcaldes de la mar* in "los pleytos de la mar y del rio" (*Recopilación de las ordenanzas de la muy noble y muy leal cibdad de Sevilla*, Sevilla, 1527, f. 54). The *alcaldes* functioned as late as 1620 (Biblioteca Nacional, *Sección de varios, ca.* 1-59-18), but there appears to be no connection between this institution and the Consulado. The *cédula* of 1543 expressly mentions the inconvenience of not having a guild merchant in Seville.

[44] Ordinances of 1556, caps. 1-2. Foreigners, menials *(criados)*, notaries, and shopkeepers were excluded. According to Veitia Linage, in order to be recognized as a *cargador a las Indias*, "basta aver cargado sola una vez" (*Norte de la contratación*, lib. i, cap. xvii, par. 28). The prohibition against foreigners was repeated in numerous laws, probably ineffectively (*R. de I.*, lib. ix, tit. vi, leyes 3-4).

[45] Ordinances of 1556, caps. 6-7.

judge of appeals, £25;[46] but the administration of the guild in Majorca was in the hands of the *defenedors* rather than the consuls. In the fourteenth century the city paid the consuls of Barcelona £40 a year and the judge of appeals £25.[47] The stipends were increased to £65 and £30, respectively, in 1475. Apparently, the remuneration of the consuls was not increased again until the end of the sixteenth century, when the pay was raised to £80. But in 1574 the council of twenty voted the consuls an additional compensation of £60 out of guild funds. Rising prices and the increased cost of living made it difficult to secure able businessmen to accept the time-consuming duties of the guild and court.[48] By comparison, the annual salary of each of the councilors of the city government moved as follows: 1379, £100; 1530, £150; 1547, £200; 1563, £250; 1617, £800.[49]

The general ordinances set the annual remuneration of the prior and consuls in Burgos as follows:

	Prior	Consul
Ordinances of 1538 (cap. 7)	8,000 *maravedís*	6,000 *maravedís*
Ordinances of 1572 (cap. 10)	20,000 *maravedís*	15,000 *maravedís*

In Bilbao, the prior's salary was always twice that of the consul. In the seventeenth century, when these emoluments were on a contingent basis, the prior's income ranged from 15,000 to 75,000 *maravedís* annually, depending upon the income of the guild.[50] Until 1593, the prior's salary in Seville was fixed at 20,000 *maravedís* and each of the consuls received 10,000; but merchants elected to these offices so often excused themselves from serving that in the latter year salaries were doubled.[51]

As time went on, the activities of the guild expanded, and the corporation acquired a large personnel. For the conduct of

---

[46] BSAL, IV, 19.

[47] Recognizing the increase in the cost of living, in 1376 a royal order increased the wages of "common carpenters" in the Barcelona shipyards from 2s. to 2s. 5d. per diem, equivalent to a rise from £25 to £30 2s. for a 250-day year (Capmany, *Memorias*, IV, 151-152).

[48] *Rúbriques de Bruniquer*, IV, 5-8; IEC, *Deliberacions, 1563-68; 1568-75*; and 1584-92.   [49] *Rúbriques de Bruniquer*, I, 77-129.

[50] See below, chap. v.   [51] AGI, Contaduria, leg. 588-589.

its economic, political, judicial, and even religious affairs, the guild employed secretaries, notaries, numerous collectors of revenues, auditors, archivists, porters, guards, constables, and other functionaries. Some of these employments were irregular or part-time, but a number of officials spent all of their time on guild business.[52] Although the number of sinecures represented by the Consulado's payroll may have been high, the institution was essentially an economic organization conducted on a businesslike basis.

Except for the purpose of electing officers, general assemblies of the guild seem to have been infrequent. Occasionally an important matter of policy or action required the express consent of the merchants in assembly, but most of the powers of the guild were delegated to the officers or to committees. Hence, in the records at least, guild life centers largely around the activities of the priors, consuls, conservators of trade, deputies, and councilors. These officials met frequently to discuss and take action on matters affecting the economic life of the guild, the community, and the nation. It is the purpose of the following chapters to examine the specific influences of the consular establishment in the three regions of Spain where the guild flourished from the twilight of the Middle Ages to the end of the Hapsburg period.[53]

[52] Thus, in Barcelona the *defenedors* and the collectors of the consular duty were full-time salaried officials, who were not permitted to accept any other employment (IEC, B*a* 192, f. 105-106).

[53] The document reproduced in Appendix V serves to illustrate the innumerable duties and responsibilities incumbent upon the consular officials in Bilbao.

CHAPTER IV

GUILD LIFE IN THE MEDITERRANEAN TOWNS

I

Medieval Italy has so long been the cynosure of scholarly investigations in economic history that the contemporaneous development of Catalonia, or any other constituent of the far-flung Crown of Aragon is often assumed to be of negligible importance. Research in the history of banking in Barcelona has belied this conclusion in one field.[1] Not a small part of the sixteenth-century political supremacy of the Spanish Empire in Mediterranean affairs was founded upon the commercial expansion of Catalonia in the thirteenth and fourteenth centuries.[2] For half a century Catalans remained in possession of the distant duchy of Athens, and appreciable trade relations with the entire Mediterranean littoral were continuous in the latter part of the Middle Ages. Catalan consuls, appointed by the city of Barcelona, resided in Bougie, Tunis, Alexandria, and Syria in the thirteenth century; and before 1500, consulates had been established in nearly fifty Mediterranean ports.[3]

The hegemony of Barcelona, among Catalan and Aragonese cities, in the development of trade and commercial institutions is matched by the unusual richness of its historical archives—dual reasons for using the problems and achievements of the merchant guild of Barcelona as the focus of the present chapter. The priority of Valencia in adopting the consular court doubtless bespeaks the quickened pace of commerce in the Valencian capital toward the end of the thirteenth century; and, subsequently, in matters maritime and commercial Valencia was perhaps Barcelona's strongest rival. What is significant for present purposes

---

[1] A. P. Usher, "Deposit Banking in Barcelona, 1300-1700," *Journal of Economic and Business History*, IV (1931-32), 121-155.

[2] R. B. Merriman, *The Rise of the Spanish Empire* (New York, 1918), I, 363-382.

[3] Capmany, *Memorias*, II, Appendix, pp. 58-67.

is the apparent inactivity of the Valencian merchant guild with respect to the promotion, protection, and regulation of trade. The lacunae in the records pertaining to the Consulado are numerous; on the other hand, important series of documents[4] fail to mention the guild in connection with matters of the greatest importance to the merchant class. The influence of the Majorcan Collegi de la Mercadería in the economy of the island-city was somewhat less important than the work of the Barcelona guild in Catalonia. The Consulado of Perpignan was an important factor in the economic life of Roussillon; but it is virtually impossible to prove that the guilds of Gerona, San Felíu, Saragossa, and Tortosa made any great or lasting contributions to the commercial development of their respective communities.

II

Primarily maritime commercial interests were represented in the early guilds, and a major activity of the Consulado, at least until the eighteenth century, was the protection of overseas trade. The slow development of national responsibility for the safety of maritime commerce has been observed in connection with the origins of the institution. Royal galleys were infrequently available for local needs; and the naval forces maintained by the Diputación General de Cataluña, or permanent executive council of the Catalan Parliament, were generally inadequate unless reinforced by other men-of-war and armed merchantmen.

The Consulado occasionally subsidized privateering in an effort to safeguard merchant shipping.[5] More often, however, the guild co-operated with the municipal government, contributing to the preparation and expense of naval expeditions approved by merchants and shipowners whose property was endangered. Time after time the armadas, fitted out by municipal and guild corporations, sallied forth to protect incoming ship-

---

[4] Such as the *Manuals de Consells*, or journals of the municipal government, which are practically complete from 1306 to 1700.

[5] BAB, Nos. 34 (1437) and 36 (1445); *Privilegis del Collegi de la Mercadería*, f. 9-10. Seamen on a privateer under orders of the guild of Barcelona (1477) were promised wages of 3 *sols* a day, or 4 *sols* if they returned with a prize (BAB, No. 30).

ping from enemy vessels; gave chase to pirates who raided the coast and burned ships in port; and took part in large-scale engagements to rid the sea of predatory sails.[6] Occasionally the Consulados of Majorca, Perpignan, and Valencia participated in expeditions projected by the guild and city of Barcelona for the defense of shipping.[7] Numerous also were the contributions of the guilds to the overseas adventures of royal naval forces, the purposes of which were more often political than commercial. But in such instances a *quid pro quo* in the form of renewal and enlargement of the guild privileges was not uncommon. It was the rule rather than the exception for the Consulado to pay substantial sums for privileges and other favors granted by the crown.[8]

On the basis of extensive correspondence with maritime centers and municipal officials, the guild sent out warnings to merchant ships of the hazards of navigation and the activities of pirates.[9] Unfortunately, among the corsairs who roamed the Mediterranean were not a few Catalans; but they were not

[6] *Dietari*, II, 311; *Rúbriques de Bruniquer*, II, 229-254 (1390-1522). Minutes of the council of twenty reveal that the Consulado of Barcelona usually paid one third of the cost of arming vessels to guard the coast and attack pirates (IEC, B[a] 200, *Deliberacions, 1538-51*); as a matter of fact, the guild frequently bore a larger share of the expenses (*Dietari*, I, 272-273; *Deliberacions, 1584-92*). In 1502 the guild borrowed £1,200, or one third of the estimated cost of arming ships to fight "the infidels" (ACA, reg. 3807, f. 91).

Similar engagements of the Majorcan guild are reported in BSAL, III, 162-166. In 1449 the municipality ceded to the Collegi the duty of 2 *diners* on each *quartera* of imported wheat in order to pay for the armada sent out by the guild in search of pirate ships (*Privilegis del Collegi de la Mercadería*, f. 12-13).

[7] AM, Barcelona, *Proces de cort de 1436*; *Libre de consell, 1395-98*, f. 72-77; AM, Valencia, *Manual de consells, 1400-1406*, f. 89-90, 102-103, 112, 155-156; IEC, B[a] 195; *Dietari*, II, 232; *Rúbriques de Bruniquer*, II, 249-251; *Colección de documentos inéditos del Archivo General de la Corona de Aragón*, III, 11-13, 189-191; *Córtes de los antiguos reinos de Aragón y de Valencia y principado de Cataluña*, IV, 368-388.

[8] In return for a grant (ostensibly a loan) of £6,000 for the preparation of an armada to defend Sicily (1460), the Barcelona guild secured the confirmation of all its privileges and the concession of new ones (ACA, reg. 3372, f. 11; IEC, B[a] 192, f. 78-82). Important ordinances prepared by the Collegi of Majorca and ratified by the king in 1449 involved a payment of £500 to the royal treasurer (*Privilegis del Collegi de la Mercadería*, f. 10).

[9] IEC, B[a] 161; B[a] 195; B[a] 200, *Deliberacions, 1552-73*; B[a] 30, *Expedientes* (a reference to three volumes, no longer extant, of "pliegos de cartas avisos de vista de buques enemigos que empiezan en 1458").

members of the guilds, nor were their activities condoned by merchants of the Consulado.[10] The exigencies of the age, such as recurrent famine, did not permit a policy of absolute non-intercourse with these seafaring freebooters. Pursuant to legislation advocated by the guilds, the master of a ship obviously not engaged in legitimate commerce was required only to swear not to harm subjects of Aragon as a condition for receiving provisions and safe-conduct in Aragonese ports.[11] Castilians and Basques, suspected of piratical practices, were forced to deposit bond with the governor of Majorca as a prerequisite of trade in the Balearics; but the requirement was waived, on recommendation of the guild, when a dearth of food threatened.[12]

As early as the thirteenth century Aragon endeavored through diplomatic channels to check the unrestrained application of letters of marque and reprisal. Agreements ratified by Barcelona and Narbonne in 1246 and 1253 provided for the indemnification of merchants, whose goods were seized by other merchants, without recourse to reprisal.[13] Although Catalan and Aragonese infringements of the freedom of the seas were not infrequent, the Consulado consistently strived to curtail privateering and to secure the enforcement of agreements, especially with French rulers, for the redress of grievances without retaliation.[14] At considerable expense agents were sent to for-

[10] Archives communales, Montpellier, armoire C, cassette 3; Archives communales, Marseille, BB. 17, f. 25-27, and BB. 23, f. 85. The Consulado and the city of Barcelona jointly agreed to pay an indemnity of 550 florins to a merchant of Burgos whose goods were destroyed by a Barcelona navigator "cosseiant per mar" (AM, Barcelona, *Clavaria, 1403-1404*, f. 135).

[11] Capmany, *Memorias*, II, 272-273 (1483); IEC, B^a 192, f. 98-99 (1493); ACA, reg. 3800, f. 188. As permitted by law, financial security was sometimes demanded (ACA, reg. 2115, f. 172; reg. 2117, f. 67; reg. 2119, f. 28).

[12] *Privilegis del Collegi de la Mercaderia*, f. 6-7 (1443); Capmany, *Memorias*, II, 232-233.

[13] R. de Mas Latrie, "Du droit de marque ou de représaille," *Bibliothèque de l'École des Chartes*, XXIX (Paris, 1868), 295-297; J. Miret i Sans, "Les represàlies a Catalunya en l'edat mitjana," *Revista Jurídica de Cataluña*, XXXI (Barcelona, 1925), 289-304, 385-417.

[14] The "marque duty" *(dret de las marcas)* was imposed on French-Aragonese trade, possibly before the end of the thirteenth century, to furnish funds for the indemnification of French and Aragonese merchants who were victims of reprisal. On the Spanish side of the Pyrenees the duty was collected by tax farmers until the end of the sixteenth century, when it was amortised by the Consulado of Barcelona (Archives

eign ports to recover ships and goods seized from Catalan traders.[15] Negotiations with foreign governments, leading to the conclusion of treaties of amity and commerce, were instigated and sometimes carried on by representatives of the Barcelona guild.[16] Masters of ships clearing Barcelona were under oath not to harm the merchants and seamen of foreign states with which such agreements were in effect.[17] Too often, a state of war destroyed much of the advantage of these accords.

Trade in the Mediterranean frequently meant intercourse with infidels which, for economic and religious reasons, suffered the interdiction of Rome. The anathema of the Church was commonly obviated by the purchase of absolution, although one of the two agreements signed by the crown and the city of Barcelona in 1373 provided for trade with Egypt without papal indulgence.[18] In 1380 the Majorcan merchants obtained royal permission to traffic in Egypt only on "vexells qui haien o

communales, Marseille, BB. 21, f. 101; BB. 24, f. 187; Archivo de la Diputación de Zaragoza, *Reg. de actos comunes de la Diputación*, No. 61; ACA, reg. 4205, f. 162; ACA, Generalidad, reg. 689, f. 99; IEC, B*a* 200, *Deliberacions, 1592-96; Constitvtions y altres drets de Cathalvnya*, III, 55-56; R. de Mas Latrie, *op. cit.*, 311-313).

[15] E.g., a payment of 100 florins "per raho de la ambaxada reginal feta al Rey d'Anglaterra . . . per beneffici de la mercaderia e signantment per recuperacio de la Galea de mossen J. Lull" (BAB, No. 34, March, 1437).

[16] ACA, reg. 4185, f. 28. Treaties were signed in 1479 and 1487 between Aragon and Provence. The Aragonese plenipotentiaries were merchants of Barcelona who carried instructions and recommendations from the guild (BAB, Nos. 30-31; IEC, B*a* 145, *Acorts; Dietari*, II, 248; Capmany, *Memorias*, II, 289-291, 298, and IV, 270-271).

In 1417 the consuls of the Barcelona guild, pursuant to the treaty between Aragon and Genoa, distributed 4,500 ducats among Catalan merchants injured by Genoese pirates, which was the indemnity paid by the Duke and Commune of Genoa (IEC, B*a* 199, *Actes e avantaments fets per la compartiment de la moneda tremesa als damnificats per Jenoveses*).

[17] AM, Barcelona, *Deliberacions, 1395-1401*, f. 20.

[18] Egypt was loosely used to signify all the lands ruled by the "Sultan of Babylon," but trade with Alexandria was the most important consideration for Barcelona merchants.

The agreement for trade in absolved ships is found in the MS *Llibre del Consolat de Mar*, Bibliothèque Nationale, Paris, MS Espagnol No. 56, f. 156-160; the one for commerce "sens absolució" is in Capmany, *Memorias*, II, 144-150. Royal duties, or penalties, were based upon dead weight of the ships, as determined by the consuls of the sea. Many *cartae absolutionis* are found in the Arxíu de la Battlía General de Cathalunya, leg. 362, 2910, and 2954. Compositions between merchants and the royal treasurer were numerous as early as 1302 (E. González Hurtebise, *Libros de tesorería de la Casa Real de Aragón*, Barcelona, 1911, I, 5-6, 10-12, 214-215, 309).

hauran absolutio del Papa."[19] War and lesser pretexts repeatedly interrupted this commerce, but it is significant that the levy on *coses vedades*, or exports to Alexandria, became in time a regular tariff.[20] In 1453 the crown covenanted with the Consulado of Barcelona to conclude a peace with the sultan, restoring commercial relations so that a Catalan consul might again reside in Alexandria. The guild represented that the Levant spice trade was the "head and beginning" of all Catalan commerce, so that the cessation of trade relations with the eastern Mediterranean meant a serious depression in Barcelona.[21]

Navigation acts in Aragon date from the thirteenth century. The first act (1227), limited to the commerce of Barcelona, prohibited the chartering of foreign bottoms for outward or inward traffic with Alexandria and Ceuta when ships belonging to natives of Barcelona were available.[22] The Consulado was directly responsible for the re-enactment of the navigation laws in the fifteenth century. One article of the agreement of 1453 with the Consulado bound the king to issue an absolute prohibition on the shipment of goods from Aragonese ports in foreign ships for a period of three years.[23] Mere anticipation of the passage of the act was said to have stimulated the shipbuilding industry, and the guild recommended its perpetuation.[24] In the

[19] IEC, B*a* 190 and B*a* 193, f. 95-96.

[20] Apparently ceded by the king to the city of Barcelona, the tariff was removed in 1454 when the guild offered to advance the crown 3,000 ducats and to subsidize the maintenance of the municipal arsenals at the rate of £25 per annum. At this time the imposition on *coses vedades* was 4 pence in the pound (ACA, reg. 1546, f. 79-80; Arxíu de la Battlía General de Cathalunya, leg. 2954; IEC, B*a* 190 and B*a* 200).

[21] Capmany, *Memorias*, IV, 241-247. Material in the *Memorias*, II, 233-235, 344-345, and IV, 284-288, 337-338, and in IEC, B*a* 190 and B*a* 193, f. 95-96, deals more fully with this subject. In the eighteenth century, when eastern Spain realized its unfavorable position with regard to the American trade, an unsuccessful effort was made to revive the Levant commerce and restore its markets to Barcelona (IEC, B*a* 139, *Expedientes*). [22] Capmany, *Memorias*, II, 11-12.

[23] ACA, reg. 2622, f. 2-6; Capmany, *Memorias*, IV, 241-247. In 1420 "Germans" and Savoyards were required to use Catalan ships to export, and the sea-consuls had the power to fix freight rates in case of disagreement between the foreign merchants and the masters (Arxíu de la Battlía General de Cathalunya, leg. 1400).

[24] IEC, B*a* 145, *Acorts, 1480-81;* Capmany, *Memorias*, II, 279-280. Interests outside of Catalonia appear to have secured the suspension of the law in 1454 (AHM, *Libre de Sant Pere*, f. 157; *Colección de varias obras . . . del Excmo. Señor Gaspar Melchor de Jovellanos*, Madrid, 1830, I, 100); but in 1459 the Consulado of Barcelona obtained the king's promise that the navigation acts would remain in force, at

sixteenth century, however, circumstances radically changed the guild's point of view. Catalan ships, typically small and poorly armed, were easy prey of Moorish pirates. After 1599 the merchants of Barcelona were required to employ native bottoms only when larger than the foreign ships available, and at least as well armed.[25] In time of war the prohibition against trade in foreign ships was invoked under heavy penalties, and to prevent freight charges from soaring, the consuls were empowered to fix maximum legal rates.[26] As early as 1465, the city of Barcelona undertook to subsidize shipbuilding,[27] but neither the efforts of the municipality nor those of the guild were sufficient to sustain and improve this important industry. The scarcity of suitable wood in eastern Spain and the comparative inefficiency of Spanish shipwrights in the sixteenth and seventeenth centuries are reasonably considered to be the chief explanations of this phenomenon.[28]

The fifteenth-century insurance and sea-loan statutes of Barcelona discriminated against foreigners. Legislation on both types of contracts was enacted in 1435, but the most complete maritime insurance laws were the ordinances of 1484.[29] The latter permitted the underwriting of foreign bottoms, which was prohibited in 1435. Increasing the maximum permissible in-

---

least until the Consulado had been refunded the £4,000 advanced for the privileges of 1453 (IEC, B*a* 192, f. 75-78).

The Majorcan guild secured the passage of a navigation act in 1511, enforcing preferential treatment for Majorcan ships in exporting from the island (*Privilegis del Collegi de la Mercaderia*, f. 22).

[25] IEC, B*a* 200, *Deliberacions, 1592-96;* Capmany, *Memorias,* IV, 321-324. Arbitrary power was conferred on the consuls to decide which ships might be employed at any given time. [26] Capmany, *Memorias,* II, 388-390.

[27] *Dietari,* II, 465-466. In 1560 the Consulado proposed to build with guild funds "one or two" large, well-armed merchantmen, but the project was apparently not realized (IEC, B*a* 200, *Deliberacions, 1552-63*). Earlier, the guild granted a subvention for the purchase of a merchant vessel, forcing the owner to promise that the ship would not be sold to foreigners or armed for piracy (IEC, B*a* 144; Capmany, *Memorias,* IV, 266-268).

[28] A. P. Usher, "Spanish Ships and Shipping in the Sixteenth and Seventeenth Centuries," in *Facts and Factors in Economic History,* p. 189.

[29] The best texts of the laws are in F. Valls, *Consolat de Mar,* III, 17-25 (sea-loan laws of 1435), pp. 33-45 (insurance laws of 1435), pp. 48-49 (1436 revision of insurance laws), pp. 51-71 (insurance laws of 1458), pp. 73-76 (1461 revision of insurance laws), pp. 77-105 (insurance laws of 1484).

surance, the city legalized the insurance of ships belonging to natives of Aragon up to seven eighths of the value; the maximum on foreign-owned hulls was three fourths. The legal maxima for insurance on cargoes similarly favored native shippers who employed native bottoms. All valuations were subject to the jurisdiction of the consuls and an appraisal committee, and every insurance and sea-loan contract had to be registered in the secretariat of the guild. Similar ordinances on marine insurance were written into the privileges granted to the Consulado of Valencia in 1493.[30]

The *defenedors* in Majorca were required to inspect all merchant ships prior to sailing and to certify that they were seaworthy. In Barcelona, the guild of bargemen *(barqueros)* was subject to the jurisdiction of the sea-consuls in the matter of lighterage fees, on the ground that exorbitant charges would otherwise prevail in emergencies and in bad weather. In general, the authority and the administrative duties of guild officials were designed to protect the interests of shippers, so that they would not incur unnecessary losses through the overloading of ships, deficiencies in their equipment, or the lack of port facilities for the safe entry and departure of vessels under varying conditions of tide and weather.[31] In Barcelona, the consuls promised in the oath of office that "once a year . . . they would inspect the galleys *(galeas e altres fustes de rems)* and the warehouse of the municipal arsenal, in order to ascertain whether the said galleys and the rigging, oars, sails, and other equipment and supplies which are, or shall be, in the said warehouse are depleted or are in need of repair."[32]

III

The guild's tariff policy was usually clear: customs barriers which impeded the trade of Catalan merchants were vigorously attacked, while duties which protected their interests were defended and encouraged. The *leuda,* an almost ubiquitous transit-

[30] ACA, reg. 3647, f. 148-153.
[31] BSAL, June, 1896, pp. 307-308; IEC, B*a* 148 and B*a* 193, f. 9; ACA, reg. 1910, f. 162-163; Capmany, *Memorias,* IV, 186-191.
[32] IEC, B*a* 192, frontispiece.

duty in Catalonia, occasioned innumerable complaints, in spite of the fact that Barcelona merchants had been granted exemption from such dues as early as the thirteenth century. The *leuda* of Tamarit, a small port controlled by the Archbishop of Tarragona, was particularly obnoxious. At various times, "in order to put an end to the extortions which . . . the farmers of the Tamarit *leuda* cause the merchants" of Barcelona, the Consulado rented and administered this duty in the name of the merchant guild.[33] Similarly, the so-called *leudas* of Tortosa were farmed to the guild for a short time in the fifteenth century; and, finally, the city of Barcelona proposed to extinguish these impositions by retiring the debts secured by the *leudas*, the guild having promised to meet one third of the cost.[34] For the benefit of the merchants of Perpignan, that guild endeavored to abolish the *leuda* imposed in the port of Colliure.[35]

The guilds were frequently at odds with the Generality of Catalonia, which was the authority for collecting the general customs in all Catalonian ports of entry. The hard-pressed deputies of the Generality were accused by the guild of undue interference with shipping and of exacting excessive duties;[36] but the merchant class of Barcelona stood by the industrialists in their fight to maintain the frequent embargoes on foreign cloth which protected the Catalan textile industry. Concern over revenue created, on the whole, antiprotectionist sentiment among the deputies of the Generality.[37]

[33] In 1477 the *leuda* was farmed for a period of twelve years at a cost of £1,350 (ACA, reg. 3391, f. 73); in 1521, 1526, and 1529, annual payments of £72 were made to the Archbishop (IEC, B^a 161-162); and in 1541 the council of twenty voted to lease the duty for three years (IEC, B^a 200, *Deliberacions, 1538-51*).

[34] BAB, No. 41; IEC, B^a 200, *Deliberacions, 1538-51*. It is not certain that the project was realized, since the matter was still being debated in 1593 and 1606 (*Dietari*, VI, 444-49, 489-493, and VIII, 315).

[35] *Llibre de privilegis de consulat de Perpinya*, pp. 122-126.

[36] AM, Barcelona, *Letres closes, 1435-36*, f. 40, 78; *Dietari*, VIII, 120, 132-133, 351-352.

[37] The Catalan Corts prohibited the importation of woolens, silks, and cloth-of-gold in 1422 (*Constitvtions y altres drets de Cathalvnya*, I, 288). In 1452, as on other occasions, the city of Barcelona prohibited by municipal ordinance the sale and *use* of all foreign textiles. The Generality demanded the revocation of these ordinances (ACA, *Dietari*, No. 6, 1456, f. 24, and *Generalidad*, reg. 665, f. 147-149; *Dietari*, II, 102).

"Unquestionably," as Professor Merriman has observed, "the most important products which Barcelona sent abroad were raw wool and manufactured cloths."[38] This conclusion is borne out by the frequency with which the guilds intervened on behalf of merchant-exporters in this trade. Complaints were promptly entered against the embargo on Catalan woolens in Naples and Sicily (1477), and steps were taken to maintain the discriminatory duties which gave Catalans an advantage over French and Genoese cloth merchants. The Barcelona guild secured the ratification of a pragmatic which imposed a tariff of 20 per cent on French textiles entering Sicily;[39] but the Consulado regarded differential duties on Catalan merchants in Genoa, Florence, and Venice as unjust and demanded the same treatment as accorded Italians in Catalonia.[40] Even the Catalan consuls in Sicily were accused of burdening merchants from Barcelona with taxes from which they claimed legal exemption;[41] while the viceroy, according to merchants of the guild, obstructed them in the collection of mercantile debts.[42] Considerable importance attached to the trade with Sicily, since it furnished credits for Barcelona's frequent imports of Sicilian grain.

For the sake of maintaining the quality of Catalan textiles and preventing the substitution of inferior grades in export shipments, the Barcelona guild lent its support to a system of marking which identified the manufacturer and the grade of his cloth.[43] At an early date the Consulado of Majorca attempted to encourage commerce in unfinished cloth. The import embargo on woolens not meeting the standards imposed by the

[38] *Op. cit.*, I, 494. The question of the relative importance of the various Mediterranean centers of the cloth and wool trade has never been satisfactorily explored. An interesting speculation is P. Clément's reference to Barcelona, "whose prosperity [in the fifteenth century] equalled, if it did not surpass, that of Genoa, its implacable rival" (*Jacques Cœur et Charles VII*, Paris, 1873, p. 31).

[39] IEC, B^a 192, f. 128-129 (pragmatic of 1519); B^a 145; *Acorts.* 1480-81; B^a 200, *Deliberacions, 1563-68*; BAB, No. 30; *Rúbriques de Bruniquer*, IV, 11, 90, and V, 189-193. In 1605 the guild protested that Catalan merchants in Sicily were treated as foreigners and forced to pay a duty of 30 per cent (*Dietari*, VIII, 165).

[40] ACA, *Generalidad*, reg. 671, f. 70; Capmany, *Memorias*, IV, 275-276 (1483).

[41] AM, Barcelona, *Letres closes, 1435-36*, f. 60.

[42] IEC, B^a 192, f. 139-140 (1542).   [43] IEC, B^a 192, f. 101.

Majorcan craft guilds was repealed so as to permit the dyeing and finishing for foreign textiles in Majorca. Their re-exportation, however, was mandatory.[44] The Perpignan guild labored to preserve foreign markets by enforcing standards of quality and honest weights for iron products shipped from Roussillon.[45]

Not only in the Mediterranean were Catalan merchants the alleged victims of commercial discrimination, but in the custom-houses of Seville and Cádiz the Consulado vociferated against the treatment of Catalans as foreigners.[46] In 1565, subsequent to the prohibition of imports of Catalan hides into Castile, the Barcelona guild publicly proclaimed the act of union (1479) of Castile and Aragon as a protest against the subjection of Catalan merchants in Castilian cities to the status of aliens.[47] Catalans never secured express permission to trade directly with America before the eighteenth century, and it is amazing that the guilds were so completely passive in regard to this potentially great interest of the merchants of eastern Spain.[48]

Agents of foreign commercial houses were required, after 1471, to register their credentials annually in the offices of the Consulado and to declare the funds of the company they represented and the investment of each of the partners. To protect Barcelona merchants, factors who exceeded their authority were

[44] *Privilegis del Collegi de la Mercadería*, f. 5-6.

[45] *Llibre de privilegis de consulat de Perpinya*, pp. 178-185.

[46] IEC, B^a 200, *Deliberacions, 1563-68*; B^a 199 (1675). The Cortes of 1542 had promised equality with Castilians to Catalans and Valencians trading in the ports of Castile (*Constitvtions y altres drets de Cathalvnya*, I, 294, 296-297).

[47] IEC, B^a 200, *Deliberacions, 1563-68*. Said the council of twenty, "de algun temps en sa en Castella, ço es en Civilla y altres parts, contra forma de la dita concordia [the marriage contract of Ferdinand and Isabella] fassen pagar als Catalans com strangers y veden la treta de les mercaderies."

[48] F. Rahola y Tremols, *Comercio de Cataluña con América en el siglo xviii* (Barcelona, 1931), pp. 12, 191-231. Under royal orders and at considerable expense to the guild, two Barcelona merchants stayed in Madrid from 1629 to 1632, conferring with state officials and other merchants on the means of encouraging commerce. His Majesty related that he had been advised, probably by the Seville guild, that what Spain needed was "el formar compañías de comercio, por la experiencia que se tiene de lo que han adelantado con él la potencia los rebeldes de Olanda" (Capmany, *Memorias*, IV, Appendix, pp. 89-92).

The Consulado was probably instrumental in projecting the Universal Mercantile Company of Catalonia, approved by the Cortes of 1702 (*Constitvtions y altres drets de Cathalunya*, I, 297-298). Political upheavals and Andalusian monopoly prevented the establishment of a trading company in Barcelona until 1755.

held personally liable for losses incurred by the nonfulfillment of contracts.[49]

From the middle of the thirteenth century, Barcelona named the consuls who represented the commercial interests of the city and of Catalonia in many foreign ports.[50] One of the earliest consulates was that of Seville, where, in 1284, the king of Castile promised Catalan cloth merchants the same privileges and exemptions as were enjoyed by the Genoese.[51] Barcelona's councilors discussed problems relating to the foreign consulates with guild officials; and the consuls, who were usually merchants, were appointed and dismissed upon recommendation of the guild. Fourteenth-century regulations for the conduct of the consulate of Alexandria were drawn up by the councilors, "haút sobre aço consell è acord moltes vegades ab los honrats Cónsols de la mar de la Ciutat de Barcelona."[52] Contemporaneously, the Catalan consul in Damascus governed the Syrian consulate on the basis of a formal agreement between him and the Consulado of Barcelona. This compact regulated the consular fees for Catalan merchants trading in Damascus and Beirut, prescribed the consul's duties in assisting merchants at the customhouses, and provided for a priest to say masses for itinerant merchants ("so that they may not have to go to mass at the house of some other consul").[53] The Consulado corresponded with the foreign consulates, as may be seen from letters of the consul in Bruges, urging the guild to intervene in securing the revocation of Flemish commercial laws obnoxious to Catalan merchants.[54] After 1586 exporters to foreign ports in which Catalan consuls resided were required to post bond with the Barcelona guild for the payment of consular dues abroad.[55]

To protect Barcelona merchants from supposedly exorbitant interest rates, particularly on bills of exchange, the Consulado

[49] Capmany, *Apéndice a las Costumbres Marítimas del Libre del Consulado*, pp. 53-55.
[50] Capmany, *Memorias*, II, 32-33, 112-113, 128. The right was confirmed even after the rebellion of Catalonia in 1640 (ACA, Consejo de Aragón, carpeta 1069).
[51] Capmany, *Memorias*, II, 45-49.
[52] *Ibid.*, II, 156-160 (1381), and 233-235 (1437); IV, 251-252 (1459).
[53] *Ibid.*, II, 174-176 (1386).   [54] *Ibid.*, II, 205-207.
[55] *Llibre de Consolat dels fets maritims* (Barcelona, 1645), f. 150-151.

entered into negotiations with ecclesiastical authorities. Thus, in 1606, the council of twenty wrote to the Pope, representing the distress of merchants who, because of the scarcity of money, were forced to pay 30 and even 40 per cent interest. Pointing to at least one mercantile failure involving liabilities of £50,000, the council urged the enforcement of a maximum rate of 10 per cent per annum.[56] At the behest of the city councilors, the Bishop of Barcelona issued an edict in 1623, which authorized a committee of six Christian merchants to fix maximum premiums, "in accordance with the abundance or scarcity of money," on bills drawn for payment at the various fairs.[57] Having protested Barcelona's twenty-four-hour law on the acceptance of bills, the consuls were empowered by the city to enact special rules on acceptance and protest, according to the circumstances of each fair.[58]

Alarmed by the alleged monopoly of the municipal bank (*taula*) of Barcelona, the guild sponsored successful opposition. Amending previous ordinances of the *taula*, "upon the supplication and request of the honorable consuls of the *lotge* of the sea and of the merchants," the city sanctioned the exchange transactions of private money-changers, but only at the rates current in the *taula*.[59] Municipal regulations governing money-changers (1397), as well as Barcelona's bankruptcy laws of 1304 and 1432, were enforced by the Consulado under the authority of the city councilors.[60]

Only one instance is at hand of the guild's attitude toward

[56] IEC, B^a 200, *Deliberacions, 1568-75; 1584-92;* and *1592-96;* Capmany, *Memorias,* IV, 327-328; *Dietari,* VIII, 281. As early as 1481 the Consulado complained that the practice of dry exchange (*cambis fictes e sechs*) had forced rates to inordinate levels (IEC, B^a 145, *Acorts,* f. 54).

[57] *Dietari,* VIII, 263-264, 266, 269, 280-281; Ripoll, *op. cit.,* pp. 172-178; *Llibre de privilegis de consvlat de Perpinya,* Appendix; Capmany, *Memorias,* IV, 333-335.

[58] Capmany, *Memorias,* IV, 311-313 (1577). According to Professor Usher (*op. cit.,* p. 144), "the earliest text [of the true mercantile bill of exchange] now extant in Barcelona is a bill of July 21, 1388." After 1450, cases involving protested bills of exchange were commonly settled in the court of the Consulado (IEC, B^a 198, *Capibrevi protestacionum factarum in curia Consulatu maris civitatis Barchinone*).

[59] *Dietari,* III, 156-161 (1499). An earlier law required the settlement at the bank of all debts in excess of £15 (*Rúbriques de Bruniquer,* II, 427). Usher (*op. cit.,* p. 35) discusses other aspects of the *taula's* attempted monopoly.

[60] Capmany, *Memorias,* II, 191, and IV, 221.

the export of specie. In 1634 the consuls attacked a ruling of the Generality which required foreigners to convert credits arising from imports into exportable goods, expressing the belief that the law was "wholly contrary to free commerce, and, instead of preventing fraud, it would encourage even greater dishonesty."[61] As a remedy for the dearth of money, the council of twenty once recommended the free coinage of gold, so that merchants might take gold to the mint and have it coined into florins like those of Florence and Genoa.[62] It is not certain whether the guild supported the city council, in 1648 and 1649, in proposing embargoes on the importation of "certain exotic wares which are of no utility whatsoever and serve only to extract from this Principality a great supply of *dobles* and other gold and silver money."[63]

The domicile of the guild and the court of the Consulado was the *lonja*, or merchants' exchange building. The municipal government built the first *lonja* of Barcelona;[64] the fifteenth-century *lonja* of Majorca, still a notable landmark of Palma, was erected by the Collegi de la Mercadería.[65] The Valencian *lonja*, commenced before the end of the fifteenth century, was the property of the city;[66] but the *loge* of the Perpignan Consulado was erected by the guild, probably early in the fifteenth century.[67] It made a difference whether the guild or the city owned the exchange building. Endeavoring to reserve the *lonja*

---

[61] *Dietari*, XI, 332-333.   [62] IEC, B*a* 145, *Acorts, 1480-81*.

[63] *Dietari*, XIV, 290, 403-404, 657-660.

[64] The *lonja* was begun toward the end of the fourteenth century, when the councilors realized that "en la Ciutat de Barchelona . . . no ha Lotge convinent ne bona, en la qual los Consols de la mar pusquen tenir Cort, e los Navegants e Mercaders . . . pusquen convenir e tractar e fer lurs contractes e affers" (Capmany, *Memorias*, II, 166, and IV, 97-98, 156; *Rúbriques de Bruniquer*, IV, 6, and V, 185). Improvements and additions to the building were financed by the Consulado as was the eighteenth-century structure, now used as a stock and commodity exchange.

[65] BSAL, I, 2; G. de Jovellanos, *Carta histórica-artística sobre el edificio de la Lonja de Mallorca* (Palma, 1835).

[66] AM, Valencia, *Manual de consells, 1480-82*, f. 192-200; and Lonja nueva, letra E.

[67] Archives Départementales, Pyrénées-Orientales, reg. B. 192; *Llibre de privilegis de consulat de Perpinya*, pp. 72-81. The Consulado of Gerona received permission to build a *lonja* (ACA, reg. 1690, f. 144), but there appear to be no records of its construction.

for mercantile uses, the Consulados of Barcelona and Majorca frequently quarreled with city officials who insisted upon storing grain belonging to the public grain administration in the merchants' business quarters.[68] On the other hand, it was not always easy to make the *lonja* the center of mercantile life. Upon recommendation of the consuls, in 1610 the Majorcan guild ruled that bills of exchange and insurance negotiated outside the *lonja* would be held invalid.[69] From the fifteenth century on the *defenedors* in Majorca and in Barcelona licensed commodity brokers *(corredors d'orella)*, who operated in the exchange, and regulated their fees.[70]

Considerable responsibility rested with the guilds for the provision of public works necessary for the safety of navigation and the encouragement of commerce. The list of such undertakings is long: the outstanding examples are the lighthouses, moles, arsenals, and dry docks which were built, maintained, or supervised by the Consulados of Barcelona and Majorca.[71] In 1492 the municipal government of Majorca surrendered to the guild authority to maintain and enlarge the breakwaters, permitting the *defenedors* to impose the mole duty *(dret de moll)* for this purpose.[72] The city collected an anchorage duty, beginning in 1439, for the maintenance of the moles, but the guild was frequently called upon for subventions. Indeed, the common view was that since the merchant class demanded harbor improvements, the funds should come from the guild treasury rather than from the treasury of the city.[73] Along the coast of

[68] *Dietari*, XI, 68; IEC, B^a 147, *Expedientes; Privilegis del Collegi de la Mercadería*, f. 20-21; BSAL, I, 4-5, and II, No. 32, pp. 10-13.

[69] BSAL, I, 4. Lamented the consuls: "essent [the *lonja*] com es, un edifici tan sumtuos y magnifich, está les mes vegades sol y sens ser freqüentat de mercaders y persones de negoci."

[70] *Privilegis del Collegi de la Mercadería*, f. 18; Capmany, *Memorias*, II, 257-260; A. Pons, *Constitvcions e ordinacions del Regne de Mallorca*, pp. 196-211.

[71] IEC, B^a 200, *Obres en les dressanes;* ACA, reg. 3800, f. 83; IEC, B^a 193, f. 9; *Dietari*, I, 389-390.

[72] ACA, reg. 3627, f. 235; AHM, *Libre del diner del moll* (several volumes of accounts, 1594-1715). The duty was imposed on exports and imports generally at the rate of one penny on the pound. In the seventeenth century the duty was farmed for an average price of about £1,500 per annum.

[73] *Rúbriques de Bruniquer*, IV, 281-295.

Catalonia several lookout stations, or towers, were constructed with subsidies from the guild.[74]

IV

Special duties on commerce financed the many activities of the guilds. In Barcelona, Perpignan, Tortosa, and Valencia the principal consular duty was the *periatge,* first authorized in 1394, "in consideration of the many expenses in the direction and defense of the mercantile art."[75] The *dret de la mercadería* constituted the most important source of income for the Majorcan Consulado. Established as an import and export duty of one penny on the pound of valuation, the tariff rose above this rate while the guild was carrying the heavy burden of the *lonja* indebtedness.[76] Since the Collegi farmed the *dret de la mercadería* almost continuously from 1450 to 1700, the account books[77] do not provide good data for the quantitative study of Majorca's commerce. In 1683 the *defenedors* complained that the guild's revenues were only half of "what they used to be" and that the *lonja* was in a deplorable state of disrepair;[78] but the magnitude of the seventeenth-century depression has not been determined. The Consulado of Perpignan leased the *periatge* to tax farmers in 1498;[79] but no account books pertaining to the revenues of the guilds in Perpignan, Tortosa, and Valencia have been found.

The *periatge* in Barcelona was an ad valorem duty, ranging from .2 per cent to 1.6 per cent, imposed on imports and exports passing through customs.[80] Although extensive accounts of the

[74] IEC, B^a 200, *Deliberacions, 1568-75* (a grant of £200 for a watchtower at Cape Creu and £300 for a similar station near Tortosa); Capmany, *Memorias,* IV, 343 (a grant of £500 "para la construcción de una fortaleza que se mandó fabricar en el cabo del rio Llobregat para defensa de Cosarios").

[75] Capmany, *Memorias,* II, 186-189; ACA, reg. 4322, f. 121; reg. 3152, f. 9; Archivo General del Reino de Valencia, *Bailia General, Letres è privilegis,* LX, f. 914.

[76] *Privilegis del Collegi de la Mercadería,* f. 2-4.

[77] AHM, *Llibre del diner de la mercadería* (several volumes, fifteenth to seventeenth century); *Privilegis del Collegi de la Mercadería,* f. 13.

[78] BSAL, I (Sept., 1885).

[79] *Llibre de privilegis de Consulat de Perpinya,* pp. 168-169.

[80] In 1627 (and probably earlier) the *periatge* was exacted "not only on merchandise and other things transported by sea directly to the port of the said city and im-

receipts and disbursements of the guild's income have been preserved, the data are not complete enough to form the basis of
an index of trade.[81] A few comparisons may be derived from
the data presented in Appendix VI. The annual income varied
widely. In 1433-34 the *periatge* yielded £5,435; in 1449-50,
only £635. The average annual income in the sixteenth century
was not over £3,000, while in the seventeenth century—a period
of rising prices—the yearly income varied from £3,000 to
£9,000.[82] Changes in the rate were responsible for some of the
variations in income; very inadequately, other changes in the
periatge receipts reflect the rise and fall of commercial activity.

The history of the financial administration of the guild
would not be accepted as proof of the business acumen of the
guild officials. Apparently, zealous and honest collectors of the
periatge demanded wages higher than the guild saw fit to pay.
The revenues fell prey to the ubiquitous tax farmer in the seventeenth century,[83] and as early as the fifteenth century the sale of
the guilds' certificates of indebtedness, secured by the anticipated
income of the *periatge*, was a frequent practice.[84] The royal

---

ported into the city through the maritime gate but also on merchandise and things
carried oversea to coastal towns of the Principality of Catalonia beyond the limits
of the said city and shipped overland into this city" (IEC, B*a* 199; *Dietari*, XI,
723-748).

[81] While it is almost certain that the *periatge* was collected from 1401 to 1714,
bating not more than ten years, accounts are available for only seventy-nine years in
this period. The principal documents are: IEC, B*a* 161-175; BAB, Nos. 32-34, 37,
and 41. Disbursements were effected at the *taula*, on orders drawn by the consuls and
the *defenedors*.

[82] Professor Usher indicates the specie equivalent of the Barcelona pound as 69.89
grains of fine gold (*op. cit.*, p. 133). In present gold prices the dutiable exports and
imports of Barcelona in the year 1582-83 were worth about $3,000,000. The guild's
income for this year (£5,040) was considerably above the average for the last half of
the sixteenth century.

[83] IEC, B*a* 200, *Deliberacions, 1584-92*. In 1644 the Consulado leased the duty for
six years for a total payment of £38,160 (*Pro syndico Logiae Maris Barcinonis contra
I. Palleia, et caeteros arrendatarios iuris pariatici*, Barcelona, 1675). The contract
price, which was reduced in leases negotiated after 1644, fell far short of the income
realized by the guild from direct administration of the *periatge* in the last decade of
the century.

[84] The evidences of debt were *censualia mortua*, or perpetual obligations similar to
rentes, which were negotiated on the basis of income. Thus, a bid of £20,000 for an
annual income of £1,000 indicated the investor's demand for a yield of 5 per cent.
They were ordinarily redeemable at the discretion of the issuer.

letters missive, which authorized borrowing, stipulated the maximum amount of the loan and sometimes fixed the interest rate.[85] At times the guilds of Barcelona and Majorca found all of their income absorbed by interest on outstanding obligations, and default followed unsuccessful efforts to borrow for the sake of meeting interest charges.[86] In 1597, its credit standing improved, the Consulado of Barcelona refunded £5,000 of obligations bearing interest at the rate of 5 per cent into 3.33 per cent certificates of indebtedness.[87]

The guilds frequently imposed duties of a temporary character, such as the so-called "manifest duty" used to defray the expenses of sending warnings and advice to merchant ships at

[85] Documents of this nature are abundant. The following deal with borrowing by the guilds of Barcelona and Perpignan: BAB, No. 32; ACA, reg. 2622, f. 16; reg. 3146, f. 123; reg. 3372, f. 11; reg. 3391, f. 73; reg. 3467, f. 11; reg. 3800, f. 83; reg. 3801, f. 66; reg. 3804, f. 27; reg. 3807, f. 86 and 91; reg. 3809, f. 135; reg. 5501, f. 60; IEC, B^a 148; Capmany, *Memorias*, IV, 282-283. The dates are 1448 to 1597.

[86] IEC, B^a 170; BSAL, III, 145-146. The Barcelona plague of 1502 retarded commerce and reduced the *periatge* income, forcing the guild to borrow £600 to meet interest charges (Capmany, *Memorias*, IV, 295-296). In 1657 it was discovered that one of the *defenedors* had made false entries on the *periatge* books and had embezzled sums which should have been paid to owners of the guild's bonds (Ripoll, *op. cit.*, pp. 254-255).

[87] The transaction—a typical one—was authorized in the following words: "Nos Laurentius Suarez . . . Consiliarius locumtenens et capitaneus generalis in Principatu Cathalonia . . . Pro parte vestrorum dilectorum et fidelium regiorum consulum, deffinitorum et consiliariis Logiae maris praesentis civitatis Barchinone fuit nobis expositum et deductum quod dicta Logia maris Barchinone facit et praestat ac facere et praestare tenetur singulis annis diversis creditoribus quam plurima censualia quaequidem consules et diffinitores . . . praeteritis temporibus pro subveniendo aliquibus necessitatibus eo tunch occurentibus manulevarunt ac super bonis, redditibus et juribus eiusdem incarricaverunt ad forum vigintiquinque mille solidorum praedictis pro mille solidis annuae pensionis pro quibus luendis et integre redimendis manulevare cupitis et intenditis quinque mille libras dictae monetae *ad alium commodiorum et utiliorem forum*, nempe triginta mille solidorum praedictis pro mille solidis dictae annuae pensionis si per nos vobis dictis nominibus licentia concedatur et indulgeatur . . . Tenore igitur presentium . . . licentiam liberam et facultatem plenariam impartimur vobis dictis consulibus . . . possitis et valeatis quibusvis universitatibus, comunitatibus, corporibus, collegiis et singularibus personis venere ac super bonis dictae Logiae maris onerare et incarricare unum vel plura censualia mortua usque ad summam seu quantitatem dictarum quinque mille librarum . . . ad forum videlicet seu rationem triginta mille solidorum praedictis pro mille solidis annuae pensionis . . ." (IEC, B^a 148). In 1477 the guild refunded 7.1 per cent *censals* into 5 per cent obligations (Capmany, *Memorias*, IV, 268-270).

sea or lying at anchor in distant ports.[88] One of the privileges
recorded in the archives of the Consulado of Barcelona bears
the caption, "Provision made by the Queen in favor of the
power of the consuls of the sea to impose duties in Flanders and
in any part of the world."[89] Sometime before 1434 the guild
imposed a duty of one *grossi* in the pound (about .4 per cent)
on goods exported to or imported from Flanders by Aragonese
subjects. It was payable to the Catalan consul in Bruges for the
account of the Consulado of Barcelona. Resisting the attempt
of the Consulado of Majorca to secure its removal, the Barcelona guild was sustained in its right to collect this tariff, which
was levied similarly in other regions where Aragonese merchants traded.[90]

No small part of the financial difficulty of the guilds arose
from the frequent call upon the merchant class for services to
the state, both in peacetime and in time of war. Births, deaths,
and marriages in the royal family had little to do with Catalan
commerce, but they adversely affected the budget of the Consulado. In 1554, to cite one of the many cases of wartime emer-
gency, Charles V called upon Barcelona for "certain pieces of
artillery." The guild (according to its own statement) furnished
"a very large piece of bronze, weighing 120 quintals, identical
and equal in weight to those which the city, the deputation of
the Generality, and the *cabildo* offered."[91] In April, 1639, the

[88] IEC, B*a* 161; B*a* 200, *Deliberacions, 1552-73*; BAB, No. 41. The Barcelona
Consulado was regularly in touch, by letter and by special courier, with Majorca and
the towns along the coast from Perpignan to Valencia.

[89] IEC, B*a* 192, f. 58. The hyperbole of official language is commonplace; needless to say, neither local nor regional authority was subordinate to that of any guild
of merchants. When the consuls wished to impose a tariff in Tarragona, they had to
secure the permission of the Archbishop: "Una regonexança feta per los Consols de la
Llotja de la mar de Barcinona al Archebispo don Enigo de que los havia graciosament
concedida licencia per cullir un dret y subsidi se era imposat per sustentacio de una
galera feta pera guardar les mars de la costa de Catalunya contra los moros cossaris
tant quant a dit Archebispo plauria" (Archivo Histórico-arzodiocesano de Tarragona,
Index, f. 642).

[90] ACA, reg. 3244, f. 95-96; IEC, B*a* 192, f. 60; Capmany, *Memorias*, IV, 226;
BAB, No. 33. The last reference deals with the receipts of £139 by the Barcelona
guild—proceeds of the sale of pepper in which the consular duty in Alexandria had
been invested.

[91] Capmany, *Memorias*, IV, 343. In 1462 the council of twenty appropriated
£1,100 for the pay of one hundred infantrymen "per acompanyar la bandera de la

crown called upon the Barcelona guild for an advance of 50,000 ducats, "until the arrival of the next fleet" from the Indies.[92] As late as 1712 the Consulado made a "donatiu gracios y voluntari per las urgencias de la guerra," but at the conclusion of hostilities Philip V robbed the guild of many of its privileges.[93]

How often the guild's advances to the sovereign were really voluntary is a moot question. The merchants of Majorca were protected from forced loans by the charter of 1409; but the degree of protection may have been slight, since "a serious war or evident famine, from which the kingdom may stand in danger of ruin," was considered an exceptional circumstance.[94]

Expenditures for religious observances and civic celebrations figured largely in the budgets of some of the guilds. For a long time the Consulado of Barcelona increased the *periatge* in order to support services in the chapel adjoining the *lonja*.[95] As administrator of the estates of wealthy merchants, this guild controlled sums, probably never large, dedicated to the succor of poor merchants, dowries for the daughters of indigent merchants, ransom for persons held by pirates, and other charitable purposes.[96] The many donations of the Collegi of Majorca to the cathedral and to convents and sundry charities imply a degree of opulence the existence of which is questionable.[97] Of course, it is not necessary to assume that when the merchants

---

Ciutat" (BAB, No. 29) and in 1683 voted subsidies of 80,000 *reals* for the defense of Catalonia (IEC, B*a* 192, f. 153-168).

[92] Capmany, *Memorias*, IV, Appendix, p. 87.

[93] IEC, B*a* 170.

[94] *Privilegis del Collegi de la Mercadería*, f. 2. In 1449 the crown ratified the following article proposed by the Collegi: "Que alguns del dit Collegi per alguna causa é rao no puxen esser forçats contra llur voluntat comprar censals sobre la Ciutat" (*ibid.*, f. 10).

[95] IEC, B*a* 200, *Deliberacions, 1584-92;* E. Moliné y Brasés, *Les Costums Maritimes de Barcelona*, pp. 348-349. The services were partially endowed by a pious navigator, Pere de Montcada, "almirall de las mars del Senyor Rey," who directed in his will, "que cascun any sie celebrat per anima sua cert Aniversari, e comprats certs draps de que sien vestits cert nombre de Pobres signantment mariners del Linatge de aquells qui ell havía sentenciats a mort" (*Rúbriques de Bruniquer*, IV, 15).

[96] IEC, B*a* 191, frontispiece; Campaner, *Cronicon mayoricense*, p. 171.

[97] BSAL, III, 145-146. The guild gave £1,000 to the Capuchin monks to enable them to carry on their suit at the Vatican for the establishment of their order in Majorca to the exclusion of the Franciscans.

paid the cost of a new altar or the salary of a priest, they were employing financial mathematics to prospective celestial residence. How often the guild rose above the primary consideration of business profits, it is impossible to say. Certainly, the major portion of its energy and resources was directed toward securing the privileged status of the merchant class and the protection of the gains of trade.

Memorializing the crown in 1702 and pointing out some of its services to the kings of Aragon in the three centuries of its existence, the guild of Barcelona asserted that it was endowed "with many and extraordinary exemptions, prerogatives, and immunities," and that "there is no proof that in any of the far-flung realms and principalities of Your Majesty, or in any others, the merchants who reside in them have greater authority than have those matriculated in the *lonja del mar*" of Barcelona.[98] This was scarcely an exaggeration.

[98] Capmany, *Memorias*, IV, 340-341.

CHAPTER V

THE GUILDS IN THE NORTHERN PORTS

I

Ferdinand and Isabella thought that the establishment of the Burgos and Bilbao Consulados would encourage the merchants of northern Spain to exploit more fully the long-established wool trade, "as one of the obvious means of adjusting their foreign obligations."[1] Exportation of Spanish wool to England began as early as the twelfth century, and in the following centuries England, Flanders, and France regularly imported the fine Castilian wools. The sheep raisers, incorporated in the politically powerful guild of the Honorable Assembly of the Mesta, secured national legislation which created vested interests in the grazing lands and sheepwalks from Old Castile to Andalusia. "The energies of the Mesta leaders," according to Klein, "had been concentrated more and more, toward the close of the fifteenth century, upon the necessity of expanding the overseas wool trade."[2]

The marketing organization comprised not only the producers but also middlemen, bankers, wool merchants, and the shipping interests which handled the wool exports. Normally, the wool was prepared for market in some interior town, was sold to merchants and exporters at the fairs, particularly that of Medina del Campo, and was carried overland in sacks for shipment from the Biscayan ports. The mercantile class insisted fully as much as the grazers upon the necessity of maintaining foreign markets, and the predominant employment of capital in the export trade may have affected adversely the development of the domestic woolen industry.[3]

[1] Julius Klein, *The Mesta*, p. 38.   [2] *Ibid.*, pp. 36-37.
[3] In an effort to encourage domestic manufactures, in 1462 Castile prohibited the exportation of more than two thirds of the annual wool clip. Charles V endeavored to lower the maximum exportable percentage to one half, but met with such vigorous protests from the Mesta and from the Burgos Consulado that he desisted (*ibid.*, p. 36).

In the absence of even theoretical interest in laissez faire and simple competition, the control and regulation of marketing and shipping were important issues in regional and local politics and a bone of contention among various private business groups. The founding of the Burgos Consulado served to accentuate the violent disagreement between Burgos and Bilbao over their respective rights in the dispatching *(afletar)* of the wool ships. Bilbao possessed the advantage of a sheltered river port, which encouraged shipbuilding and navigation, but the town was largely dependent upon the Castilian hinterland for export goods. Although more than a hundred miles from the nearest port, history, location with reference to the grazing regions, and royal favoritism made Burgos the most important wool depot, with a merchant class specializing in the purchase of the clip from Castilian grazers and the preparation and financing of wool for export. Until late in the fifteenth century the organization of shipping all along the Cantabrian coast tended to be subordinated to the demands of the Burgos exporters. However, the natural advantages of Bilbao, coupled with a nascent trade in iron manufactures (especially anchors, cables, and nails), weakened the hegemony of the Castilian city; and before 1500 a considerable amount of Burgos capital seems to have migrated to Bilbao.[4]

The conflict had its repercussion, and possibly some of its origins, in Flanders, where "Spanish" merchants were differentiated from traders of "the coast of Spain," i.e., of Biscaya and Guipúzcoa. Following a quarrel between the Basques and the Castilians over the use of a chapel, separate guilds and consulates for the two groups of merchants in Bruges were established about the middle of the fifteenth century.[5] In 1465 the two "nations" entered into an agreement regarding the division

---

[4] T. Guiard y Larrauri, *Historia del Consulado y Casa de Contratación de Bilbao,* I, 11. The voluminous transcriptions of documents serve to make Sr. Guiard's history valuable reference material and an excellent guide to sources.

[5] AC, Bilbao, *Reg. 1 de memoriales, y representaciones,* No. 1; AM, Bilbao, *cajón* 14, reg. 2, No. 6; García de Quevedo, *op. cit.,* p. 27; Guiard, *op. cit.,* I, xliv-xlix. Castilian merchants elected the four "cónsules de la nación de España"; Basque and Guipuscoan merchants chose the four "cónsules de la costa de España y de Vizcaya," in accordance with a royal decree of 1455.

of duties on goods imported into Flanders in Spanish ships, under which the Castilian consulate received about two thirds of the revenues. But in 1493 the city of Bruges granted to the Nación de Vizcaya certain trading rights and exemptions which were not shared by Castilian merchants.[6] Resentment over the steady rise of Bilbao's commerce inspired Burgos to push its claims for the establishment of the Consulado in the Castilian capital.

Prior to 1494, municipal ordinances prohibited exports from Bilbao or any port of Old Castile, Biscaya, or Guipúzcoa except in ships chartered by the merchant guild of Bilbao.[7] But, under the terms of its first privilege, the Consulado of Burgos secured the right to charter vessels sailing from all the northern ports, including those of Biscaya and Guipúzcoa, provided the prior and consuls notified the wool merchants of Segovia, Vitoria, Logroño, Valladolid, and Medina de Rioseco of the time and place of sailing. The pragmatic of 1494 did not clearly grant the Burgos guild a monopoly, but little doubt existed of Burgos' ambition to acquire exclusive control of the wool transport. The bitter complaints of merchants in Alava, Biscaya, and Guipúzcoa forced revisions of the Burgos charter in 1495 and 1496. Ostensibly, Burgos and Bilbao thereafter were to enjoy equal rights in regulating shipping, but the causes of friction between the two cities and guilds were not eliminated.

The compact of 1499 between the Consulado of Burgos and the merchant guild of Bilbao[8] was the first of a series of written agreements by which the two commercial rivals attempted to settle their differences. The Burgos guild received the exclusive right to charter the wool ships for Flanders, Nantes, La Rochelle, and England. The wool ships for Flanders were to form

[6] Guiard, op. cit., I, xlix-lvi.

[7] AM, Bilbao, ca. 14, reg. 4, No. 1; Guiard, op. cit., I, lxxxiii-lxxxviii. Cartas de afletamiento y averías are reproduced in Guiard, op. cit., I, 68-84. The principal part of the contract, which was signed by the ship's owner, or master, and officials of the guild, concerned the payment of export duties (averías) to the guild. The guild verified the master's bills of lading and approved, and sometimes fixed, the freight rate for each shipment.

[8] AC, Burgos, leg. 139; reproduced in Guiard, op. cit., I, 16-19. See also Larruga, Memorias, XXVIII, 197 ff.

one annual fleet. (Early in the sixteenth century, two annual fleets were customary.) The prior and consuls of Burgos were authorized to select all the ships comprising the fleet, although they were bound to choose some bottoms from Bilbao. Officials of the Bilbao guild took charge of the freightment of iron *(hierros y aceros)*, reserving one third of the tonnage for the merchants of Burgos. Both guilds had authority to fix freightage on the chartered vessels.[9]

Although the agreement of 1499 was to remain in force for twenty-five years, its application was almost immediately a fresh source of trouble. In 1505 the Bilbao guild complained that Burgos was striving to boycott Bilbao's shippers, and on two occasions the crown issued feeble orders to the Burgos guild to desist from monopolistic practices.[10] The petition for the establishment of an independent Consulado in Bilbao was in part a protest against the jurisdiction claimed by Burgos over shipping in Bilbao's port. However, in 1512, a year after he consented to the erection of the Bilbao Consulado, the king granted new privileges to the Burgos guild, placing in the hands of the Castilian merchants a virtual monopoly over wool shipments from every northern port between Fuenterrabia (east of San Sebastián) and Corunna.[11]

This serious threat to Basque shipping prompted the Bilbao guild to acquiesce in nearly all the terms proposed by Burgos as conditions of a new commercial accord. In 1513 the two guilds signed an agreement, similar to that of 1499, which remained in force for twenty years and was prorogued in 1533 for a period of twenty-five years.[12] Shortly after 1533 new dissensions arose. The arrogance and obstinacy of the Bilbao Consulado, it is said, thwarted all efforts to adjust the differences; but in 1553 a new pact was consummated. Bilbao surrendered to

[9] So far as this agreement was concerned, the jurisdiction of the Burgos guild and its right to impose consular duties extended to the merchants of Santander, Laredo, Logroño, Segovia, Valladolid, and Medina de Rioseco; similarly, Bilbao's jurisdiction comprehended Alava, Guipúzcoa, Vitoria, and all of Biscaya.

[10] AM, Bilbao, ca. 1, reg. 2, No. 62 (1505 and 1511).

[11] *Cédula* of Jan. 31, 1512, in the Ordinances of 1538, caps. 34-35.

[12] AM, Bilbao, ca. 14, reg. 2, No. 2; AC, Burgos, leg. 139; Guiard, *op. cit.*, I, 24-26.

the Burgos guild the right to charter the wool ships, while the merchants of Burgos agreed to place one half of their wool shipments on vessels belonging to natives of Bilbao.[13] The arrangement did not produce a lasting peace; but the decadence of Burgos, which set in before the end of the century, made further negotiations of this nature supererogatory. What remained of the wool trade in the seventeenth century was almost entirely handled by the merchants of Bilbao. Burgos was probably clutching at a straw in those sections of the Ordinances of 1572 which deal with the chartering of wool ships.[14] Most extraordinary was the proposal of the municipality and guild, in 1625, to make Burgos the sole port of entry for all foreign trade to the Biscayan coast.[15]

García de Quevedo found that 119 merchants were present in the guild assembly of December 22, 1535; but only eight merchants, constituting a majority of the guild membership, attended the general assembly in 1661.[16] From April, 1567, to January, 1569, over 1,000 marine insurance policies were registered in the Consulado, and the policies for twelve months ordinarily filled a register of 1,000 pages. Only one register was used for all the policies issued between 1594 and 1619.[17] It is difficult to believe that Burgos had only 823 householders (vecinos), including clergymen and widows, in 1616;[18] but its almost complete loss of commercial importance is undeniable. Nor did any of the measures adopted by the guild, the municipality, or the central government succeed in reviving the city during the seventeenth century.

[13] Guiard, op. cit., I, 27-28; García de Quevedo, op. cit., p. 69.

[14] Ordinances of 1572, caps. 36-39. Under penalty of 2 doblas a sack of wool, members of the guild were prohibited from exporting wool except in ships chartered by the prior and consuls. As late as 1617 the crown approved an arrangement between the guilds of Burgos and Bilbao, whereby the Burgos Consulado agreed to give up certain rights to intervene in the administration of averías in Bilbao, provided the Bilbao guild would collect the duty on goods belonging to members of the Burgos guild at one half of the customary rate (Guiard, op. cit., I, 298-301). Another agreement was projected in 1653 (AC, Bilbao, Reg. 1 de escrituras, No. 2).

[15] Academia de la Historia (Madrid), Est. 20, gr. 3ᵃ, No. 29.

[16] García de Quevedo, op. cit., pp. 56, 96.

[17] AC, Burgos, legs. 37-44, 60-61, 66; García de Quevedo, op. cit., pp. 83-84.

[18] Larruga, op. cit., XXVIII, 124. A contemporary document reported a population of "mas de 5000 vecinos" about 1550 (García de Quevedo, op. cit., p. 77).

From very early times much of the prosperity of Burgos was bound up with the success of the biennial fairs in Medina del Campo, but the fairs lost ground rapidly after the middle of the sixteenth century. The Consulados of Burgos and Seville were called upon to recommend measures for their revival, and various panaceas were tried. In 1583 the crown increased the number of fairs to three a year, and enjoined the settlement at Medina del Campo of all bills of exchange payable during the one hundred days' duration of the fairs.[19] In 1601 the crown transferred the ancient fairs of Medina del Campo to the Castilian capital, granting the prior and consuls of the guild authority to examine the credentials of merchants and to issue licenses for trading. Four fairs a year were planned, and the guild was empowered to fix the terms of payment and interest rates on bills of exchange negotiated at each fair.[20] In a few years the fairs were restored to Medina del Campo. As in the sixteenth century, repeated moratoria on payments and prorogation of the fairs, at the order of the crown and sometimes at the insistence of the guild, discredited the fairs and the commercial reputation of Burgos.

In a memorial to the crown, published in 1616,[21] the city proposed new panaceas: to compel foreign merchants to bring all imported wares directly to Burgos; to prohibit all merchants from trading with foreigners in the ports of Biscaya and Guipúzcoa, in order to prevent the export of money; to establish a customhouse in Burgos; and to place all trade under complete jurisdiction of the Burgos Consulado. Finally, in 1673, Burgos petitioned unsuccessfully for the organization of an "emporio, estanco, y feria de las lanas" in the Castilian city for the exclusive trade in wool exported through Cantabrian ports.[22] The

---

[19] AGS, Diversos de Castilla, leg. 48-15; AM, Bilbao, ca. 2, reg. 1, No. 14.

[20] García de Quevedo, *op. cit.*, pp. 86-95. Actually, the first fair was not held until March, 1602. See also C. Espejo and J. Paz, *Las antiguas ferias de Medina del Campo*, esp. pp. 281-317.

[21] Reproduced in Larruga, *op. cit.*, XXVIII, 123-135.

[22] Guiard, *op. cit.*, I, 517. Cf. also AM, ca. 15, reg. 21, No. 14, "Dos memoriales dispuestos a nombre de este Señorío y villa, para presentar a su Mag. en razon del Comerzio de lanas que intentaba la ciudad de Burgos fuese a la villa de Santander" (*ca.* 1726). Material in Larruga, *op. cit.*, XXVII, 290-321, and XXVIII, 1-76, in-

economist and finance minister, Francisco Centani, sided with the guild and city in supporting the idea of a wool staple in Burgos. It was held out as a remedy for the unconscionably low prices which foreigners paid for Spanish wool and as a means of preventing the export of specie, declining tax revenues, poverty, and several other social and economic ills.[23] When the fairs were returned to Medina, new ordinances provided that a prior and consul elected by merchants present at each fair should constitute a tribunal for hearing commercial complaints arising during the fair. This Consulado, or fair-court, thus seems to have replaced the Consulado of Burgos in one of the spheres of its long-established jurisdiction.

II

The Burgos-Bilbao rift was but one segment of a wider economic conflict involving (1) merchant-shippers who desired to purchase carrying services and warehouse and harbor facilities on the most advantageous terms, and (2) the maritime interests in the towns along the Biscayan coast whose prosperity largely depended upon the volume of goods passing through their harbors. At times the merchants of Burgos appear to have been successful in playing off one port against another. Thus, as early as 1453 the Burgos guild contracted with the city of Santander to secure preferential treatment for Burgos merchants in wool shipments from that port.[24] A century later (1547) the guild signed an agreement with the town of Portugalete (below Bilbao, at the mouth of the Nervión River), stipulating the conditions under which Burgos merchants would export their wool through the port of Portugalete in preference to Bilbao.[25] The Burgos guild enjoyed the right to supervise the administration of customs duties, with the understanding that the duty of 1 *maravedí* a sack on exported wool and the tax of 1 ducat on each departing ship would be devoted to the maintenance of the

cludes proposed bylaws for a company to be formed by the Consulado for the "gobernación de dicho estanco y ferias."

[23] Larruga, *op. cit.*, XXVII, 297-300.

[24] García de Quevedo, *op. cit.*, pp. 39-40.

[25] AM, Bilbao, ca. 38, reg. 6, No. 61; AC, Bilbao, *Reg. 1 de Escrituras*, No. 1.

mole. Burgos promised that one half of the wool exported to
Flanders would go on ships belonging to residents of Portugalete. Little advantage could have been gained by Burgos from
this contract, since the harbor of Portugalete was incommodious
and Bilbao was usually successful in challenging the jurisdiction
of Portugalete over shipping from the estuary of the Nervión.[26]
The city of Santander and the Burgos guild signed a similar
compact in 1564.[27] In return for favorable treatment in the
matter of tolls and promises to maintain the roads over which
the wool traveled to Santander, the Burgos merchants agreed
to use ships of natives of Santander for one quarter of their
shipments from that port. Tantalizing as were the attempts to
attract or force Bilbao's trade to other ports, the guild usually
withstood the competition and political skulduggery of Bilbao's
commercial rivals.[28]

Less successful were the efforts of the guild to stem the
rising tide of taxes on the Biscayan traffic in wool and iron.
Although Bilbao claimed exemption, under the *fueros* of Biscaya, from royal duties on exports of iron, the crown levied such
tariffs, at least as early as 1629, and in 1692 increased the specific
duties 100 per cent.[29] After several increases, by 1667 the royal
duties on wool exports consisted of the following tariffs:

(1) two ad valorem duties amounting to 11½ per cent;
(2) three tariffs totaling 6 *reals* silver per *arroba*; and
(3) a tariff of 4 ducats per 10 *arrobas*.

Both the merchant guild and the Mesta protested vigorously, not
only against the burden of the duties, which were said to be
almost equivalent to the value of the commodity taxed, but also

---

[26] Guiard, *op. cit.*, I, 64-67, 336-338. Bilbao and Portugalete entered into an
agreement in 1585, whereby the river port was permitted to charter two vessels for
every one sailing from Portugalete.

[27] AM, Santander, leg. 3, No. 55; García de Quevedo, *op. cit.*, p. 71.

[28] Bilbao was successful, in 1666, in preventing merchants from using Vitoria as
an inland port *(puerto seco)* for the payment of wool duties prior to shipment from
San Sebastián (Guiard, *op. cit.*, I, 517). At the instance of town and guild, the crown
likewise denied the petition of the seacoast town of Castro Urdiales for permission to
establish a depot for wool exports (AC, Bilbao, *Reg. 1 de facultades reales*, No. 2;
Guiard, *op. cit.*, I, 301-302).

[29] Guiard, *op. cit.*, I, 346-347, 522-523.

against the excessive meddling and delays arising from the administration of the wool tariffs by tax farmers.[30] But the chronic bankruptcy of the Hapsburgs, as much as the "ruthless shortsightedness" of royal officials and tax farmers, underlay the policies which resulted in "taxing the wool trade practically out of existence."[31]

Navigation acts generally met with the approval of the Burgos guild. In line with legislation then effective in Castile, the charter of the Consulado prohibited the prior and consuls from contracting for the use of foreign vessels whenever Spanish bottoms were available.[32] Bilbao, heavily dependent upon imports of foodstuffs, appreciated that some assurance of return freight was needed to attract foreign imports in the desired volume. When native ships were idle, presumably because of the competition of foreigners, the guild clamored for the enforcement of restrictions on foreign shipping.[33] But in 1528 the Biscayan government induced the crown to repeal a law which prohibited the use of Portuguese ships when native bottoms were available;[34] and, upon recommendation of the guild, foreign ships were permitted to export iron up to the value of their inward freight receipts.[35] An arrangement between the Consulado of Bilbao and Portugalete (1573) permitted the chartering of French ships on terms only slightly less favorable than those applicable to Basque merchantmen.[36]

Upon the insistence of the Burgos guild, which complained of a dearth of large ships, the *cédula* of January 31, 1512, authorized the Consulado to restrict the shipment of one half of the exports from the northern ports to vessels of two hundred

---

[30] In 1627 the 10 per cent (ad valorem) duty on wool exports was farmed for 18,800,000 *maravedís* (one half in silver, one half in vellon), and the duty of 4 ducats per 10 *arrobas*, for 28,900,000 *m.* (*Assiento del Licenciado García de Yllan*, Madrid, 1627). See AM, Bilbao, ca. 12, reg. 8, No. 165, and reg. 10, No. 202.

[31] Klein, *op. cit.*, p. 46.

[32] Several navigation acts (e.g., 1499) laid down an absolute prohibition against exporting in foreign ships; but their inobservance was almost chronic (AM, Bilbao, ca. 4, reg. 4, No. 192).

[33] AM, Bilbao, ca. 37, reg. 17, No. 113 (1541); AC, Bilbao, reg. 1, ca. 3, No. 25 (1609).   [34] Guiard, *op. cit.*, I, 130-131.

[35] AC, Bilbao, reg. 1, ca. 3, Nos. 8 and 29 (1588-1619).

[36] Guiard, *op. cit.*, I, 33-34.

tons *(toneles)* or more.[37] The guild alleged that a period of peace had encouraged the use of small ships, making it difficult to organize the wool fleets. It is doubtful that this law had a significant effect on shipbuilding. Of profounder influence on the practices of the industry were the physical conditions of harbors and rivers where vessels plied. The agreement between the Bilbao guild and Portugalete (1573) stipulated that only ships of from thirty to sixty tons should be used in trade with Nantes, since it had been learned by experience that larger vessels were unable to navigate the channel of the Loire River.[38] Rising prices and a prolonged period of business uncertainty, according to the Consulado of Bilbao, deterred the employment of capital in the building of large ships; and with laws discriminating against the use of small vessels, shipbuilding was at a standstill at the opening of the seventeenth century.[39]

In a measure the guilds shared the prevailing distrust of foreign merchants and foreign ships as media for the unlawful export of money. As early as 1477, municipal ordinances of Bilbao charged the guild with the responsibility of registering the imports and licensing the exports of all foreigners, in order to prevent the drain of "gold and silver and coined money."[40] But circumstances forced Bilbao to welcome a considerable traffic with foreigners, especially in time of a dearth of provisions, and the guild strenuously resisted the attempts of Burgos to secure more stringent laws on the residence and business relations of foreigners along the Basque coast.[41] In the seventeenth century the Consulado was instrumental in securing royal licenses for continuing trade with certain French ports during periods of war between Spain and France.[42] Apparently, only jealousy of the prerogatives of the guild-court and fear of a possible loss of revenue from port services prompted the Consulado to oppose

[37] Ordinances of Burgos, 1538, cap. 34.

[38] Guiard, *op. cit.*, I, 33.

[39] AC, Bilbao, reg. 1, ca. 3, No. 21; AM, Bilbao, ca. 14, reg. 2, No. 6 (1607-1652).   [40] Guiard, *op. cit.*, I, lxxxiv.

[41] *Ibid.*, I, 295-298. Burgos insisted that foreign merchants should be compelled to live at least "20 leagues inland" (Larruga, *op. cit.*, XXVIII, 128-132).

[42] Guiard, *op. cit.*, I, 385.

the establishment of English, Dutch, and French consulates in
Bilbao.[43]

Early in the sixteenth century the crown established an office
of registry in Biscaya to administer the laws against the export
of money, horses, cattle, and other proscribed goods. Foreign
traders were ordinarily required to post bond to the effect that
they would export in "fruits of the land" the equivalent in value
of merchandise imported by them.[44] The Bilbao guild violently
opposed the administration, if not the principle, of these statutes.
The excesses of the royal officials and the unequal enforcement
of the laws in different ports caused Bilbao to lose trade at the
expense of her neighbors.[45] The office of the contraband judge
(juez de sacas) entailed certain emoluments for notarial services; and, in 1641, the guild was able to eliminate some vexatious
practices by purchasing the notaryship at a cost of 6,000 ducats.[46]

Strenuous measures were also taken by the Consulado of
Bilbao to curb the excesses of the Commissioner of the Inquisi-
tion (Santo Oficio). The principal function of this guardian of
public morals was to inspect imports in search of proscribed
literature. Not content with thorough examination, the commissioner habitually delayed the unloading of cargoes and demanded fees in contravention of orders from the Tribunal de la
Inquisición. Eventually, the guild found it expedient to pay the
commissioner a "retainer" of 50 ducats a year and to agree to
a fixed schedule of moderate fees to be imposed on goods subject to inspection.[47]

[43] Ibid., I, 304-311.
[44] AC, Bilbao, Reg. 1 de pragmaticas reales: Premática en que se amplia la ley
diez, libro sexto, título diez y ocho de la Nueva Recopilación, que trata, que el dinero
que procediere de las mercaderias, que entran en estos Reynos de fuera dellos, se
emplee en otras de los naturales (Madrid, 1626).
[45] AM, Bilbao, ca. 2, reg. 1, No. 2 (1514); Guiard, op. cit., I, 47-50. Foreign
ships, advised of their strict enforcement in Bilbao, avoided this port and went to San
Sebastián or "otros puertos de mayor libertad."
[46] AC, Bilbao, reg. 1, ca. 3, No. 39; Guiard, op. cit., I, 266-274, 282-284.
[47] AC, Bilbao, Reg. 1 de escrituras, No. 13; AM, Bilbao, ca. 4, reg. 4, Nos. 188-
189; ca. 12, reg. 10, No. 203: El muy noble . . . Señorío de Vizcaya, villa de Bilbao,
y su Casa de Contratación, representan las razones . . . en orden a que se reconzca el
modo irregular, y escandaloso de que ha vsado, y usa Don Domingo de Leguina,
Comissario nombrado por el Santo oficio . . . (Bilbao, n.d.); Guiard, op. cit., I, 1,
45-47, 288-295.

Piracy and reprisal continued through the sixteenth and seventeenth centuries to exact their toll on legitimate commerce. One of the normal expenses of the Consulado of Burgos, according to the Ordinances of 1538 (cap. 21), was the cost of recovering ships illegally seized. The Bilbao guild not only took legal action to recover such property, but on one occasion ransomed a vessel captured by French pirates.[48] It was the duty of the prior and consuls, who maintained intelligence with foreign ports, to warn shipping of the presence of corsairs; and not infrequently the guild provided convoys.[49] As in the Middle Ages, the most efficacious measures consisted of arming vessels to capture or destroy the pirate ships; and to a limited extent the guilds of Burgos and Bilbao co-operated in such enterprises. Even though chartered under the authority of the crown, the cost of arming vessels to attack pirates most often fell directly on the merchants who paid the *averías* for this and other purposes of their guilds.[50] The Consulado of Bilbao also contributed to the military defense of the town when invasions by land were feared, as in 1590.[51]

III

Of paramount importance to the successful regulation of overseas shipping was the establishment of rules for the insurance of vessels and cargoes. The drafting and the enforcement of insurance laws were almost exclusively prerogatives of the Consulados of Burgos and Bilbao. The insurance laws of Burgos, drawn up with the advice and approval of the most experienced merchants of the guild, comprise forty-two chapters of the Ordinances of 1538. The statutes prescribed the exact form for policies on merchandise,[52] and required the registration of

[48] AC, Bilbao, *Reg. 1 de cuentas* (1561); Guiard, *op. cit.*, I, 37 (1556).

[49] Guiard, *op. cit.*, I, 248, 262-265.

[50] AC, Bilbao, reg. 1, ca. 7; Guiard, *op. cit.*, I, 37-38. In 1691 the Consulado received permission to borrow money for the purpose of chasing French pirates from the coast; but the guild did not go through with the venture, alleging that the enemy ships were too numerous (AC, *Reg. 1 de facultades reales*, No. 3).

[51] Guiard, *op. cit.*, I, 37-40.

[52] Ordinances of 1538, cap. 48. A revised form adopted in 1542 is reproduced in García de Quevedo, *op. cit.*, p. 236; and a printed contract form used in 1553 is in AC, Bilbao, *Reg. 1 de Ordenanzas*, ca. 18. Ten volumes of registries of policies from 1565-1616 are preserved in the Archivo Consular, Burgos.

all contracts before a notary of the Consulado. The insurer, whose risk could not exceed 90 per cent of the value of the goods insured, was bound to honor claims upon the demand of the insured, although the latter might be required to furnish bond "to render justice to the insurers, in the presence of the prior and consuls." Other articles of the 1538 laws deal with the valuation of goods, contributions of insurers in case of jettison, and the time limit for paying premiums.

The insurance laws in the Ordinances of 1572 set forth variations of the general policy which should apply to insurance in the American trade. They also include the official form of policies for the insurance of bottoms *(casco de nao)* and rules for the insurance of slaves on the voyage from Africa to America.[53] It is most significant, however, that the new laws permitted the prior and consuls to fix maximum premiums, which they might increase or decrease "according to the changes of circumstances."[54]

Bilbao's first marine insurance laws were drafted by the *fiel* and *diputados* and a committee of captains, masters, and merchants elected in the assembly of the guild. Although ratified by the guild in 1520, presumably they failed to secure royal confirmation.[55] Almost two thirds of the ordinances approved in 1560 deal with maritime risks and insurance. A declared purpose of the statutes was to obviate the "great variety" of policy forms and contracts in order to lessen litigation. The ordinances prescribed separate policy forms for the insurance of merchandise and of hulls. Maximum legal coverage on bottoms was limited to 80 per cent, because of the conviction of guild officials that complete coverage encouraged negligence in the shipping of goods and in the management of ships at sea. The terms under which the ship, and its freight receipts *(fletes)*, the cargo, and the insurers had to contribute under the general average *(avería gruesa)* rule, were set forth in great detail. Heavy

---

[53] Slaves were insured as merchandise. As the ordinary policy would not cover loss from the spoiling of perishable commodities, so the insurance of a slave would not cover death from natural causes, nor from injuries inflicted by other slaves.

[54] Ordinances of 1572, caps. 43-85.

[55] Reproduced in Guiard, *op. cit.*, I, 579-582.

penalties were established for infraction of the ordinances. Thus, a fine of 100 ducats was fixed for insuring subsequent to the loss of goods on which insurance was sought. Anyone who falsely reported the loss of a ship in order to collect a claim had to return the sum thus collected and pay a fine of one thirtieth of the amount. The guild's treasury received one third of the fine.[56]

Excepting insurance policies, the bill of exchange was the most important mercantile instrument whose use the guild found it expedient to regulate. The Bilbao Ordinances of 1560 (cap. 74) are limited to the observation that bills of exchange should have the force and prestige of public documents. In the course of the seventeenth century a plethora of disputes in the Consulado brought forth a special ordinance on bills of exchange in 1672.[57] Bills negotiated in Bilbao, or payable therein, had to be protested for nonpayment within twenty days after maturity. The payee might then either return the bill to the maker or take action against the acceptor. In either case the creditor received the amount of the debt with interest at the rate of .5 per cent monthly from the maturity date of the bill.

Disputes persisted, and a new law on bills of exchange came out in 1677.[58] This limited the number of days within which the payee had to present the bill for acceptance. By an ordinance of 1688 the guild adopted a statute of limitations with respect to domestic drafts.[59]

Among the expressed objectives of the foundation of the Burgos Consulado was the establishment of more effective jurisdiction over the foreign agents, or factors, of merchants residing in Spain. The charter of the Consulado made it mandatory for

---

[56] Ordinances of 1572, caps. 23-71. It is significant that a party condemned by the prior and consuls to pay an insurance claim might not enter notice of appeal until he had paid the claim (cap. 53).

[57] *Hordenança, hecha por la Casa de la Contratación, . . . que trata en raçon de los pagamentos, y protestos de letras . . .* (Bilbao, 1691).

[58] *Hordenança, hecha por la Casa de la Contratación, . . . Por la qual se añadieron diferentes declaraciones de los terminos de los pagamentos, y protestos de letras, que se dan en esta Villa para las partes de Castilla, y otras de estos Reynos de España, a la ordenança antecedente, del año de 1669* (Bilbao, 1691).

[59] *Ordenanza de la Casa de Contratación, . . . que trata en razon de vales, y libranzas . . .* (Bilbao, 1691), cap. 1.

all factors to return to Burgos and render an accounting to their principals and to submit to the jurisdiction of the prior and consuls, regardless of their usual place of residence. The provision was reinforced through the ratification (1494) by the Commune of Bruges of certain articles proposed by the Spanish consulate in the Flemish town, including the provision that "Spaniards who acquire citizenship in Bruges, or marry there, shall continue to be obligated to return to Spain and render their accounts, and if they refuse, the consuls of our Nation [Castile] shall have authority to imprison them."[60] In 1526 the king of France authorized the prior and consuls of Burgos to apprehend on French territory the factors of Burgos merchants, provided they did not possess French naturalization papers.[61] Spanish consuls in Flanders were similarly required to present their *avería* accounts during the fairs at Medina del Campo for audit by the prior and consuls of Burgos and four other Spanish merchants.[62]

IV

Trade promotion in its many ramifications was perhaps the most constant function of the prior and consuls, excepting only their judicial duties.[63] Toward the close of the sixteenth century Bilbao spent certain sums in Nantes and elsewhere, "so that the commerce of this town [Bilbao] would not go to San Sebastián or Laredo, as it had commenced to go."[64] What manner of persuasion was employed does not appear. Both Burgos and Bilbao were justly concerned with the reputation of Spanish wool in foreign markets and drew up ordinances to control the quality of the commodity. About 1535, however, the complaints multiplied that the wool was "mixed with dirt and oil and trash."[65]

In vain the Consulado of Bilbao endeavored to secure permission for direct trade with the New World, especially after

[60] García de Quevedo, *op. cit.*, pp. 44-45.

[61] Larruga, *op. cit.*, XXVIII, 213-214.

[62] *Cédula* of July 21, 1494, establishing the Burgos Consulado.

[63] The document reproduced in Appendix V illustrates the ordinary and extraordinary duties incumbent upon the principal guild officials.

[64] Guiard, *op. cit.*, I, 56. [65] *Ibid.*, I, 122-123.

the independence of Portugal prevented the Basques from using Lisbon as an entrepôt for American trade. In 1646 the guild sent emissaries to the General Assembly of the Señorío of Biscaya, urging the Assembly to petition the crown for sanction of direct shipping from Bilbao to Buenos Aires. If such a petition ever reached the ears of His Majesty, he did not receive it with favor; but the Dutch and English continued to bring Spanish colonial products to Biscaya.[66] In 1668 the Queen corresponded with the guild concerning the formation of a Spanish Company of Armed Commerce, but intrigues at Court killed this project, and the Basque merchants obtained no important privileges in the American trade until the formation of the Caracas Company in 1728.[67]

Through the instrumentality of the Consulado the merchants and shipowners of Bilbao and Burgos planned, constructed, superintended, and paid for virtually all of the improvements and aids to navigation in the port of Bilbao and the approaches thereto. Frequently, legal arrangements for the use of public and private property had to be made by agencies of government; but the chief burden of projecting and financing these improvements rested upon the guilds.

As early as 1502, experts employed by the Consulado of Burgos reported the necessity of changing the course of the river or constructing a canal in order to reduce the swiftness of the current and prevent the silting of the bar near Portugalete.[68] The Bilbao guild, intermittently with financial aid from the Burgos Consulado, carried through the recommended work, and throughout the sixteenth century spent large sums on the river and canal. An employee of the Bilbao Consulado was assigned to prevent the unloading of sand ballast where it would obstruct navigation. The guild also employed an inspector (*veedor*) of ballast for outgoing ships to prevent short-weighting and overcharging for lastage purchased by foreign ships.[69]

[66] *Ibid.*, I, 445-450.
[67] AC, Bilbao, *Reg. 1 de cartas órdenes*, No. 5; Guiard, *op. cit.*, I, 246; R. D. Hussey, *The Caracas Company, 1728-1784* (Cambridge, Mass., 1934), pp. 20-64.
[68] Guiard, *op. cit.*, I, 102-103 (reproducing part of a technical report); AM, Bilbao, ca. 12, reg. 10, No. 201; AC, Bilbao, reg. 1, ca. 3, Nos. 33-34.
[69] Guiard, *op. cit.*, I, 356.

A large share of the moles at the mouth of the river were constructed and kept in repair by the Bilbao guild, which received financial support from the Burgos guild and the town of Bilbao. The repair and replacement of the breakwaters, piers, and quays were a constant preoccupation of the Consulado, especially following the rather severe inundations of the valley of the Nervión. Control of the bar below Portugalete was a particularly difficult problem. Although vessels of six and seven hundred tons appear to have passed the bar with ease, early in the seventeenth century vessels of eight hundred tons found the crossing dangerous. The depth of the deepest channel was then from 8 to 10 *codos* or 14.5 to 18 feet, approximately, at high tide.[70] Regular soundings were made by the *piloto mayor*, an official of the guild.

The difficulty of crossing the bar virtually forced every ship bound for Bilbao to demand a pilot before entering the port. When the Consulado found that inexperienced individuals, claiming to be pilots, were responsible for the loss of several ships, guild officials drew up ordinances for the examination and licensing of pilots. After 1562 no one was permitted to pilot a ship across the bar or take the vessel up the river to Bilbao unless he possessed the pilot's certificate issued by the Consulado.[71] Though licensed, a pilot who ran a ship aground or caused it to founder was liable to imprisonment and criminal action.[72] Pilots and other functionaries who assisted in the mooring and docking of ships collected fees regulated by the guild.[73]

[70] AM, Bilbao, ca. 37, reg. 6, No. 62, "Capitulado con el Prior y Consules de Burgos sobre la Barra de Portugalete y fábrica de muelles" (1558); Guiard, *op. cit.*, I, 103-107, 348-355.

[71] AC, Bilbao, *Reg. 2 de Ordenanzas*, No. 8 (pilotage ordinances approved by the crown in 1562). The ordinances and specimen *títulos de piloto* are reproduced in Guiard, *op. cit.*, I, 59-61, 326-331, 571-574, from the originals in AC, Bilbao, C. 1, reg. 12, Nos. 1-262.

[72] *Ordenanza de la Casa de Contratación . . . que trata en razon de vales . . .*, cap. 3. In 1663 the *piloto mayor* and other pilots were responsible for running four ships on the bar. Four persons were drowned, and the losses amounted to 200,000 *pesos* (Guiard, *op. cit.*, I, 363).

[73] AC, Bilbao, *Reg. 1 de escrituras*, No. 63: *Memoria de los derechos que se estilan, y acostumbran pagar a los pilotos de la Barra de Portugalete, y a los maestres de chalupas, por la entrada, y salida de los navios . . . conforme a un auto de buen govierno, proveido por los señores Prior, y Consules de la Universidad, y Casa de Contratación de esta Villa, en quinze de Septiembre del año de 1685* (Bilbao, 1691).

Mainly to prevent pillage, the prior and consuls, immediately upon the receipt of news of a disaster in the port or along the coast near Portugalete, were required to hasten to the scene and take charge of all property.[74] The naval equipment owned by the Consulado and employed in the emergencies of shipping included cables and rigging, and other auxiliary stores. The guild maintained a quarantine storehouse *(lazareto)* near Portugalete for the deposit of goods coming from plague-ridden countries, notably England.[75]

In the seventeenth century the Bilbao Consulado made substantial contributions to the improvement of the wagon roads leading into Bilbao. As a condition of such grants, the guild negotiated with neighboring towns for relief from transit tolls for cargoes of wool and provisions en route to Bilbao.[76]

The home of the Consulado was the Casa de Contratación or *lonja*. The Consulado of Burgos owned a *lonja* and apparently leased several smaller buildings as the business of the guild increased.[77] The first Casa de Contratación of Bilbao, erected about 1515 on the Plaza Mayor, was demolished as a result of the flood of 1593. It was rebuilt a few years later; but after the destructive flood of 1651 the town and guild erected a new edifice for the joint use of the two corporations. An inventory of the furnishings, works of art, and ornaments in the quarters of the guild suggests liberal patronage of the arts as well as considerable affluence in some periods of the guild's history.[78]

"More noteworthy and unusual than all these faculties and distinctions, without doubt, is that which from remote times the Consulado possessed of performing the duties of Postmaster-General *(Correo mayor)* and, as such, of dispatching letters."[79]

[74] *Ordenanza de la Casa de Contratación . . . que trata en razon de vales . . . ,* cap. 4.   [75] Guiard, *op. cit.,* I, 107-108, 363-364.

[76] AM, Bilbao, ca. 14, reg. 2, No. 8; ca. 14, reg. 15, No. 1, "Escritura de acuerdo y capitulación entre Bilbao, su Casa de Contratación, y la ciudad de Orduña" (1681).   [77] García de Quevedo, *op. cit.,* pp. 56-57.

[78] AC, Bilbao, *Reg. 1 de títulos de pertenencia,* No. 1; AM, Bilbao, ca. 14, reg. 2, No. 10, "Tasación y valuación que hicieron maestres peritos de el sitio y materiales de la Casa perteneciente a la Universidad y Casa de Contratación" (1676); Guiard, *op. cit.,* I, 235-240, 550-554.   [79] García de Quevedo, *op. cit.,* p. 76.

The privilege extended only to the correspondence of members of the Burgos guild;[80] but it involved the Consulado in litigation with Raimundo de Tassis, who claimed to have a royal monopoly of all postal services. Finally, the guild paid De Tassis about 2,000 ducats for the waiver of his claim.[81] Similarly, in Bilbao the guild purchased the office of Correo mayor from the De Tassis family, and the Casa de Contratación served as a post office for guildsmen and business houses. The carrying of letters was ordinarily accomplished by private parties under contract to the guild, which subsidized some routes for the sake of promoting trade.[82]

From time to time the crown found the merchant guilds convenient instruments for anticipating or supplying the deficiencies of royal revenues. When Charles V was preparing to make war on France (1543) he asked the Consulado of Burgos for a loan of 70,000 ducats, a sum so large that the merchants responded with considerable reluctance and delay.[83] The Bilbao guild was held responsible for raising 2,000 ducats, or one sixth of a forced loan imposed on the town of Bilbao for the support of a royal armada in 1631;[84] but, by and large, the regional statutes, or *fueros*, of Vizcaya estopped forced loans as well as other impositions of the Spanish crown.

Duty to God and to the poor was not a trifling burden on the mind of the prior and the purse of the guild. The corporation paid for the masses which were ordinarily a prerequisite of a guild assembly for elections. Among the alms and offerings required annually of the Burgos Consulado were: four *fanegas* of wheat, four *cántaras* of wine, and two sheep for the Monastery of St. Francis in Burgos; identical offerings for each of nine other monasteries and convents; two *fanegas* of wheat, two *cántaras* of wine, and one sheep for poor convicts in the city jail.[85]

[80] Ordinances of 1572, cap. 16.   [81] AC, Burgos, legs. 149 and 154.

[82] Guiard, *op. cit.*, I, 108-110, 367-369.

[83] Larruga, *op. cit.*, XXVIII, 212; García de Quevedo, *op. cit.*, p. 54.

[84] AC, Bilbao, *Reg. 5 de cuentas*, No. 34.

[85] Ordinances of 1538, cap. 4. The religious institutions also received donations of "fish and sardines" from the guild during Lent. Alms in kind were later com-

Among the religious works supported by the Consulado of Bilbao was the Church of San Antón, where the guild had its private chapel. Several other religious and charitable foundations received support from the guild.[86]

V

Tariffs and other levies on trade and commerce provided the guilds with financial resources. From "time immemorial"—not always a long time in Spanish thought—the Burgos guild levied duties on the trade of its members. Not all of the guildsmen paid without protest, but in 1514 guild officials secured a royal decree confirming their right to impose duties and closing the courts to suits over exemptions claimed by members of the guild.[87] The schedule of duties was published in the Ordinances of 1538. Most of the rates were specific duties on the exports and imports of Burgos merchants; about fifty dutiable commodities were enumerated. Naturally, the most important levy was the duty on wool exports. Every sack of wool for Flanders paid 2 *dineros de gruesos*, equivalent to 10 *maravedís*; a sack of wool exported to any other region paid 12½ *maravedís*. Normally, the wool duties were collected by agents of the guild in foreign ports and remitted to Burgos in bills of exchange.[88]

The rates were generally higher under the Burgos Ordinances of 1572. The diminished wool trade had increased, rather than decreased, guild expenses, according to the framers of the new statutes. In an effort to produce more revenue, the duty on wool shipped to Flanders was increased to 15 *maravedís* a sack.[89] Only one book of accounts (1625-1701) has been pre-

muted to money payments, total contributions of 150 ducats being specified in the Ordinances of 1572, cap. 3. This was more than the combined salaries of the prior and consuls.

[86] Guiard, *op. cit.*, I, 555-560. According to Guiard, the Consulado gave something to the city for the support of educational institutions, and in 1595 "trató de instalar por sí un colegio de doctrina y gramática, y para este efecto se tuvo correspondencia con el doctor Larragan, de Alcalá de Henares" (*op. cit.*, I, 240). In the eighteenth century the Consulado supported an ambitious program of technical education for the youth of Bilbao.

[87] Ordinances of 1538, cap. 21.   [88] *Ibid.*, cap. 22.

[89] Ordinances of 1572, cap. 28. The ordinances signalize the duty of the Spanish consuls in Flanders, described as "inferiors de esta Universidad," to proceed against agents of the guild who were remiss in forwarding the wool duties to Burgos.

served, and it bears witness to the almost complete cessation of revenue-producing activity during the seventeenth century.[90]

The Bilbao guild likewise enjoyed the "ancient" privilege of taxing commerce for the support of its work in protecting and encouraging trade and navigation. Ordinances approved in 1518 permitted the Consulado to impose a bottomry duty of one-half *maravedí* a ton on vessels clearing Bilbao and specific duties on wool, iron, and other exports and imports. Both foreign and native merchants paid the duties of the Bilbao guild.[91]

The monies collected by the Bilbao guild were commonly referred to as the *averías*; but not all of the various *averías* were duties, strictly speaking. In its original sense, *avería* meant damage or, by extension, compensation for damages incurred in connection with the transporting of goods by sea. Specific payments for certain conventional port services were included in the *averías* collected on outgoing shipping.[92] The *averías* imposed on incoming vessels and their cargoes included sums collected by the guild for the benefit of the master; that is, charges levied on the shippers to reimburse the master for certain expenses incurred in sailing from a foreign port and for damages and losses suffered en route to Bilbao. In accordance with the ordinances of the Consulado, the owners of the ship as well as the shippers and insurers might be held responsible for contributions under the rules of general average *(avería gruesa)*.[93]

---

[90] AC, Burgos, leg. 72; García de Quevedo, *op. cit.*, p. 94.

[91] Guiard, *op. cit.*, I, 575-579; AC, Bilbao, reg. 1, ca. 3, No. 5. The export duties were paid by the ship's master at the Casa de Contratación in Bilbao, and the master was reimbursed by agents of the shippers upon delivery of the goods.

[92] *Cartas de afletamiento y averías* in the sixteenth century regularly specify the exaction of *averías* "por sebo [tallow], mangas [wind-sails?], y chapas [metal plates?], y claos [nails] y baxada de la ribera y leman y piloto de la salida de la barra y *otras aberias ordinarias y acostumbradas.*"

[93] Guiard, *op. cit.*, I, 84-101, 338-350. The following is a typical entry showing the *averías* allowed the master: "Al maestre se le dieron 267 reales por sus averías que hizo en la ribera de Nantes a la salida conforme el padron que truxo hasta entrar en la barra de Portugalete en esta manera: 12 R. las misas de Santa Clara; 28 rs. por el padron; 33 rs. por los derechos de la probostad, carta de afletamiento y obligación; 120 rs. por el pillotaje de la ribera de Nantes, cebo, y mangas y una gabarra que tuvo para alijar en la dicha ribera; 60 rs. por el pillotaje y dos pinacas que tomo en la barra de Portugalete; 8 rs. por las nuevas y traer de las cartas; 6 rs. por el barco de la visita de Santo Oficio" (AC, Bilbao, *Reg. 3 de cuentas*).

The amount allowable for the *avería gruesa* was determined by appraisers, ap-

Frequently, temporary duties were approved for extraordinary expenses of the guild;[94] but by the end of the sixteenth century the principal *avería* for the support of guild activities became an ad valorem duty of 1 *maravedí* on each ducat (375 *maravedís*) of valuation. Throughout the seventeenth century the gross income from this duty was prorated among the various functions and beneficiaries of the guild. The scheme of distribution effective in 1658 was as follows:[95]

Objects	Proportion of total revenues
Religion and charity	
Santos y pobres*	1/16
San Antón†	1 per cent
Improvements and promotion	
Caminos y ribera‡	1/16
Universidad¶	about 72 per cent
Emoluments	
Prior and consuls	1/12
Treasurer	1/48
Secretary	1/48
Overseer *(andador)*	1/48

* *Santos y pobres:* for poor relief, masses, relief of shipwrecked sailors, especially those robbed by pirates, and poor merchants. Relief of foreign seamen robbed at sea appears constantly in the accounts after 1600 (Guiard, *op. cit.*, I, 252-253).

† San Antón: Besides the chapel, the guild maintained the burial ground for foreign seamen in this parish (Guiard, *op. cit.*, I, 93).

‡ *Caminos y ribera:* improvements on roads, harbor, and moles.

¶ *Universidad:* general purposes of the guild.

---

pointed by the guild, thus: "al navio *Santa Ana* . . . procedente de La Rochela, se le dieron de sus averías además de lo usual lo tasado de su pérdida en el temporal que corrió, es a saber, sal arrojada al mar (moderado su valor en cien rs.), un cable (tasado en ciento diez rs.), un barco (idem en ciento cuarenta y cinco), una barrica de vino y dos fustes vacíos (veinte)" (Guiard, *op. cit.*, I, 340).

[94] Guiard, *op. cit.*, I, 91-92. An *avería extraordinaria* was imposed in 1535 in order to raise 9,000 ducats for removing the sandbank at Portugalete, and during the last half of the seventeenth century an extraordinary duty of 1 *real* in the ducat was levied for the purpose of dredging the river channel (AC, Bilbao, *Reg. 10 de cuentas*).

[95] AC, Bilbao, *Reg. 7 de cuentas*. Here is a typical entry: "En la Casa de la Contratación desta billa de Bilbao a 29 de agosto de 1612. El capitan San Joan de Fano, Fiel y Pera Fernandez del Campo y Joan de Belarro, Consules de la dicha Universidad contaron las averías del nabio nombrado la Maria de San Vicente, maestre Min de Campana que vino de Terranova con pescado bacallao y pago 60 Reales que se reparten en esta manera: Dinero de Dios, 10 maravedís; Santos y pobres, 127 m.;

Sixteenth-century account books are rare,[96] but records showing the income of the guild are complete for the seventeenth
century with the exception of one year. That the figures reveal
anything more than a general picture of the commercial activity
of the port of Bilbao may well be doubted. Officials of the
guild admitted that they took no pains to verify the declared
values of dutiable merchandise; probably the income from a
few specific duties was included in the entries for the ordinary
avería, which was an ad valorem duty of about .26 per cent; and
the seventeenth century was a period of monetary disorder and
inflation. For these reasons, the yearly fluctuations in the revenues of the guild furnish a decidedly weak index of trade.
However, the following comparisons may be of some value.

In the six fiscal years between 1590 and 1596 the Consulado's average annual income was about 607,000 *maravedís*.
In the first twenty-five years of the next century the receipts
from the ordinary *avería* averaged approximately 565,000
maravedís per annum. For twenty-four of the twenty-five years
between 1626 and 1651 the average yearly income was 725,000
maravedís; and in the twenty-six year period, 1651-77, the
revenues averaged 1,850,000 *maravedís* a year. In the last
quarter century, 1677-1701, the average annual income of the
guild was about 2,555,000 *maravedís*.[97]

Hardly a vigorously thriving town in this century of Spanish
decadence, Bilbao, nevertheless, continued to be actively engaged
in maritime commerce. Another proof of its failure to reach the
nadir experienced by other commercial centers of the Peninsula
may be found in the records of the *dinero de Dios* duty, a trifling
tariff (for charitable purposes) of 10 *maravedís* on each vessel
entering and clearing the port of Bilbao. Some obvious errors
have crept into the accounts, exemptions were not rare, and the

Universidad, 1,041 m., Caminos y beneficio de Ria, 127 m.; Papel y tinta, 190 m.,
Thesorero y registro, 190 m., Diligencias en beneficio de la Casa, 253 m.; Persona de
Portugalete, 34 m.; Andador, 51 m.; Sant Anton, 17 m."

[96] Apparently the guild's income for 1562-63 was 154,230 *maravedís*; for
1563-64, 297,259 *m.*; and for 1564-65, 293,410 *m.* (AC, Bilbao, *Reg. 1 de cuentas*,
Nos. 1-11).

[97] AC, Bilbao, *Registros 1-11 de cuentas de averías*.

rate was halved for a short period; but the minimum number
of ships which paid the *dinero de Dios,* calculated as one tenth
of the receipts in *maravedís,* furnish additional evidence of the
volume of Bilbao's shipping in the seventeenth century. On the
average, 209 vessels per annum paid the duty from 1601 to
1626; in the period 1626-51, the number was only 184 per
annum; in the next quarter century the figure rose to an annual
average of 211; and in the last twenty-five year period, the
average number of ships paying the duty was 213.[98]

The demise of Hapsburg rule created only a brief period of
transition in the Señorío of Biscaya, and the commercial institutions of Bilbao, unlike those of eastern cities, were virtually un-
affected. The relative prosperity of the town continued into the
eighteenth century, and within a few years the guild discovered
the need for a complete revision of the sixteenth- and seventeenth-century consular ordinances. After several years of study
and drafting on the part of committees appointed by the guild,
the ordinances were submitted to the crown. The approval of
the Bilbao Ordinances of 1737 was a landmark in the development of Spanish commercial law equal in importance to the
appearance and acceptance of the medieval *Llibre del Consolat
de Mar* and the adoption of the national commercial code of
1829.[99]

[98] AC, Bilbao, *Registros 1-11 de cuentas.* In 1643 the Consulado claimed that
more than seventy ships a year put in at Bilbao exclusively for wool cargoes (Guiard,
op. cit., I, 514).

[99] T. Guiard Larrauri, M. Torres López, and A. Elías y Suárez, *Las Ordenanzas
del Consulado de Bilbao* (Bilbao, 1931).

CHAPTER VI

THE SEVILLE GUILD AND AMERICAN TRADE

I

Agitation for the establishment of the guild[1] in Seville began as early as 1525. Reasons for opposing an Andalusian commercial organization similar to the existing guilds of Burgos and Bilbao are not apparent. Eventually, increasing dependence upon the merchants of Seville for support of the naval services incident to trade with the Indies compelled the crown to grant the request of the Cargadores a las Indias. In June, 1543, the Comercio de Sevilla petitioned for the organization of a convoyed trade fleet,[2] which promised to necessitate large expenditures for ships and armaments; and in August of that year the merchants received permission to incorporate as a guild. The rapid growth of commerce with the New World and an increase in litigation beyond the ability of the Casa de Contratación to adjudicate[3] with the dispatch desired by merchants furnished important motives for establishing the guild-court.[4]

II

By steps which are generally familiar to students of Spanish history, Seville became practically the exclusive emporium for the American trade and the House of Trade, the chief instru-

---

[1] Universidad de los Cargadores a las Indias was the corporate name of the guild, but it was commonly referred to as the Comercio de Sevilla as well as the Consulado. The word gremio was seldom used (R. de I., libro ix, título ix, ley xxiv).

[2] C. Fernández Duro, Armada española, I, 430; C. H. Haring, Trade and Navigation between Spain and the Indies, p. 71.

[3] Since 1511 the jueces oficiales of the Casa had determined cases on freight, insurance, partnerships, contracts, and commissions, "sumariamente sin sigura de juicio, solamente la verdad sabida," observing the procedure of the Consulado of Burgos (Colección de documentos inéditos relativos al descubrimiento, conquista y organización de las antiguas posesiones españoles de Ultramar [hereinafter cited as Documentos de Ultramar], V, 305-306).

[4] J. de Solórzano Pereyra, Política indiana, libro vi, cap. xiv, 22-23; Veitia Linage, Norte de la contratación de las Indias occidentales, libro i, cap. xvii, 1-3; R. de I., 9.6.1.

ment for the state regulation of commerce, navigation, and emigration. Whether the river port fell heir to this royal favor by design or by chance,[5] the result was to create vested interests whose dislodgment required almost two centuries. In 1529 the colonial trade was opened to the principal Spanish ports,[6] although ships departing from these points had to return directly to Seville. Despite the onerous terms of this privilege, which discouraged most of the towns from attempting to enter the American trade, the Seville guild brought about the revocation of the law in 1573, having convinced the crown that Biscayan ships returned surreptitiously by way of Portugal and evaded the payment of Spanish customs.[7] In 1667, when Málaga again sought permission to trade directly with America, the contentions of the Seville guild that such a privilege would encourage interloping, permit exports to enemies in time of war, and defraud the treasury were complacently accepted by the king.[8]

Cádiz never ceased to insist upon its superior fitness as a terminus for the overseas trade. Concessions, chief of which was the erection of the Juzgado de Indias in 1535,[9] permitting limited exportation from Cádiz, were wrested from the crown in the sixteenth century. The increasing tonnage of ships em-

[5] The ease of defending an inland port was an important desideratum. On the other hand, Seville was chosen "not because of superior maritime facilities, for Cádiz had much the better harbor, but probably because Seville happened to be the wealthiest and most populous city of Castile" (Haring, *op. cit.*, pp. 7-8).

[6] Excepting those within the Crown of Aragon. The ports habilitated were Corunna, Bayona, Avilés, Laredo, Bilbao, San Sebastián, Cartagena, Málaga, and Cádiz (R. Antúnez y Acevedo, *Memorias históricas sobre la legislación y gobierno del comercio*, Appendix, pp. i-v).

[7] AHN, *Cedulario índico*, 36-69-48; Antúnez, *op. cit.*, Appendix, pp. vi-ix; G. de Artíñano, *Historia del comercio con las Indias*, pp. 62, 77. Legally, ships from other ports might join the Indies fleet in Seville or Cádiz; but the guild recommended the vessels to be licensed for the voyage to America and fixed tonnage quotas (*R. de I.*, 9.35.2).

[8] Antúnez, *op. cit.*, Appendix, pp. ix-xvii. It was frankly admitted that the reason for not granting a similar request from Gibraltar was "el no enflaquecer las flotas, y causar a la Universidad de los Cargadores de esta ciudad [Seville] el perjuicio de disminuirle su comercio y contratación."

[9] Removed to San Lúcar de Barrameda in 1666, the Juzgado was restored to Cádiz in 1679 in return for a tribute of 80,250 *escudos* (BM, 1323.k.14.31; *R. de I.*, Vol. III [1774 ed.], f. 161-162). Commerce originating in either Cádiz or San Lúcar was still subject to the "ordenanzas y leyes" of the Seville Consulado (*ibid.*, 9.5.20).

ployed in colonial trade, rendering the Guadalquivir River hazardous to navigation, perhaps contributed more than any other factor to the impairment of the Sevillan shipping monopoly. Furthermore, the silting of the bar facing San Lúcar de Barrameda served both to handicap access to the river and to forestall the transfer of the Andalusian privileges to San Lúcar, the natural seaport of Seville.[10] After 1680 American transports were required to make Cádiz the beginning and the end of the transatlantic voyage,[11] and in 1717 the Casa de Contratación was permanently removed to the Atlantic seaport. For years the merchants of Seville intrigued, mostly in vain, to throttle the Cádiz trade and to restore the American commercial monopoly to its sixteenth-century fountainhead.[12]

While Spain and Portugal were united, the crown, "adopting the selfish views of the Consulado of Andalusia," consistently excluded the Portuguese from trade with America;[13] but the guild's petition to apply the policy of exclusion to native-born sons of non-Spanish subjects was apparently unheeded.[14] Intercolonial trade considered prejudicial to mercantile interests of Seville was generally interdicted. When, under guise of

[10] AM, Cádiz, *Reales órdenes i papeles sobre la conservación del comercio en Cádiz*; BPC, *Papeles escriptas del comercio de Cádiz y Sevilla*; BM, C. 62.i.18 (95), *Por parte de la ciudad de Cádiz, informando . . . de las conveniencias y utilidades que se seguiran de despachar en su puerto y bahia las armadas y flotas*; *Representación al Rey . . . que haze . . . la muy noble ciudad de San Lúcar de Barrameda, sobre desvanecer los obices que vulgarmente suponer para la entrada de las armadas*; A. Girard, *La rivalité commerciale et maritime entre Séville et Cadix*.

[11] Sevillan shippers, however, retained the right to employ two thirds of the tonnage in the American trade (Antúnez, *op. cit.*, pp. 6-10).

[12] BM, 1323.k.15 (1-9); *Memorial de la civtat de Sevilla . . . expresando los grandes perjuizios que a los intereses de su Magestad y a la causa publica se siguen residir en Cádiz la Casa de la Contratación, el Consulado. . . .*

[13] G. Scelle, "The Slave-Trade in the Spanish Colonies," *American Journal of International Law*, IV, 621. In 1589 the guild complained that twenty-one Portuguese ships entering Tierra Firme were destroying the market for Spanish goods entering with the fleet. The guild demanded the confiscation of Portuguese wares and their reshipment to Spain (AHN, *Cedulario índico*, 35-71-85). The same exclusive attitude was taken by the guild in opposition to the establishment of a trading company permitting Flemish subjects of the Spanish crown to traffic in Hispaniola and Puerto Rico (R. D. Hussey, "Antecedents of the Spanish Monopolistic Overseas Trading Companies," *The Hispanic American Historical Review*, IX, 15-18).

[14] BM, 1324.i.11 (6); 1323.k.15 (32), *Explicación de la vltima determinación del Real y Supremo Consejo de las Indias, en el pleyto entre el Comercio de España, y los hijos de estrangeros, nacidos en estos dominios*; Haring, *op. cit.*, p. 108.

provisioning the province of Rio de la Plata, imports into Buenos Aires were reshipped to Peru, "with grave harm and prejudice to the commerce of Seville," a customhouse was erected at Tucumán and a 50 per cent duty imposed on goods entered at Buenos Aires for re-export to Peru.[15] Numerous prohibitions curbed the trade of the Philippines with the American colonies, principally for the sake of protecting the merchants of Seville from the competition of Asiatic textiles.[16]

It was an open secret that merchants of the guild habitually trafficked with foreigners in Seville, acting as intermediaries for the shipment of exotic wares to the colonies and furnishing channels for the exodus of treasure brought back from the Indies. Primarily because of this lucrative arrangement, the Andalusian exporters supported the national policy of excluding aliens from direct commerce with America. The *navios de permiso* from the Canaries were repeatedly denounced by the guild, since foreign merchants were patently using the islands as an entrepôt for illegal trade with the Spanish Indies.[17] The Consulado, in fine, subscribed to the current opinion in the seventeenth century that the decadence of Spanish economy was attributable to interloping, which the government had been powerless or unwilling to check.[18] But, in their undoubted eagerness to maintain monopolistic advantages in supplying European goods to America, the guild merchants invited the competition of more aggressive traders. Frantic efforts to bolster the monopoly by limiting the volume of legal exports served only to increase the incentive for foreign competition.

[15] *R. de I.*, 8.14.1, 10, 12; Antúnez, *op. cit.*, pp. 122-125; Haring, *op. cit.*, pp. 142-143. Because Peruvian treasure crossed the Andes and made its way to interlopers in Buenos Aires, in 1659 the Seville guild urged closing this fine port (E. J. Hamilton, *American Treasure and the Price Revolution in Spain*, p. 36, n. 1).

[16] BM, 1323.k.14 (28); M. Colmeiro, *Historia de la economía política en España* (Madrid, 1863), II, 405-406; E. J. Hamilton, "Spanish Mercantilism before 1700," in *Facts and Factors in Economic History* (Cambridge, Mass., 1932), p. 238; Haring, *op. cit.*, pp. 145-147.

[17] *R. de I.*, 9.30.23; Artíñano, *op. cit.*, pp. 67-68; G. Scelle, *La traite négrière aux Indes de Castille*, I, 593-594. According to Veitia Linage (*op. cit.*, pp. 245-247), trade from the Canaries to America was entirely prohibited in 1647; ten years later it was reopened, and, if they did not carry bullion, ships were permitted to return to Tenerife instead of Seville. Of course, the guild protested energetically.

[18] Veitia Linage, *op. cit.*, 2.5.13-20.

III

Relations between the Consulado and the Casa de Contratación were close, continuous, and consequential. As a matter of routine, or under specific instructions from the king, the Casa consulted guild officials concerning trade regulations, the selection of vessels to comprise the merchant fleets, and the organization of the all-important convoys. Ordinarily, officials of the Casa sought the advice, if not the consent, of the prior and consuls on recommendations for legislation, while the heads of the guild customarily assisted in the administration of the multitudinous measures which implemented the commercial policy of the monarchy.[19] The intervention of the guild in the governance of the armadas which protected the flotas and galleons is the salient example of the administrative, financial, and quasi-political activity of this corporation of merchants.

The first effort on the part of the government to defend the nascent American trade from piracy and privateering appears to have been made in 1521 when the Emperor, outraged by the loss of ships returning from the Indies, ordered the preparation of an *armada de defensa*. Irregularly, during the next two decades, similar armadas were commissioned, especially to guard incoming treasure ships around Cape St. Vincent.[20] Constantly in touch with the movements of shipping and the hazards of navigation, after 1543 officers of the guild assumed the primary responsibility for informing His Majesty of the requirements for protection. Recognizing the interests of private shippers as well as the need for reliance on their financial support, the king

[19] *R. de I.*, 9,2,1, 7; Veitia Linage, *op. cit.*, 1.17.50. Direct correspondence with the sovereign was maintained by agents of the guild in Madrid. In 1584 Juan Carrillo received 50,000 *maravedís* "por aver servido de secreto de dicho Consulado, escriviendo las cartas a su Magestad" (AGI, Contaduría, leg. 588-589); earlier, the guild sought to have the consular duty of one-half *maravedí* increased to 2 *maravedís*, "por la grande necesidad que esta Universidad tiene de bolso para informar a su Magestad de las cosas que a su real servicio convengan" (BPC, *Libro de cartas del Consulado* . . . *1559-1562*, f. 28).

[20] Veitia Linage, *op. cit.*, 2.4.3-4; *Documentos de Ultramar*, XIV, 222. Contracts with a group of Sevillan shippers for *armadas contra cosarios* were made in 1522 and 1525 (Fernández Duro, *op. cit.*, I, 422-423), and an armada was equipped in 1526 "at the expense of 67 merchants of Seville and 12 other individuals" (*Documentos de Ultramar*, XIV, 56).

usually empowered the prior and consuls to assist royal officials in the preparation and dispatch of the armadas.[21]

Although, soon after 1525, vessels were forbidden to sail singly, the Council of the Indies issued many licenses for *navios sueltos* in the face of the guild's protests.[22] The fleet system— the compulsory sailing of all merchantmen in annual or semi-annual fleets convoyed by men-of-war—was originally adopted as a war measure;[23] but by 1561, after repeated attacks on the treasure galleons and continued agitation by the guild, the system became a permanent feature of Spanish commercial policy. Repeatedly, in correspondence with the crown, the prior and consuls went on record in favor of rigorous control over the size and number of merchant ships and men-of-war, their armaments, crews, cargoes, and time of sailing, and approved severe punishment for infringements of the meticulous trade rules.[24]

While thus endorsing the restrictive system, the guild sought ways to escape the excessive cost of protecting the Indian trade.[25] Instead of subsidizing commerce for the sake of colonial expansion, the Spanish sovereign regarded the defense of merchant shipping as a particular benefit, and for two centuries or more practically the entire cost of the armadas was met by the *avería,* or convoy-tax, which was an ad valorem duty on goods

[21] Academia de la Historia, *Colección de Muñoz,* LXXXVII, f. 96; AGI, Contaduría, leg. 420-421 (*cédula* of March 11, 1564, in response to petitions from the guild, admitting the prior and consuls to the administration of eight *galeras* sent out to defend treasure ships from Moorish corsairs). In 1576 the consuls were summoned to court to parley with the king "sobre hacer nuevo asiento en lo de las galeras" (AGI, Indiferente general, leg. 2,366).

[22] AGI, Ind. genl., leg. 2,366; Haring, *op. cit.,* pp. 205-206. When licenses were not available, unfavorable weather and acts of God were advanced as pretexts for the unheralded arrival of *navios sueltos* from America (*Ordenanças para remedio de los daños . . . de los descaminos y arribadas maliciosas de los navios que navegan a las Indias*).

[23] In 1553, at the behest of the guild, the crown provided for two Indies fleets, one in January and the other in September, each to be convoyed by two warships. This arrangement was to be effective for the duration of the war with France (*Colección de documentos inéditos relativos al descubrimiento, conquista y organización de las antiguas posesiones españoles de América y Oceanía* [hereinafter cited as *Documentos de Indias*], III, 513-514).

[24] BPC, *Libro de cartas del Consulado . . . 1559-1562,* f. 113; R. de I., 9.30; Veitia Linage, *op. cit.,* 1.17.34; Fernández Duro, *op. cit.,* I, 438.

[25] *Documentos de Indias,* III, 512-520: a letter from the guild (1554), proposing two *naos de armada* and one dispatch boat for each fleet, instead of four men-of-war.

carried to and from America. First imposed at 1 per cent in 1521, the tariff ranged as high as 7 per cent in the sixteenth century. On account of a long delay in the Indies, in 1596 the rate on the return voyage was set at 14 per cent; but the protest of the guild that this would ruin trade brought the assessment down to 7 per cent, the deficit being carried over to a subsequent administration. The *avería* on passengers and slaves was a head-tax of 20 ducats.[26]

Detailed ordinances for the administration of the *avería* were promulgated in 1573. Recognizing the vital interests of the merchants in the cost of provisions, personnel, and armaments, the ordinances instructed officials of the Casa to confer with the prior and consuls in estimating the requirements for each convoy and the *avería* rate which should yield sufficient revenue. The collector *(receptor)*, the controller of purchases *(veedor)*, and other officers of the administration were named by the Casa in consultation with the guild.[27] In 1580 the king advised the Casa to take no action concerning armadas "without the agreement of the Consulado."[28]

Discrepancies in the *avería* rate, possibly inefficiency in provisioning the *armadas*,[29] continued evasions of the duty,[30] and the laxness of officials of the House of Trade created dissatisfaction with the early *avería* administration. Through the *asiento*,

[26] *R. de I.*, 9.9.8; Veitia Linage, *op. cit.*, 1.20.11, 14. Extraordinary *averías* were imposed for special contingencies. Thus, in 1549, advised that eight armed ships had sailed from Dieppe to intercept the incoming Spanish fleet, the prior and consuls requested the immediate preparation of an armada and permission to "echar nueva avería para tener artillería y municiones para semejantes casos" (Fernández Duro, *op. cit.*, I, 436).

[27] AGI, Ind. genl., leg. 2,366; *R. de I.*, 9.9.5, 7, 11, 17 and 9.8.68; Veitia Linage, *op. cit.*, 1.20.9; Haring, *op. cit.*, pp. 73-75.

[28] BPC, *Inbentario protocolo del archivo del Consulado*, No. 109.

[29] *Documentos de Ultramar*, XIV, 290. Too numerous checks on the purchase of supplies (*R. de I.*, 9.16.33-35) may have impeded the efficiency which they were designed to promote. In 1629 Alonso de Carranza claimed that officials of the Casa paid twice as much for arms and provisions as the guild paid when administering the avería under contract (*Ajustamiento i proporción de las monedas*, Madrid, 1629, p. 323); but "little, if any, basis" has been found for this charge (Hamilton, *American Treasure and the Price Revolution in Spain*, p. 187, n. 2).

[30] In spite of prohibitions on the statute books, the armed galleons frequently carried goods which escaped duties; and, at first, there were several loopholes for avoiding the tax (Haring, *op. cit.*, pp. 74, 217).

or exclusive contract for the preparation and dispatch of armadas and flotas, demands for a more centralized supervision and undivided responsibility for the management of the *avería* were recognized. In possession of the *asiento* for at least thirty-six years between 1591 and 1642,[31] the Seville guild assumed the major responsibility for the conduct and defense of transatlantic shipping. The *asiento*, officially negotiated through the Council of the Indies, stipulated the reciprocal obligations of the crown and the contractors, or *asentistas*. Typically, in the case of contracts with the guild, the prior and consuls pledged their corporation to provide annually a specified tonnage in merchantmen and a minimum number of men-of-war and messenger ships *(avisos)*:[32] to provision and arm the infantry and seamen on the armada; and to pay out of the *avería* all expenses incurred in providing such services and protection for the trade as the *asiento* required. Bond was exacted for the performance of the contractor's obligations. In the seventeenth century the *asentista* was also obligated to make an annual payment to assist in the liquidation of debts incurred by previous unprofitable administrations.[33] The *avería* rate for the term of the contract was specified in the *asiento*; if the contractors, collecting the duty at this rate and meeting all their obligations, were able to show a profit, the gains were distributable among those who "participated" by

[31] The first *asiento* with the guild was signed in 1591, but seems to have become effective during the quadrennium 1594-97; another four-year contract was made in 1598 (*Documentos de Ultramar*, XIV, 60-64). *Asientos* with individuals or partnerships (e.g., with Juan Nuñez Correa in 1603: BM, C.62.1.18.56) may have been made for some years prior to 1608, when the guild signed a contract for six years (*Documentos de Ultramar*, XIV, 35). Subsequently, the following (and possibly other) *asientos* were taken by the Consulado: 1614-17 (*Documentos de Ultramar*, XIV, 74-78); 1618-20 (BM, 8223.d.28); 1621-27 (AGI, Contaduría, leg. 588-589); 1628-33 (AGI, Ind. genl., leg. 2,688); 1634-36 (AHN, Consejo de Indias, leg. 20, 182); 1640-42 (AGI, Ind. genl., leg. 2,688). Printed copies of the last four *asientos* are in the sources indicated.

[32] The *avisos*, dispatched immediately upon the arrival of the fleet in America and in Spain, at first carried only official letters and dispatches (AHN, *Cedulario índico*, 16-247-236; R. de I., 9.37.1, 5, 6), but under some of the seventeenth-century *asientos* the guild was permitted to ship on its own account forty tons of produce on each *aviso* (AHN, *Cedulario índico*, 30-51-62).

[33] The *avería* administration fell badly behind in payments, owing 68,000,000 maravedís in 1614 when the debt was funded at 5 per cent. The *avería vieja* was an annual payment of 60,000 ducats from current income for the exclusive purpose of paying interest and retiring these obligations (Veitia Linage, *op. cit.*, 1.20.8).

contributing to the initial capital fund and guarantee.[34] Incidentally, the *asiento* usually provided that *caballeros* as well as merchants might participate without detriment to their noble rank.

On the expiration of the 1618-20 *asiento*, the guild negotiated a renewal for six years. Merchants of Cádiz, however, were clamoring for the right to participate in the *avería* administration; and when the Seville guild refused to grant Cádiz a one-quarter interest in the contract, the *asiento* was awarded jointly to a group of Cádiz merchants and the seamen's guild (Universidad de Mareantes) of Seville. In March, 1621, for reasons which have not been ascertained, the contract was returned to the Seville merchant guild.[35]

The administration of the 1621 *asiento* was rescued from financial embarrassment by loans from the *lonja* funds of the Consulado, the total debt on this account having risen to 16,-722,855 *maravedís* in 1628.[36] The *asiento* of 1640-42 was terminated in 1641; for the dispatch of one fleet, meagerly laden, exhausted the *avería* funds and the credit of the contractors.[37] During the next two decades, while the Casa took charge of the armadas, a precipitate decline in the imports of treasure, increasing evasions of the duty, and maritime disasters pushed the *avería* rate to exorbitant levels.[38] The order of June 7, 1644, which pledged the crown not to raise the *avería* above 12 per cent,[39] and the reduction of the tariff on gold to 2 per cent (1649) were impotent to produce sufficient revenue for the proper organization and protection of the overseas trade. Finally, following the abolition of the compulsory registration of treasure (1660), a new form of *asiento* was assumed by the

---

[34] Veitia Linage, *op. cit.*, 1.20.35-45; R. de I., 9.9.17.
[35] AGS, Contadurías generales, leg. 3,024; AGI, Ind. genl., leg. 2,688; *Documentos de Ultramar*, XIV, 79, 95-96.   [36] AGI, Contratación, leg. 1,077.
[37] AGI, Contratación, leg. 181; Veitia Linage, *op. cit.*, 1.20.44-45.
[38] Veitia Linage (*op. cit.*, 1.20.47) reports rates on imports of 99 per cent in 1653; of 49 per cent in 1656; of 31.75 per cent in 1659.
[39] R. de I., 9.9.43. The law was revoked in 1655. In 1644-45, to cite an example of the financial difficulties of the fleet system, the expenses of the Tierra Firme armada were 229,289,625 *maravedís*, whereas the *avería* at 12 per cent yielded only 189,195,947 *m*. Including the New Spain fleet, the *avería* deficit in this fiscal period came to 104,624,498 *m*. (AGI, Contaduría, leg. 590-591).

guilds and merchants of Spain and America. Fixed annual assessments replaced the old *avería*, while the royal treasury advanced about one fifth of the cost of guarding and convoying the trade fleets. This system of the *dotación fija* involved expenditures of 790,000 ducats in 1667. After lengthy consultations with the Seville guild, the president of the Casa assessed the Andalusian exporters 171,000 ducats, which was 21,000 ducats more than the king's contribution; and the remainder of the *dotación fija* was made up of levies on the merchants of Peru (350,000 ducats), New Spain (90,000 ducats), and New Granada and Cartagena (29,000 ducats).[40] Although this system remained in force—on the statute books at least—until the close of the century, in emergencies the guild sent out additional warships for patrolling and for strengthening the regular armadas, financing the undertakings through special *averías*.[41] As late as 1688 the Consulado sought to obtain complete control over the flotas and armadas, promising to finance the project without recourse to state funds if the guild were granted monopolies in the slave trade and in the export of quicksilver.[42]

IV

The *registros*, or official registers of all goods and precious metals carried by the fleets, served the dual purpose of uncovering illegal shipments and of providing bases for customs duties. The affidavits *(relaciones juradas)* of shippers were generally accepted by the officials who compiled the registers; except under presumption of fraud, goods were not unpacked for count or inspection.[43] Royal *cédulas* issued at the request of the guild repeated the injunction against detailed examinations, suggesting that officials and tax farmers were prone to exceed their authority.[44] Although the guild's subvention of 200,000 ducats in sup-

[40] AHN, Consejo de Indias, leg. 20,185; AGI, Contratación, leg. 643; BM, 1323.k.14 (8); *Traslados de quatro cédulas reales . . . tocantes a la contribución y repartimiento de averías, para la dotación, y caudal fixo de los despachos de las reales armadas y flotas;* Veitia Linage, *op. cit.,* 1.20.48-51; Haring, *op. cit.,* pp. 80-82.

[41] Academia de la Historia, Est. 24, gr. 5a, B132; AGI, Contratación, leg. 192B, No. 21.

[42] AM, Cádiz, *Reales órdenes i papeles sobre la conservación del comercio,* No. 2.

[43] *R. de I.,* 8.16.17 and 9.33.4.

[44] AGI, Ind. genl., leg. 2,366, and Contratación, leg. 870.

port of the "cavalcade for the Queen of Hungary" (1629)
purchased exemption from submitting sworn statements of
goods shipped to the Indies,[45] the merchants continued to complain of tax farmers who were overzealous in examining goods
for tariff purposes. Supported by officials of the House of Trade,
the guild contended that the destruction of trade would result
from making public the kinds and quantities of goods ready for
shipment to the colonies.[46] After the middle of the century, it
became the practice to value goods on the basis of the gross
weight or bulk of shipment, with little or no regard to the
quality of the merchandise.[47] The rule in America—often vi-
olated, judging by complaints of the Consulado—was to base
values on the average prices prevailing during the month following the arrival of the fleets.[48]

The penalties of confiscation of property and perpetual exile
for the importation of unregistered treasure were applicable to
the prior and consuls, if convicted of abetting the evasion of
registration.[49] Since the guild often interceded on behalf of
those prosecuted for possession of unregistered bullion, securing
pardons or a mitigation of the penalties, and, finally, had a hand
in the abolition of compulsory registration, plainly the Consulado failed to share fully the mercantilist preoccupation of the
state to prevent the drain of specie to foreign parts. In deplor-
ing the fact that 500,000 *pesos* of Peruvian treasure annually
leaked out to China through the port of Acapulco,[50] the guild

[45] Veitia Linage, *op. cit.*, 1.18.5-6; Antúnez, *op. cit.*, Appendix, pp. xxv-xli. Possibly this was a temporary favor. A *cédula* of March 13, 1640, ordered "que no se le
pidan relaciones juradas de lo que se embarca en flota *este año* (AHN, *Cedulario
indico*, 243-732a-494).

[46] AGI, Contratación, leg. 870, No. 9; Antúnez, *op. cit.*, Appendix, pp. xli-xlvi.

[47] An *arroba* of goods for Tierra Firme was valued at 5,100 *maravedís* and an
arroba for New Spain, at 3,400 *m*. (AGI, Contaduría, leg. 643; Veitia Linage, *op.
cit.*, 1.18.5-6).

[48] AGI, Contaduría, leg. 643; R. *de I.*, 8.16.8; AHN, *Cedulario indico*, 35-45-54.

[49] R. *de I.*, 9.33.57. As the guild intervened in the appointment of silver masters
and had authority to veto the formation of partnerships of silver merchants, oppor-
tunities for collusion existed. With heavy imports of treasure, the office of silver
master was lucrative. In 1616 the Consulado denounced the attempt of silver masters
to increase their fees 25 per cent as a "conspiracy" (AGI, Contratación, 2ª sección,
leg. 798, No. 9).

[50] Hamilton, *American Treasure and the Price Revolution in Spain*, p. 37, n. 2.

was doubtless more concerned over the loss of trade than for the exodus of gold and silver. While condemning the frequent sequestrations of private treasure,[51] self-interest induced the guild to proffer its services in arranging for the delivery and coinage of the seized metal and in negotiating the securities by which the owners were indemnified.[52] When the king sequestered 299,330,939 *maravedís,* representing one eighth of the private bullion on the 1620 fleet, the Consulado appointed the *receptor,* purchased German copper for the coinage of vellon, and paid off the importers of the specie.[53] A few years later (1627), the prior and consuls petitioned the Cortes, decrying the delay in the coinage of a two years' shipment of American silver and protesting the irreparable injury to business from the slow process of minting one-half *real* and two-*real* pieces *(plata sencilla)* instead of the customary four- and eight-*real* coins.[54] A priori, we might expect mildly inflationary sentiment among merchants of the guild. Tomás de Cardona, who for twenty-five years campaigned for a 25 per cent debasement of gold and silver,[55] was an agent of the Consulado in negotiating the *avería asiento* of 1628. Alonso de Carranza, Cardona's able publicist, claimed furthermore that Admiral Francisco de Mandoxana, onetime prior and consul, whole-heartedly agreed with the advo-

[51] Hamilton, *op. cit.,* p. 37, n. 5. In 1544 the king apologized to the Consulado for the necessity of sequestering 180,000 ducats and promised to take possession of the treasure "con menos dampno de los dueños, especialmente de los mercaderes, para que ninguno venga en quiebra y todos puedan continuar sus tratos." He offered better terms than formerly: merchants might elect for payment in terminable *juros* at 18 *mill al millar* (about 5.5 per cent), or in life annuities, or in drafts payable in the Indies (AGS, Contadurías generales, leg. 3,052).

[52] E.g., the agreement of 1565 for the delivery of 400,000 ducats of private treasure in exchange for *juros* (AGI, Contratación, leg. 710). On behalf of mariners and shipowners the seamen's guild sought exemption of the specie representing wages and freights, but the merchant guild insisted upon equality of treatment (AGI, Contratación, leg. 192B).

[53] AGS, Contaduría mayor de cuentas, 3ª-4ª época, leg. 1,305.

[54] *Actas de las Córtes de Castilla,* XLV, 465-469. Alleging that the coinage of small denominations was designed to prevent their exportation, the guild maintained that the coins were overweight and more desirable to foreigners than the *plata doble,* "y asi el remedio que parece inducir la ley viene a cambiar en provecho de los contra se induce." But at the same time the guild stated that *plata doble* commanded a premium of 3 per cent over *plata sencilla!*   [55] Hamilton, *op. cit.,* p. 66.

cates of debasement.[56] Inflationist sentiment among the Seville merchants doubtless led the Consulado to recommend, in 1617, the reduction of the tariff on gold[57] and to subsidize the quick-silver mines of Almadén, when foreign supplies of this metal were difficult to obtain.[58]

The deficiencies of Indian labor for exploiting the mines and fields of the New World impelled the crown to modify the early legislation which prohibited the carrying of Negro slaves to the colonies. From the second quarter of the sixteenth century slaves were exported under royal licenses, generally sold at 30 ducats for each Negro. The rapidly increasing business furnished an important source of revenue, making it attractive to farm the licenses under monopolistic *asientos de negros*.[59] As early as 1552 the guild endeavored to secure control of the monopoly, alarmed by the clandestine mercantile trade of foreigners in possession of licenses to traffic in Negroes.[60] Throughout the seventeenth century the Consulado denounced the unfair competition of goods illegally carried to the Indies on slave ships with the legitimate exports of Sevillan merchants and vehemently opposed granting the *asiento* to foreigners.[61] For a century or more the guild was powerless to provide a remedy because of its inability to assume the *asiento* on terms as favorable to the crown as those offered by private, usually foreign, *asentistas*. Only for five years (1676-81) were the prior and

---

[56] Carranza, *op. cit.*, p. 387.

[57] *Documentos de Ultramar*, XV, 11-12; R. de I., 9.9.44.

[58] AGI, Ind. genl., leg. 2,730.

[59] The first *asiento* was awarded in 1528 for a period of four years (G. Scelle, "The Slave-Trade in the Spanish Colonies," *loc. cit.*, pp. 619-620). The seven-year contract with Fernando de Ochoa in 1552 (AGI, Ind. genl., leg. 2,366) appears to have been abrogated at the instance of the Consulado (G. Scelle, *La traite négrière*, I, 205-206). Although laws of 1572-73 in the *R. de I.* (8.15.18) refer to the then effective *asiento* with the Seville guild, no records have been found of its administration. An *asiento* with the prior and consuls was projected in 1590, but did not go into effect (AGI, Ind. genl., leg. 2,829; Scelle, *op. cit.*, I, 341-343, 799-809).

[60] AGI, Ind. genl., leg. 2,366; BPC, *Libro de cartas del Consulado . . . 1559-1562*, f. 52. The theologian, Tomás de Mercado, who defended the "just" capture and sale of Negroes, testified that merchants of the guild had large investments in the slave stations of Guinea (*Summa de tratos y contratos*, Sevilla, 1587, lib. ii, cap. 20).

[61] AGI, Ind. genl., leg. 2,829 and 2,839; Veitia Linage, *op. cit.*, 1.25.17; Scelle, "The Slave-Trade in the Spanish Colonies," *loc. cit.*, pp. 623, 628-629.

consuls in possession of the Negro *asiento*, and then they found
it impossible to deliver the required 10,000 "tons" of blacks.[62]
The ease of smuggling slaves into the colonies had by this time
practically dried up the demand for licenses for legal entry.[63]

The prior and consuls enforced the maritime insurance laws,
which formed a part of the guild's general ordinances.[64] The
exact form of several types of contract was prescribed, following
recommendations of the Consulado. Guild officials had complained that the marine insurance business had "begun to decline" because underwriters were frequently obliged to pay un-
justifiable claims. To remedy abuses, the laws prohibited the
insurance of freight receipts, military stores, and rigging, and
limited the amount of insurance to two thirds of the value of
the vessel. Infractions of the statutes called for a penalty of
50,000 *maravedís*, one half of which was payable to the guild's
treasury.

Sea-loans *(dineros a cambio)* on a ship reduced propor-
tionately the insurable value. The limit for such loans was fixed
at one third of the ship's value in 1587, but was increased to a
maximum of two thirds in 1621.[65] The loans had to be approved by the prior and consuls and registered in the consulate.
According to Veitia Linage, the laws were considered stringent,
and violations were so numerous that the guild finally urged
their revision, especially to permit larger loans to slave traders
seeking capital in Seville. The Consulado was required to maintain a register of ships lost in the American trade,[66] and the

[62] AGI, Ind. genl., leg. 2,839-40; Contaduría, leg. 643. The Consulado acquired
the contract upon the failure of the *asentista* who signed a five-year *asiento* in 1674.

[63] Furthermore, Spaniards had been so effectively cut off from sources of supply
that the guild sought permission from the Council of the Indies to buy *piezas de
esclavos* from the Dutch in Curaçao. In 1679 the Consulado's *asiento* was subrogated
in favor of Juan Barroso del Pozo (AGI, Ind. genl., leg. 2,840; Scelle, *La traite
négrière*, I, 621-640, 831-836).

[64] Ordinances of 1556, cap. 27-60; also reproduced in *R. de I.*, 9.39, in Capmany's
Apéndice a las costumbres marítimas del Libro del Consulado, pp. 121-134, and in
Haring, *op. cit.*, pp. 344-353 (incomplete). The preamble states that the number of
underwriters had declined because of the excessive number of fraudulent claims.
The laws were drawn up, undoubtedly by guild officials, "para que el trato y comercio
se extienda más."   [65] Veitia Linage, *op. cit.*, 2.19.4.

[66] Ordinances of 1556, cap. 22. Artíñano notes that "el famoso registro de Lloyd
inglés tiene aquí su ilustre abolengo" (*op. cit.*, p. 55).

prior and consuls possessed both administrative and judicial functions in connection with the salvaging and restitution of shipwrecked property.[67]

V

Partial control of the *averia* funds and complete authority over several categories of tariffs on the India trade made the guild, particularly in the seventeenth and eighteenth centuries, an influential financial institution as well as an important fiscal agent of the crown. Ordinary expenses of the Consulado (i.e., "masses and alms,[68] lawyers' fees and the emoluments of solicitors, procurators, and notaries, mail, porterage, porters, and other similar items") were paid out of the income from the consular duty of *una blanca al millar* (.05 per cent) on exports.[69] In addition, the guild derived substantial revenue from the sale of notarial offices and privileges *(escribanías)*.[70] When the volume of trade was large, the revenues from these duties exceeded current expenses, and investments were made in various obligations secured by national and local taxes.[71] The "hard times" of the seventeenth century are reflected in the sharp shrinkage of the guild's revenues. From an average of 400,000 *maravedís* in the last quarter of the sixteenth century

[67] Cases of this nature are described in AGI, Contaduría, leg. 643; Contratación, leg. 120; Ind. genl., leg. 2,366.

[68] In 1585 the guild spent 89,080 *maravedís* on "limosnas y misas" for the security of the fleet; and 54,000 *maravedís* purchased 800 masses for "el buen viage de los galeones" in 1606 (AGI, Contaduría, leg. 588-589).

[69] Ordinances of 1556, cap. 20-21. In 1603 the duty was increased to 1 *maravedí* (.1 per cent) and maintained at this rate until abolished in 1712. It was payable by "él que huviere más de un año que trata en las dichas Indias, o él que cargare de nuevo mas cantidad de 1,000 ducados en una o mas veces" (AGI, Contratación, leg. 61).

[70] The Consulado enjoyed a proprietary right in the appointment of three classes of notaries in the Indies trade: *escribano mayor de armadas y flotas, escribanos de nao,* and *escribanos de raciones.* Their duties are described in R. de I., 9.6.48; 9.10.24; 9.16.22; 9.20.1-2, 7-8, 15-16, 22; 9.40.6. See, also, Veitia Linage, *op. cit.,* 1.27. Typically, the Consulado sold *títulos de escribano* to the highest bidders, the purchasers securing the exclusive right to the perquisites of the offices (AGI, Contaduría, leg. 588-591; BPC, *Libro de escrivanias de todas las flotas y armadas, 1570-1586*). *Títulos* for some ships were sold on a tonnage basis (AGI, Contratación, leg. 120).

[71] Particularly *juros* secured by the *almojarifazgo mayor* (general customs), the *almojarifazgo de Indias,* and the *alcabalas* (sales taxes) of Seville. The guild also owned real estate in Triana, a suburb of Seville. For one period, September, 1634, to June, 1640, the guild reported an income from its investments of 11,389,983 *maravedís* vellon (AGI, Contaduría, leg. 590-591).

and nearly 500,000 in the following quarter century (the rate having been doubled), receipts from the consular tariff fell to about 300,000 annually in the second quarter of the seventeenth century and to little over 100,000 in the last half of the century. The *escribanías* produced 450,000 *maravedís* per annum in the period 1576-1600, about 550,000 in 1601-25, and 980,000 in 1626-50, but dropped to annual averages of 785,000 and 365,-000, respectively, in the last two quarter-centuries.[72]

Comparative affluence of the guild and of its members tempted the crown on many occasions to exploit their resources and credit to alleviate the almost chronic embarrassment of the royal treasury. Voluntary subsidies *(donativos graciosos)* for military and political exigencies were not uncommon,[73] and forced loans and advances to the exchequer were recurrent.[74] Large sums were raised by the sale of the guild's interest-bearing certificates *(escrituras)* to merchants and institutional investors; and to retire these obligations, the Consulado received authority to impose a new tariff or to prorogue some duty established in connection with a previous crown debt.

The *lonja* duty of a third of 1 per cent on goods entering and leaving Seville was first imposed in 1582 to finance the construction of the *lonja,* the merchants' exchange and domicile of the Consulado (now the Archives of the Indies).[75] The

---

[72] Data by five-year periods are furnished in Appendix VI.

[73] E.g., the donation of 30,000 ducats and 2,000 *quintals* of biscuit for the defense of Cádiz in 1625, and the 350,000 *escudos* "por via de donativo gracioso para las asistencias y mayor defensa de la monarquía" in 1689 (AHN, Consejo de Indias, leg. 20,209).

[74] E.g., the loan of 300,000 *pesos escudos* in 1699 to drive the Scotch from Darién, not only to avoid the "imponderables perjuicios" to trade but also, the Consulado agreed, to preserve "la pureza de nuestra sagrada religión" (AHN, Consejo de Indias, leg. 21,330; AGI, Contaduría, leg. 643). Similar instances are recounted in the MS "Apunte exacto de las expresiones de benevolencia con que siempre han honrado los señores Emperador, y Reyes de España a su Tribunal del Consulado, y Comercio de Andalucia" (AHN, Consejo de Indias, leg. 20,209) and in Veitia Linage, *op. cit.,* 1.17.53.

[75] AGI, Contratación, leg. 858, and 5,014. Both the *lonja* duty and the *infantes* duty were collected on imports by land and by sea and on exports overseas. The Council of the Indies fined the guild 44,000 ducats in 1664 for collecting the duties on outward shipments overland (AGI, Contratación, leg. 120). After 1717 they were levied in Cádiz and Seville. Accounts for the last half of the seventeenth century

guild borrowed freely on the security of this revenue, not only for construction purposes, but also for making urgent advances to the king.[76] Though still unfinished, the *lonja* was put into use in 1598; but the so-called *lonja* duty was collected at least until 1826.[77]

The *infantes* duty of 1 per cent, similar in form to the *lonja* tariff, was imposed in 1632 in connection with the Consulado's subsidy of 360,000 ducats for the maintenance of five hundred infantrymen *(infantes)*.[78] This impost, scheduled to expire in 1638, was perpetuated by royal decree in 1637 and burdened with a debt of 800,000 ducats, the amount of a subsidy demanded of the guild for certain state purposes.[79] Both the *lonja* and the *infantes* duties were imposed by the guild through the first quarter of the nineteenth century.

Another phase of guild financing was the product of the widespread evasion and nonenforcement of the thousand and one trade regulations. Laws to the contrary notwithstanding, unregistered imports, contraband trade, and other forms of illicit commerce did not often incur the statutory penalties. Instead, and perhaps not without a close calculation of the net gain to his treasury, the king repeatedly compromised with Spanish merchants, permitting the guild to negotiate for general pardons *(indultos)* or compositions.[80] Generally, the purchase price of the *indulto* was prorated among the merchants who had shipped illegally; since their bargaining position was obviously weak,

---

and for all of the eighteenth century are in AGI, Contaduría, leg. 590-591, 597-600, 602-623, and 643; Ind. genl., leg. 2,343-344, 2,353-357, and 2,359-364.

[76] E.g., the loan of 90,000 ducats for the fortification of Gibraltar and Ceuta (AGI, Ind. genl., leg. 2,352).

[77] AGI, Contratación, leg. 1,077 and 4,553; Haring, *op. cit.*, p. 325.

[78] AGI, Contratación, leg. 5,014. In 1596 "sirvió el Consulado y Comercio con 100 soldados a su coste, en la imbación de Cádiz" (AHN, Consejo de Indias, leg. 20,209, No. 6).

[79] AHN, Consejo de Indias, leg. 20,182; AGI, Ind. genl., leg. 2,352; Contratación, leg. 858 and 5,014. The guild also made a *servicio gracioso* of 589,000 ducats in 1637.

[80] Representative cases are: AGI, Ind. genl., leg. 2730, "Expediente sobre el indulto que solicitó el Consulado de Cadiz de la carga del navio de azogues del cargo de D. Juan de Cordoba" (1699); a composition of 140,000 *pesos* for contraband trade, and one of 76,000 *pesos* in 1676 for shipments of "ropa de Francia" to Tierra Firme (AGI, Contratación, leg. 5,100; BM, 1323.k.14.14; Veitia Linage, *op. cit.*, 1.17.53).

foreigner merchants in Seville sometimes paid the lion's share of the composition.[81]

One important *indulto,* amounting to 206,000 ducats, was financed through the sale of certificates of indebtedness signed by the Consulado and hypothecated on the so-called *Balbas* duty, a new tariff of 1½ per cent on imports from America.[82] Other compositions in the seventeenth century bear the earmarks of forced loans or, at best, schemes whereby the crown anticipated revenues and passed on to the Consulado the responsibility of imposing and collecting the taxes. Occupied by military affairs in Catalonia, in 1695 Charles II hastily borrowed 500,000 *pesos* from the guild and granted the merchants permission in advance to ship "goods of illicit commerce."[83] Increasingly, both court and Consulado recognized the necessity of dependence upon foreign sources to satisfy colonial demand, and foreign traders were welcome in Seville and other marts so long as they employed Spanish merchants as intermediaries and middlemen. Needless to say, the merchant guild stoutly defended the policy of excluding foreigners from direct trade with the Indies.[84]

Loans of 400,000 ducats, in 1625, to equip an armada of ten galleons and three *pataches* for patrolling the Mar del Sur gave rise to an extraordinary *avería* of 1 per cent, called the *toneladas* duty.[85] This was prorogued as the *Balbas* duty in

[81] The economic and diplomatic status of French merchants in this respect are adequately discussed in A. Girard, *Le commerce français à Séville et Cadix,* pp. 272, 277-281, 286-328.

[82] AGI, Ind. genl., leg. 2,741; Contaduría, leg. 641-42; AHN, Consejo de Indias, leg. 20,177, 20,209, and 21,776. The affair arose from the discovery of attempts to defraud the fisc: "que haviendo tenido S. M. a bien de perdonar al comercio de Sevilla . . . los delitos que contra ellos se pudiesen averiguar consecuente a la denuncia que hizo Christobal de Balbas, siendo factor de Tierra Firme, y la acusación puesta por el Sr. Fiscal sobre las fraudes que en el año de 1624, cometió en la condución de crecida cantidad de mercaderias a la misma Provincia en la flota de Gaspar de Acevedo." First imposed at 1 per cent, the *Balbas* duty was raised to 1.5 per cent in 1634.

[83] AGI, Contratación, leg. 628-629; BM, 501.g.4 (4) and 1323.k.14 (19).

[84] BM, 710.b.27 (6): *cédula* of Dec. 25, 1616; 1323.k.14 (18): *provisión* of the Audiencia of Santa Fé, Dec. 2, 1706.

[85] AGI, Contaduría, leg. 643. In this connection, a *cédula* of March 16, 1626, instructed "que el Consulado administrase la lavor de 400,000 ducados en vellon que se fabricavan en la casa de la moneda de Sevilla para el apresto de la Armada del Sur" (BPC, *Inbentario protocolo del Archivo del Consulado,* No. 252).

1627, but another *toneladas* impost was instituted in 1645 as a result of the Consulado's loan of 200,000 ducats for military needs in Catalonia.[86] The guild made this latter subvention under protest, bewailing the penury of the merchants of Seville and of the Consulado; in contrast, toward the close of the sixteenth century comparative prosperity had prompted the guild to propose purchasing the farm of the general customs *(almojarifazgo mayor)* and the *almojarifazgo de Indias,* provided the king would renounce for ten years the sequestration of treasure.[87]

The Consulado of Cádiz inherited the liabilities as well as the privileges of the Seville guild and continued to administer various imposts on the Indies trade throughout the eighteenth century. Indeed, the labyrinthic history of these tariffs, notably the *lonja, infantes,* and *Balbas* duties, runs well into the nineteenth century. The preceding century was replete with suits against the Consulado for the payment of principal and interest on obligations which, it seems, should have been retired. At least one important *Balbas* creditor had not been satisfied in 1825, and the heirs of other seventeenth-century purchasers of the guild's certificates were taking steps to collect from the Real Hacienda in 1852.[88]

Probably no phase of the guild's conduct served to arouse criticism and to undermine its prestige as much as did its financial administration. If not incompetent to judge the ability of trade to bear taxation, the prior and consuls were blinded to the primary objectives of the guild organization by the importunities of His Majesty's treasurer. Audits of the guild's accounts for the sake of verifying the claims of its numerous creditors revealed "a chaos of confusion," attributed both to malfeasance and to the perpetuation of tariff duties beyond the time required to extin-

[86] AHN, Consejo de Indias, leg. 20,185. As far as may be ascertained from unsatisfactory account books, this *toneladas* duty was removed later in the century. So was the *Balbas* duty, although its creditors had not been paid off. Records of the collection of both tariffs are in AGI, Contaduría, leg. 594-596, 643, and Contratación, leg. 858 and 4,553.

[87] BM, Add. MSS 28,369; AGI, Ind. genl., leg. 2,366.

[88] AHN, Consejo de Indias, leg. 20,177 and 21,331.

guish indebtedness, assuming efficient administration.[89] The climax came in 1705, when a sweeping investigation resulted in claims for the restitution of almost three million *pesos* by guild officials in control of the consular treasury between 1689 and 1705. Perhaps because the king's ministers in the House of Trade had been as remiss in their obligations as the prior and consuls, the officers of the guild were completely exonerated, in 1718, and declared to be "fieles y buenos ministros de los Consulados." Significantly, some of the funds in question were found to have been appropriated for "diferentes efectos del real servicio."[90]

On the other hand, the existing conditions made it inevitable that the guild should employ its strongest weapon, money, in attempting to secure royal assent to measures deemed desirable by the dominant mercantile sentiment. In view of the "repeated and urgent financial straits of the crown,"[91] the voice of the guild was perhaps too audible in the councils of government; in the matter of the slave trade as in other affairs "the blind confidence placed in the advice of the Consulado was . . . one of the great errors of the Spanish monarchy."[92] As has been pointed out, "in practice, if not in theory," the merchants associated in the Seville Consulado "resembled the exclusive trading companies of the same period in England and Holland."[93] Most of their policies reflected an inordinate ambition to maintain an economy of scarcity in Spain's colonial possessions through the exclusion not only of foreigners but of all Spanish merchants not affiliated with the Andalusian guild. Even when secure in their privileges, officials of the Consulado feared the depressing influence on prices of "excessive" exports by their

[89] AGI, Contratación, leg. 61; AHN, Consejo de Indias, leg. 20,209; Biblioteca Nacional, Madrid: *Discurso informativo por el Consulado de la ciudad de Sevilla.*

[90] BM, Add. MSS 21,449, f. 61-83; 1323.k.14 (26); and 1323.k.14 (14); AHN, Consejo de Indias, leg. 20,185, and *Cedulario índico,* 40-209-209; AGI, Contratación, leg. 858, No. 4; Larruga, *Historia de la Real Junta de Comercio,* II, 2575-2588.

[91] Artíñano, *op. cit.,* p. 61.

[92] Scelle, *La traite négrière,* I, 557. An aspirant to the presidency of the House of Trade, the Marquis de Varinas, charged that officials of the Casa were mere tools of the prior and consuls, who could afford to spend 50,000 *pesos* in bribes more readily than His Majesty could disburse 10 *pesos* (*Documentos de Ultramar,* XII, 95-98, 100-102, 104-108).   [93] Haring, *op. cit.,* p. 137.

own membership; and, among other things, they ignored the economies of larger freighters in the transatlantic trade in order to forestall navigational objections to the use of Seville as a terminal port.[94] Having but slight interests in the ownership of merchant vessels, members of the guild approved the practice of fixing maximum freight rates, but they opposed price-fixing in the American markets for European goods.[95] The ability of the merchants of Seville to convince the crown, until late in the eighteenth century, that their interests were identical with those of Spain and her colonies is a significant commentary on the prevailing economic and political thought of the age.

[94] AGI, Ind. genl., leg. 2,688 (asiento of 1640, art. 41); Contratación, leg. 122.
[95] AGI, Ind. genl., leg. 2,366; Antúnez, op. cit., pp. 169-170.

CHAPTER VII

CRITIQUE OF THE GUILD-COURT ORGANIZATION

The Spanish Consulado, especially during the first four centuries of its history, combined the attributes of a commercial-maritime court and of a guild merchant. Thus, the functional structure comprised judicial, administrative, regulatory, and executive powers. These powers were only partially segregated, so that often the priors and consuls were at once trial judges, executive officers with quasi-public authority, and "watchdogs" of the economic interests of the merchant class. The intermingling of these separate functions in the hands of a relatively small officiary suggests the characterization of the Consulado as an integrated guild and guild-court.

I

The court of the guild came into existence because the maritime and mercantile classes, above all the entrepreneurial segments of these two business groups, wanted a tribunal of this type. Numerous allegations of the deficiencies of the existing judicial facilities were employed to show that the consular court was indispensable to the encouragement of business undertakings. But no proposals seem to have been made for reorganizing the so-called ordinary courts for the better handling of commercial disputes, discarding certain formalities and time-consuming procedure in deference to the desires of merchant-litigants. Only the larger and more influential centers of trade secured the privileges necessary for the establishment of the guild-court; obviously, then, the institution was not quite indispensable to industrial and commercial pursuits. In no case did the court of the consuls prove to be the touchstone of uninterrupted prosperity, and in the last analysis the exact influence of a commodious judiciary upon the ebb and flow of business activity is hardly determinable.

In all probability the founders of the early guild-court were in part motivated by a spirit of independence, that is, by the desire simply to free the merchant class from the larger degree of social and political responsibility inherent in the pre-existing judicial system. Similarly, but to a lesser degree, the merchants found in the Consulado the advantages and immunities afforded the clergy by ecclesiastical courts. Both clerics and merchants were suspicious of lay lawyers and of judges outside their own ranks. As religion was generally more highly esteemed than business pursuits, only at a relatively late date in the Middle Ages were the merchants able to realize their particularistic ambitions. Special tribunals for particular social and economic groups were not sanctioned indiscriminately, but the power and wealth of the clergy and the merchants were sufficient to enable these two classes to acquire separate judicial processes. By pragmatic tests, such institutions may be adjudged useful if they serve the classes for which they are created without substantially injuring other groups. In the main, the Consulado was useful and even desirable so long as it served the ends of equity and justice, as these concepts were understood by merchants. For seldom were non-merchants brought before its bar, and for the occasional litigant unfamiliar with its principles and practices (the widow or the minor, for instance) the state endeavored to insure adequate safeguards.

The vitality of the medieval ideas and institutions that germinated in Iberian soil during the Middle Ages is well known, but longevity has not always been synonymous with continued usefulness. Essentially, the consular court functioned in the eighteenth century as in thirteenth-century Valencia, where the revival of the Consulado a few years ago was acclaimed as a tribute to the wisdom of the remote past. Anyone who stands in the shadow of the Cathedral and watches the time-honored Tribunal de les Aigües of Valencia settle disputes over irrigation rights must recognize the inherent utility of informal and summary procedure in certain types of cases affecting property. Modern attempts to expand the sphere of commercial arbitration tacitly invoke principles of equity which, though older than the Consulado, were nurtured long and usually well by the medieval guild-court system of Spain.

On the other hand, only partial success rewarded the merchants' endeavors to secure justice with economy and dispatch. We have already observed the nature of the principal obstructions to the efficient conduct of the guild-court in the early period. What seems to stand out as the most persistent fault was the failure of the consular judges to establish a precise and universally recognized area of jurisdiction. Increasingly, in the last century of its existence, the Consulado failed to measure up to the high standards upon which its institution was predicated, and the conflict of jurisdiction was even more acrimonious than in its early years. Threatened with the loss of jurisdiction except in actions in which both plaintiff and defendant were matriculated merchants, the Consulados defended themselves, at great expense, by preparing lengthy briefs on the sources and the scope of their judicial authority.[1] In 1819 a conference of representatives from several Consulados agreed that jurisdictional disputes had undermined the prestige of the consular court and almost destroyed the very foundations of commercial justice.[2]

As early as the seventeenth century the Consulado of Majorca experienced difficulty in enforcing the procedural code with respect to the summoning of merchant associates (adjuntos) because of the habitual absence of "practical individuals of business affairs" from the vicinity of the court. As a last resort,

---

[1] Archivo de la Audiencia Territorial de Barcelona (hereinafter, ATB), *Registro de órdenes, 1781-88,* f. 44; *idem, 1791,* f. 146; *idem, 1792,* f. 1.

[2] ATB, *Registro de órdenes,* 1819, f. 24-36. Disputes involving the Consulados of Barcelona, Burgos, and Cádiz were declared to be most serious. "Las competencias," the committee averred, "han tomado un cuerpo y son tan multiplicadas en el día que la sabiduria del gobierno no puede desentenderse de su influjo en la moral pública, y en las fortunas de los hombres de bien. Todo litigante de mala fe que no puede sacar partido en el tribunal correspondiente, elude la fuerza de la ley acojiendose a una jurisdicción distinta."

members of the guild's council of twenty were compelled to serve as *adjuntos* whenever summoned by the consuls.[3] But compulsory service was not a remedy for the defects of the court, as the conviction grew that merchants were too often unqualified to sit in judgment on many types of actions. Thus, the judge of appeals in Barcelona complained bitterly that inexperienced merchants were allowed to determine decisions in matters "at times so intricate and baffling that the keenest merchant is unable to get at the bottom of the case." Eventually, the consular courts at Barcelona and Valencia were reformed so as to admit as *adjuntos* salaried officials, elected for a four-year term, one of whose necessary qualifications was legal experience.[4] An anonymous critic of the Consulado of Cádiz, writing about 1760, expressed the "heresy" that there is no necessary connection between familiarity with the practical matters of business and the ability to decide fairly in contentious articles of commercial contracts.[5] Although these remarks savor of special pleading, they attest an undercurrent of doubt and criticism which was not confined to any consular court in particular:

> Nothing is more common among merchants and traders than the belief that they understand judicial matters, and to speak with authority on points of law and to take it for granted that with their native reason and intelligence they may pass sentence without difficulty on affairs upon which the most intricate suits turn and in which justice is most obscure; censuring continually even the most carefully studied points over which the legal advisers of the Consulado and appellate tribunal have sweated in order to reach a decision and nullifying it with only the agreement of two or three of the merchants.
>
> Often such cases involve foreigners, wherefore not only are the decisions of these intrusive jurisconsults odious, by virtue of their incorrigible ignorance of the correct administration of justice for nationals, but also prejudicial to the honor of the nation. . . .

---

[3] BSAL, I, 4, and VI, 308 (1610-1615).

[4] *Real cédula, de 24 de junio de 1797, por la qual se sirve S. M. crear adjuntos quadrienales para el Tribunal de Alzadas o de Apelaciones del Consulado de Comercio de Cataluña* . . . (Barcelona, n.d.).

[5] BM, Egerton MS 513, f. 158-168. "Es copia *mui, mui* reservada," according to a marginal note.

The memorial went on to show how inept the consuls proved to be at handling verbal cases, with consequent delays; while other evidence tends to confirm the view that too frequently the Consulado failed to achieve promptness in the disposal of many suits.[6]

In the eighteenth century Spain was economically more interdependent than were Aragon and Castile in the preceding era, and the absence of a uniform commercial law was a hindrance to interregional trade. Many of the Consulados, operating under heterogeneous privileges and ordinances, were aware of this obstacle. As early as 1766 the Barcelona guild submitted to the national Junta General de Comercio the project of a uniform commercial code, and other Consulados made similar recommendations for the codification of commercial law.[7] No significant action was taken before the end of the century.

Joseph Bonaparte planned to draft a commercial code for Spain, but political events thwarted his intentions.[8] A commission appointed in 1821 made a thorough study of existing commercial law, examining all the ordinances and privileges of the Consulados, especially those of Bilbao, and the French Commercial Code of 1807. The recommendations of this body bore fruit in the first Spanish Código de Comercio, promulgated on May 30, 1829. The Código abolished the Consulados and erected in their stead uniform Tribunales de Comercio. Although the judges of this new tribunal retained the titles of prior and consuls, they were appointees of the crown rather than representatives or officials of the merchant guild, and they were bound to conduct the courts under the terms of a uniform commercial law.[9]

[6] ATB, *Registro de órdenes, 1790*, f. 105. "Parece, Señor, increible," wrote an exasperated litigant to the crown, "que en un Tribunal de Comercio el cual por sus atribuciones y leyes . . . se halla desembarazado de las ritualidades y formulas . . . haya podido prolongarse por tanto tiempo el fallo de la citada causa . . . un asunto tan sencillo que podia y puede ser terminado en menos de una hora" (ATB, *Registro de órdenes, 1816*, f. 78-79).

[7] IEC, Bª 82; ATB, *Registro de órdenes, 1798*, f. 3-6, 57-65.

[8] AAH, Fomento, leg. 975.

[9] *Código de comercio, decretado, sancionado, y promulgado en 30 de mayo de 1829: edición oficial* (Madrid, 1829); L. Benito y Endara, *Contestación a las preguntas relativas a derecho mercantil* (Madrid, 1915).

II

Except for an interval of quiescence under Philip V, the guild merchant (now generally known as the Junta de Comercio) expanded its activities during the eighteenth century. Both individually and in union with the Junta General de Comercio in Madrid, the guilds applied their resources to the encouragement and improvement of industry, agriculture, commerce, and navigation.[10] Under Charles III the number of Consulados was increased with a view to stimulating economic activity; until the nineteenth century, when the guilds lost their ancient prerogatives one by one, the mercantile institution continued to be influential in various phases of local, regional, and national economy.

Our attention is now directed, however, to the place of the merchant guild in Spanish economic life prior to 1700. For these centuries a paramount question is the relation of the guild to the municipality. "It could be said," Guiard y Larrauri believes, "that occasionally Bilbao was its Consulado." Even when qualified, such a statement tends to exaggerate the importance of the guild. Although the preceding chapters have attempted to depict the varying scope of guild influence with respect to time and place, they have not revealed an instance in which the identity of the municipal corporation was merged with that of the guild. The extraordinary number of royal and guild interests and institutions in Seville, where the Consulado was at least as active as in Bilbao, tended to obscure the work of the city government but did not destroy its significance. In all cases, many spheres of municipal administration were beyond the purview of the guild (e.g., certain public works and taxes, sanitation and public health, poor relief); furthermore, the city authorities were often adamant in face of the desires and demands of the merchants and their guild.[11] To view the Con-

[10] Larruga, *Historia de la Real Junta de Comercio* (a MS in twelve volumes, now in the Biblioteca del Ministerio de Hacienda, Madrid). Several investigators have searched in vain for the archives of the Junta General de Comercio.

[11] A curious, if unimportant, example of this comes from Barcelona. In 1598 Jaume Pou, a matriculated merchant, was convicted of fraudulent withdrawals from the *taula*. The consuls interceded on his behalf, endeavoring to persuade the coun-

sulado as simply an important department of municipal government, enjoying of course considerable autonomy in finances,[12]
internal organization, and business policies, would not do vi-
olence to the facts in many instances, especially where the guild
was associated with relatively unimportant commercial centers
like Gerona and San Felíu. Usually the municipality itself
sought the royal franchises which created the guild organization; and it is apparent that the desire to be relieved of certain
duties, rather than the importunities of the merchant class,
impelled the city fathers to request the bestowal and the frequent
enlargement of the guild prerogatives. The Spanish experience,
in this respect, parallels English guild history. There, according to Gross, the guild merchant "was the department of town
administration whose duty was to maintain and regulate the
trade monopoly. This was the *raison d'être* of the gild merchant of the twelfth and thirteenth centuries; but the privilege
was often construed to imply broader functions—the general
regulation of trade and industry."[13]

After all, the merchant guild was but one of many occupational and professional organizations, functioning within the
framework of the municipality, which were characteristic of
town economy in the medieval and early modern periods. In
Barcelona, the forms and purposes of the "corporative régime"[14]
were clearly defined. There the consuls of the sea were similar
in functional relationships to the consuls, or *promens,* of numerous craft and professional guilds. Living under ordinances approved by the entire city council, each guild enjoyed certain
exclusive prerogatives in a particular sphere of economic life.
Each craft association was represented in the municipal council,

---

cilors to assent to the commutation of the death sentence "per levar la infamia gran
que de la exequtio de la dita sententia havia de redundar a ell mateix, a sos parents y
amichs y *a tot lo estament mercantivol.*" The councilors declined, and Pou was hanged
(*Dietari,* VII, 132-133).

[12] See, for example, the *Allegación en drecho, en favor del Magistrado de la Lonja
de la Mar . . . de que no deve dar cuenta en el oficio de Maestre Racional . . . del
drecho de periatje* (Barcelona, 1634).

[13] C. Gross, *The Gild Merchant* (Oxford, 1890), I, 43.

[14] So styled by M. González y Sugrañes, *Contribució a la historia dels antichs
gremis dels arts y oficis de la Ciutat de Barcelona* (Barcelona, 1915), I, xvii.

where general affairs of the city were debated and voted upon, and to a lesser extent in the executive council of the *consellers*. Superficially, representation was proportional; but actually tradition, royal fiat, and power acquired through financial resources were weighty factors. In the case of Barcelona, representation of the several social groups was mandatory, so that the executive council invariably drew one of its members from the ranks of merchants, while other business and professional groups furnished one or more of the five (after 1641, six) *consellers*.[15] In its fifteenth- and sixteenth-century form the grand council, or Council of One Hundred, was similarly representative, the merchant class having regularly one fourth of the total membership. In accordance with the law promulgated in 1455, the *jurats* were drawn by lot from panels arranged to produce the following professional and occupational distribution:

Group or Guild	Number of Jurats
Burgesses, including physicians and lawyers	32
Merchants	32
Notaries	14
Apothecaries, druggists, and cloth dealers	10
Surgeons	6
Chandlers, silversmiths, tailors, bridlemakers, shoemakers, blacksmiths, wool-dressers, and clothiers	16 (2 each)
Carpenters, potters, stonecutters, wool weavers, linen weavers, tanners, cotton dealers, curriers, bladesmiths, coopers, crossbow makers, glovers, auction brokers, gardeners, butchers, bargemen, mattressmakers, and fustianmakers	18 (1 each)
Total membership, Council of One Hundred	128

The utility of such systems of representation and division of authority is a function of time and circumstance. In Spanish experience, perhaps the greatest drawback was the inflexibility

[15] Capmany, *Memorias*, II, Appendix, pp. 67-72. In 1510 the *consellers* were drawn from six panels, or *bosses*, made up as follows: first *conseller:* 14 noblemen *(caballeros)* and 20 burgesses *(ciudadanos honrados)*; second *conseller:* 11 noblemen and 13 burgesses; third *conseller:* 12 noblemen and 13 burgesses; fourth *conseller:* 24 merchants; fifth *conseller:* 18 notaries public, 4 royal notaries, 13 apothecaries, 2 chandlers, 9 surgeons, and 94 craftsmen representing 31 guilds.

of class lines and the perpetuation of class prerogatives without regard to changing economic and social needs. Excepting Spain's novel experiences in exploiting her New World possessions, the study of the Consulado to the close of the seventeenth century fails to yield much evidence of significant differences in institutions and attitudes between the Middle Ages and modern times. But the guild's lethargy, traditionalism, and resistance to innovation were fully matched by the inertia and indifference of the church, the nobility, and the crown itself.

The guild organization, even in the Middle Ages, was not alone in its efforts to secure adequate protection for merchant shipping; but it is safe to say that without the concerted aid of mercantile groups the limitations imposed by duress and piracy upon normal maritime intercourse would have been greater. Practically, the guild's action took the form of measures of defense, such as convoys; and it is not clear that guildsmen contributed anything to the development of the idea that an international right, or law, should guarantee the safety of unarmed, nonbelligerent merchant ships.

In the American trade, guild responsibility for the security of shipping and the character of navigation was doubtless too great. The administrative and financial interdependence of trade and naval affairs obstructed the development of a sovereign naval force and the advancement of the arts of navigation. The inordinate toll of shipwrecks in the sixteenth and seventeenth centuries suggests that the Spanish monopolistic system overnourished the avarice of merchant exporters and shipmasters. "It was a great lottery, this American commerce. Both preferred to take a long chance, with the prospect of enormous winnings."[16] The role of gold in the sweepstakes of trade was of extraordinary importance for the Spaniard, both merchant and prince. The *auri sacra fames* was felt in England, where mercantilist policies at least laid sound technological bases for the merchant marine and the royal navy; but only Spain possessed the direct means of indulging that enervating passion.

[16] Haring, *op. cit.*, p. 294.

Public works sponsored and maintained by the guilds represented, for the most part, a unique and permanent contribution of mercantile organization to economic betterment. Such improvements might have been secured through general taxation and administration by public authority, but the disproportionate demands upon public revenues of the military and monarchical establishments often hindered the acquisition of funds for promotional and developmental functions. At times, the clergy as a class, as well as the merchants, was called upon to furnish money for needed public works. Considering the financial status of the monarchy in the seventeenth century, it was perhaps fortunate that these groups did not contribute more to the public exchequer, since it is remarkable that they had anything to spare for the promotion and maintenance of commerce.

The financial ventures of the guilds were not always profitable, or wise. The merchants of Seville (for instance) repeatedly overestimated the yield of duties on the American trade and hypothecated revenues to a degree hardly creditable to their business judgment. Furthermore, privileges and exemptions secured by the guilds in connection with their participation in imposing and administering public, or quasi-public, revenues constituted a species of favoritism generally repugnant to the concept of what was most advantageous to the realm as a whole. But it is fitting to recall that the English privileged companies, similarly and for a long time successfully, withstood the opposition of interlopers, who were simply those merchants who pleaded for "open" foreign trade.[17] All this is understandable in the light of the common guild ideal of a sort of town-centered autarchy. Indeed, the attitude of the guild was not unlike that of modern chambers of commerce with respect to local "prosperity"; but the Spanish guild had more influence and authority in matters affecting the national interest than has any chamber of commerce.

The Consulado, in early Italy as well as in Spain, has not been generally recognized as a type of guild merchant in

[17] W. Cunningham, *The Growth of English Industry and Commerce in Modern Times* (Cambridge, 1903), Pt. I, pp. 214 ff.

treatises dealing with mercantile organizations in western Europe. "Merchant guilds *(Kaufmannsgilden)*," according to Doren, "are all those permanent, associative organizations in which merchants come together primarily for the protection of their special mercantile objectives, in which the purpose of the union is associative regulation and the advancement of trade, but not a real associative-capitalistic enterprise and proportionate sharing of the individual member in the common profit."[18] The Consulado eminently satisfied these conditions. Furthermore, considering the universality of the needs and purposes giving rise to the guild organization, it may well be questioned that the guild (except in name) was "in its typical form a specifically German institution."[19] The usual sphere of activity of the Spanish Consulado differed somewhat from the principal interests of the typical English guild merchant. For instance, the Spanish guildsmen were only incidentally concerned with the practices of the retail trader, who was generally excluded from the guild merchant. Yet the narrow, restrictive, and provincial attitudes and aims of the two organizations were substantially similar. In England, these purposes were attenuated and defeated at a relatively early date by the upsurge of liberal economic ideas, and the few guilds that survived to modern times were unimportant. No such transformation was effective in Spain, where fear of competition, love of privilege, and devotion to tradition were the hallmarks of guild philosophy until the abolition of privileged mercantile establishments in the nineteenth century.

[18] A. Doren, "Untersuchungen zur Geschichte der Kaufmannsgilden des Mittelalters," *Staats- und socialwissenschaftliche Forschungen*, XII, Heft 2 (Leipzig, 1893), 44.   [19] *Ibid.*, p. 5.

APPENDICES

I. Charter of the Consulado of Valencia

Source: *Aureum opus,* f. 33.

The charter is one paragraph of a general privilege entitled
"De franquitate lezde ac aliorum iurium, de officio consulum
maris et eorum electione, iuramento et potestate," and issued at
Valencia, the calends of December, 1283.

Item statuimus et ordinamus quod in Valentie sint duo consules:
qui anno quolibet sint electi in festo Natalis Domini per probos
homines maris: et presentati coram nobis vel iustitia Valentie: qui
consules postquam electi fuerint et presentati incontinenti teneantur
iurare in posse dicti iustitie quod bene et fideliter se habeant ad fideli-
tatem nostram in offitio consulatus: volentes quod illi qui electi fuerint
sciant de arte seu usu maris et terminent contractus et dissentiones
inter homines maris et mercatores qui iuxta consuetudinem maris
fuerint terminanda prout est in Barchinona fieri consuetum.

The Catalan version of the above document is found in the
MS *Llibre del Consolat de Mar* (f. 100), in the Municipal Archives of Valencia.

Item statuim e ordenam que en Valencia sien dos consols que sien
elegits cascun any en la festa de Nadal de nostre senyor Iesu Christ
per bons homens de mar e presentats davant nos o davant lo iusticia
de Valencia los quals Consols apres que seran elets e presentats encontinent sien tenguts iurar en poder del dit iusticia que be e feel-
ment se haien a feeltat nostra en loffici del consolat. E volem que
aquells que seran elets sapien del art e us d'mar e determenen los contractes e discenssions entrels homens de mar e mercaders que segons
la usança o costum de mar seran determenadors segons que es acostumat fer en Barchinona.

II. Election Procedure in Barcelona and Bilbao

A. Barcelona: Rules for Election of Council of Twenty and Other Officials, Adopted in 1500

Source: IEC, B^*a* 192, f. 103-105.

Nos Fernandus . . . Desijant lo be a endreça de la mercaderia e
que las coses a aquella tocantes e havent sguart sien be ordenades e

regides, a setze dies del mes de Nohembre del any passat de Mil quatrecents noranta nou, a supplicacio dels consellers de la nostra Ciutat de Barcelona, Statuhim, ordenam e provehim que lo consell quis diu de vint, defenedors, collectors, advocats, scrivans, sindichs, guardes e verguers de la casa de la lotja de dita Ciutat tots temps que fos cas e loch de haver se crear e fer algu de aquells se fessen a sort trahent se per dits consellers dels sachs dedicats o assignats pera dits officis ço es de alguns sachs fets per los offitis de la dita Ciutat en la forma e segons largament en lo privilegi per nos dit dia atorgat es contengut, e com apres siam stats supplicats per part dels consols de la mar, defenedors de la mercaderia e prohomens mercaders de la dita Ciutat que per mes be de la mercaderia nos plogues atorgar a ells dits consols, deffenedors e mercaders que per al dit consell de vint e offitis demunt dits se fessen les bosses necessaries distinctes e sepa-rades de aquellas del offitis de la Ciutat e aquelles stiguessen en lo dita casa de la lotja e de aquelles en son cas y loch se fessen les extrac-tions necessaries per los dits consols en e per la forma devall scrita, deduhint nos moltes rahons per les quals nos sia paregut e par con-decendre a atorgar a dits consols, defenedors e mercaders la dita insaculacio en e per la forma devall scrita.

Perço et als de nostra certa sciencia delliberament e consulta, revocant e havent per revocada la forma donada per nos en dit privilegi a dits consellers atorgat dit dia quant a dit consell de vint e officis demunt dits seran declarades, provehint, statuint e ordenant que les dites bosses stiguen dins una caxa en la qual haia cinch tancadures de diverses guardes e clavs de les quals cascun Consol e defenedor ne tinga una e la quinta lo scriva de la casa, e cascun any lo dia que los consuls novells juraran e entraran en posessio de llurs officis e lo dia apres seguent en presencia dels dits defenedors e scriva e del consell de vint qui aquell any sera stat fins aquell dia o de la maior part de aquells facen obrir dita caxa e de la bossa per nos manada fer, intitulada bossa primera dels mercaders per al consell de vint, sien tretes per hun fadri de edat de set fins en deu anys dotze redolins ço es hu apres altre obrint lo qui primer sera tret e axi per orde cascun redoli e les persones los noms de les quals eran trobats scrits en lo pergami qui sera en cascun redoli sien de dit consell de vint per aquell any venidor.

E apres sien tornats dits pergamins e lo sos dins la dita bossa e apres encontinent en lo orde mateix oberta la bossa altra dels mer-caders, intitulada bossa segona dels mercaders per al consell de vint,

sien trets huyt redolins e aquells los noms dels quals se trobara scrits
en dits redolins sien per semblant de dit consell de vint per al dit any
e axi apres cascun any sia mudat e tret lo dit consell en lo forma
demunt dita. Provehint, statuhint e declarant que dins lany nos
puga fer mutacio de dites persones de consell sino en cas de mort o de
absencia o de malaltia, per la qual aquell tal no pogues esser en consell
axi empero que en loch de mort sen puga traure altre en dita forma
en presencia dels consols, defenedors e consell per lo temps qui restats
fins a la fi de dit any e per los absents o malalts se traga en dita forma
e los qui exiran sien de consell tant con diuara la absencia o malaltia
per que sera trets e no mes.

E mes avant statuhim e ordenam que dit dia cascun any sia tret
hun defenedor axi que dels dos defenedors qui son en la dita casa
cascun any seu mut hu e nomes axi com fins aci es estat acostumat e
lo que se haura a mudar se traga lo hun any de la dita bossa primera
dels mercaders pera consell de vint e laltre any de la segona bossa de
mercaders pera dit consell, començant e trahent lo present any lo
defenedor de la dita primera bossa.

Mes statuim e ordenam que en cas de vaccatio de collectors o
collector del dret de periatge se traga lo qui haura esser collector o
collectors de la dita bossa intitulada bossa segona de mercaders pera
consell de vint, la qual extractio se haia a fer dins huyt dies apres ques
sabra dita vaccacio en presencia dels dits consols, defenedors e consell
o la maior part de aquells per hun fadri en e per la forma demunt dita.
E semblant forma ordenam se serve quant se haura a fer advocat,
trahent lo de la bossa intitulada de advocats. E lo semblant sia fet
quant se haura provehir de scriva de la lotja e consell de vint e o dit
sindich de dita lotja trahent cascu dells en la forma demunt dita de la
bosa intitulada de scriva e de sindich e lo semblant orde sia servat
quant se haura provehir de guardes de mar per lo dit dret e o de
verguer o verguers de la dita casa, trahents aquells e cascu dells de la
bossa intitulada de guardes o de verguers. . . .

Mes com les dites bosses sien stades fetes de manament nostre e
en aquelles e cascuna de aquelles sien stats mesos los redolins ab los
noms de les persones nos han paregut abils e suficients per provehir
per al temps sdevenidor volem, statuhim e ordenam que de cinch en
cinch anys en los mes de abril avans del dia de la festa del glorios
sanct March evangelista los consols qui lavors seran e los defenedors
de la mercaderia ab cinch mercaders dels dotze qui seran de consell
aquell any trets de la primera bossa, los quals cinch a la sort ab

lengues de paper sien trets dels dits dotze, tots instats en presencia del
scriva de la casa prestat per ells primer jurament de tenir secret lo qui
venera e farera e de metre e embossar persones sufficients e ydones
obren les dites bosses e descusen la cedula que en cascuna bossa sera
cosida en la qual es scriva la nomina dels embossats e vista dita nomina
per ells en loch dels morts sien mesos per los dits consols, deffenedors
e cinch prohomens o per la maior part de aquells si nos concorda ne
altres en redolins en forma semblant en les dites bosses e aquells
affigits en dita cedula e aquella sia tornada a cobren dita bossa. . . .

B. AN ELECTION IN THE CONSULADO OF BILBAO

The following document[1] is representative of the numerous
actas de elección preserved in the consular archives of Bilbao:

Election of the year 1600: In the House of Trade of this honored
town of Bilbao, on Monday, the eve of St. James' day, July 24,
1600, the mass of the Holy Ghost having been said in the Church
of San Antón, where it is customarily said, and other arrangements
having been made for the gathering of the captains, shipmasters, and
merchant-traders belonging to the said Corporation for the purpose
of electing the *fiel* and consuls for the coming year 1600 [*sic*], the
following persons met in the House of Trade between eight and
nine o'clock in the morning: Dr. Francisco de Verastegui, *corregidor*
for His Majesty in this seigniory of Vizcaya, and Juan de Albear
Salazar, *fiel*, and Juan Ortiz de Saracha and San Pedro de Adaro,
consuls, and Juan de Varnechea, and Juan de Zumelzu . . . and other
merchants who for the great number of them are not here named.

And when they were thus assembled in the House of Trade I,
Juan Cacho de Herrera, royal notary public of this town and secretary of the House of Trade, read and proclaimed the ordinances
which deal with said elections, and having read and declared them,
I received the oath of the *fiel* and consuls and merchants upon a silver
cross and upon the gospels which were written in a missal, charging
them with the significance of the oath, so that they would name for
the office of *fiel* two persons and for consul, four other individuals,
who were competent and qualified. Jointly and severally they
promised and swore to do this, and after having taken the oath in
this manner, the *corregidor* and the *fiel* and the consuls went into an
anteroom of the assembly hall and, summoning the merchants one

[1] Translated from the Spanish text in Guiard, *op. cit.*, I, 534-535.

by one, they received the votes of each of them; and having taken down the votes, they came out into the hall, and in front of everyone the votes were tallied. And it was found that those who had the most votes for *fiel* were Hernando Hortiz de Allende and Juan de Çubiaur, whose names I, the secretary, inscribed on two slips of paper of the same size. The slips having been folded, they were placed in an earthen pot in which they were turned upside down, from top to bottom, and when they had been shaken up, a boy was called in, and he drew out one of the slips, and when opened, the name of Hernando Hortiz de Allende was found to be written on the slip; so that he was elected first *fiel*. And then the boy took out the other slip and it was opened and on it was written the name of Juan de Çubiaur, who was elected second *fiel*.

And then on four other slips of the same size were inscribed the names of Bernave de Alvia and Pedro de Aldecoa and Francisco de Novia and Domingo de Ceceyaga, who were the ones having the most votes for consul. And the slips were placed in the same pot, and after they had been shaken up several times, a boy was called in and he withdrew one of the slips, and upon opening, the name of Bernabé de Alvia was found written on it; and he was elected first consul. . . .

[Similarly, the second, third, and fourth consuls were selected.]

And all the officials were determined in the above form, in the presence of all, and with this the election of *fiel* and consuls was concluded, the witnesses being Lope de Basurto y Acha and Juan de Landaverde and Juan de Villavaso, residents of this town.

III. Cases in the Court of the Consuls

A

The following document, reproduced without alteration of form, spelling, or punctuation from a manuscript in the Institut d'Estudis Catalans (B*ª* 199), is the citation of a typical case in the Consulado of Barcelona.

> Die Jovis xii mensis Julii anno
> a nativitate domini MDLxxi
>
> Consols misser Juan Amell Doctor
> en quiscun dret
> M*º* Joan Garriga mercader

Promens

Francesch Guiamar Berthomeu
Romaguera Bertran Jaume
Sala Joan Canyella Bastistagori

Parts

Mattheu Cervera droguer y
Barthomeu Fabregues olim
patro de nau y altres mercaders
qui applicar hi volran
ciutadans de Barchinona agents
de una part

Pere Homs patro patro de nau
anomenada Santa Maria y
Sant Christophol natural
de la vila de Blanes bisbat de
Gerona defferent de la part altra

Sobre la differentia o questio vertent en la present cort entre dites parts sobre la demanda feta per dits Matheu Cervero y y Barthomeu Fabregues a dit patro instants y demanants lo dany se feu en certs cuyros de dit Cervero e ab tres fills de formatge de dit Fabregues les quals robes aporta dit patro sus dita nau de Cerdenya assi. E lo dit patro Homs Responent dient que lo dany prengueren los cuyros y dits formatges lo prengueren per la causa del mal temps corregueren conformenara con testimonial de Blanes que deposa dit patro en lo present magistrat.

B

The following decisions of the consuls and of the judge of appeals of the Consulado of Majorca are reproduced from the MS *Sentencies de la Cort del Consulat*, No. 13, f. 5 (Archivo Histórico Regional de Mallorca).

Sentencia donada per los honorables Consols.

Com fos questio e contrast devant los honorables en Guillem Ortola Ciutada e Iohan Nadal mercader Consols lany present dels actes e negocis mercantils entre en Gabriel Bruy patro ho senyor de una carauela de una part demanant e lo discret Nanthoni Piris notari en curador per los dits honorables Consols donat en aquesta questio per la absencia den Pere Soriano son cunyat ço es que lo dit Gabriel

Bruy demanava nolit de quoranta botes que li foren fermades e donades per en Pere Soriano aci en Mallorqua per portar de Morvedre aci plenes de vi segons se mostra en hun contracte per ell produhit. E en contrari lo dit Anthoni Piris en lo dit nom en contrari deya no esser tengut en pagar sino lo nolit de tretze botes que lo dit patro havia portades plenes ab la dita caravela e que de les buydes noy era tengut. E com fos en alguna cosa per aquelles fos tengut deya no poder esser en altre tingut que en deu lliures quo lo dit Suriano se havia imposades de pena segons forma del dit contracte. No resmenys deya no esser hi tengut per quant lo dit patro no havia servat co e que era tengut fes co es consignar lo vi a ell dit Anthoni Piris e axi mateix que li haura a dar raho de certs draps que per lo dit Soriano foren carregats aci en Mallorques sobre la dita caravela. E mes deya ell esser crehedor en los bens del dit Soriano en gran quantitat per la qual se volia retenir lo preu del dit vi. E lo dit Bruy replicant deya que lo dit nolit li havia esser pagat integrament per totes les dites xxxx botes com per aquella causa e sots aquella sperança la dita caravela havia fet lo dit viatge e no per altre com per ell no ha stat de carreguar totes les dites xxxx botes sino per los factos del dit Suriano produhuit certs protests fets contra aquells co es que li donassen compliment del dit carrech. E quant al consignament damunt dit responia que ell havia seguit co que per los dits factos era stat fet e que los dits draps eren stats liurats als dits factos segons ques mostrava en les dits protests. E hoides les dites parts aple de tot lo que dir e alleguar han volgut los dits honorables Consols lo nom de nostre senyor deu Ihesu Xrist humilment invocat de consel dels honorables en Pere de Veri e Guillen Linas promens de voluntat de les dits parts presos tots en una concordans e en res no discrepans pronuncien sentencien e declaren que lo dit patro sia pagat complidament e integra e tot lo nolit de les dites xxxx botes al for e nolit per ells concordat pus per ell no ha stat de carreguar e aportar tot lo dit carrech com axis mostra per dits protests e encara per dues letres dels dits factos dirigides al dit Soriano a paga e solucio del qual nolit condampnen lo dit Piris en lo dit nom e que lo dit patro sia primer en lo vi de les dites xiii botes. Levant ne empero primer totes les mesions que lo dit Piris haura pagades aci per lo dit vi absolent e liberant lo dit patro de les demandes a ell fetes per lo dit Anthoni Piris com per les dites letres e protest se mostra ell no esser en culpa alguna nenguna de les dites parts en despeses condempnant. Guillen Ortola. Iohan Nadal. Pere de Veri. Guillen Linas.

Ffonch lesta publicada e promulgada la dita sentencia de manament dels dits honorables Consols de la mar presents en Gabriel Bruy patro de fusta de una part e lo dit discret Nanthoni Piris notari en lo dit nom de la altra presents per testimonis en Pere Cernera e Iohan Solsona Vergues dels dits honorables Consols a xxxi de Iuliol any M CCCC lxxvii a hora de vespes.

Sentencia per lo honorable Iutge dapells donada.

E lo honorable en Matheu Riera Iutge dels apells dels actes e negocis maritimes e mercantils de la present Ciutat e Regne de Mallorqua vista la apellacio de paraula devant ell introduhida per lo discret en Anthoni Piris notari com a curador donat en aquestio per la absencia den Pere Soriano e encara com acrehedor pretes en los bens de aquell de certa sentencia per los honorables Consols donada entre en Gabriel Bruy patro de fusta ho cert navili de una part demanant e lo dit descret Nanthoni Piris notari en los dits noms de la altra deffenent e demanant sobre certs nolits que lo dit Bruy demanava de botes ha portades per lo viatge de Morvedre vista la dita sentencia dels dits honorables Consuls e hagut lur parer per que havien dada la dita sentencia segons forma de Capitol de Consolat hoidies les parts aple e los greuges per lo dit Piris en los dits noms plenament deduhits be considerats atteses les coses attenedores e les coses vehedores vistes lo nom de nostre Senyor deu Ihesu Xrist humilment invocat de consell dels honorables en Pere Vilalonga Ciutada e den Manuel de Thomas Pardo mercader promens de voluntat de les parts presos en una concordans e en res no discrepans pronuncia sentencia declara mal esser stat per lo dit Anthoni Piris en los dits noms de la dita sentencia apellat e be per los dits honorables Consols esser stat sentenciat e declarat lo dit discret Nanthoni Piris en los dits noms mal appellat en despeses condempnant. Matheu Riera., Manuel de Thomas Pardo.

Ffonch publicada la damunt dit sentencia de . . . .

IV. The Jurisdiction of the Consuls of Valencia

Source: AM, Valencia, *Llibre del Consolat de Mar.*

Quin poder han los consols largament.

Los consols de la ciutat de Valencia han tot poder ordinari e conexenca de tota questio o contrast que sia en la dita ciutat e regne de aquella entre qualsevol persones civilment per raho de fusta de mar.

Axi com naus, lenys e altres vexells e roba que fos en los dits vexells
o encara de nau fraig encare esdevengur per raho de empera feta per
lo batle o son lochtinent. De totes questions que son de nolit e de
dampnatge de robes que sien carregades en vexell. De cambis e de
assegurament de diners e de robes. De questio de compra e venda
de mercaderia venguda per mar o per ops de navegar per mar e dels
preus de aquella. De loguers de mariners de part de nau afer o
daltre vexell. De encantar. De feyt de git. De totes comandes
feytes de naus o de penys o altres vexells d'diners o de robes entre
mercaders ab patron o mariners o entre aquells mercaders patrons o
mariners ad invicem o separadament. De totes comptes de mercaderia
e de comanda entre qualsevol persones que halen contrast de comptes
e de questio o contrast d'mercaderies ab alfondeguers o entre aquells
in inuicem per raho de comandes e carregaments e descarregaments.
De deute degut per algu que haia manlevat pera ops de vexell a
exerciar o a ops de vexell. E de roba trobada en mar deliura o en
plaia. De armaments de naus o de lenys o de altres vexells. E de
tots coses preses o comprades o prestades dells o per ops dels vexells e
o per copannya de aquells. E generalment de totes altres coses o
contractes los quals han acostumat e acostumen fer a conexer los
consols de Barchinona. E de totes coses contengudes en les costumes
de la mar. E segons que en aquelles es declarat. Les quals costumes
e capitols se serven per tots los consolats del mon e los capitols dels
quals per orde son los ques seguexen.

V. Guild Affairs and Problems

The following translation[2] may serve to illustrate concretely
the variety of problems to which the priors and consuls were
expected to give their attention. The document is a memorandum prepared by the officials of the Bilbao Consulado for the
use and guidance of their successors in office:

Memorandum given to Juan de Larragoiti, *fiel-prior*, and Juan
Antonio de Jarabeitia and Bernardo de Landa, consuls of the House
of Trade in this honored town of Bilbao, concerning the status of
the business and related matters in which Mateo de Montiano, *fiel-
prior*, and Domingo de Lasarte and Benito de Rucabado, consuls
during the past year 1670, until July 25, 1671, leave their Consulate:

[2] Based on a document in Guiard, *op. cit.*, I, 544-548.

In the matter of the Commissioner [of the Inquisition] no news has been given out; evidently, there is some new development, since the naming of another Commissioner has not been decided upon.

There is pending in Madrid a petition, entrusted to Joseph de Lacuesta, for the confirmation requested of His Majesty, in the name of the Consulado, of his decree providing for a stay in the collection of and actions on bills of exchange this year; and concerning this letters have been written to the President of Castile and to the Dutch ambassador, so that he [*sic*] might interpose his influence. It is known that the *corregidor* of this seigniory [Vizcaya] obtained a report of the proceedings in this affair, in order to discover whether the confirmation would lead to any harm or would be advantageous; and he reported favorably. To pay for the expenses of this undertaking there was remitted to Joseph de Lacuesta a letter of credit which Juan de Larragoiti drew on Gregorio de la Cuesta, so that what he should have received for this as well as the amount received for the royal notarial certificate for the secretary of the company of Francisco de Galbarriatu will have to be refunded to Juan de Larragoiti.

For the affairs of the Consulado in Madrid a new agent has been named in the person of Joseph de Lacuesta. The unsatisfactory correspondence of Francisco de Zabala and his everlasting procrastination in every matter he was requested to handle have furnished many motives and just causes for this step. When he encouraged the Consulado to seek relief from certain injurious articles in the wool tariff—which were limited to six articles of the greatest importance since they include the 5 per cent silver payment and duties on undressed lambskins, reduction of the *ballines* [?], the six months' period of grace for the payment of duties at inland customshouses, and others—on behalf of the Consulado a letter was addressed to the Honorable Assembly of the Mesta [the grazers' guild] at the time of their meeting, in the hope that the Assembly would see fit to use their influence, since it was known that they were vitally interested and have contributed one half of the costs of this representation, having instructed their agent in Madrid, Felipe de San Medel, together with the agent of the Consulado, to get the petition presented in the Royal Council. The letter was forwarded to Zabala but he neglected to deliver it, replying that a reliable individual advised him not to and that the Assembly of the Mesta would never spend a *maravedí* but would give only their acquiescence. Nevertheless, so that he would not fail to undertake a matter of such great benefit to the Consulado, 1,000 *reals* in silver were sent to him and a gratuity of 500 *reals* was sent to the general agent of the Mesta to give him an incentive for the undertaking.

Holding out the expectation, from one post to another, that he would commence preparing the petition, while each day he was searching for some document or other, Zazala, it is known, changed his intentions, while enjoying the friendship of the farmer of the customs. Consequently, nothing has been started. In case it seems appropriate to take some action, although it may be only in connection with the 5 per cent payment and the lowering of the duty on hides, it will be possible to write to the Assembly of the Mesta when they hold their September meeting, remitting the letter to Joseph de Lacuesta for him to deliver to the Assembly in due season. Zabala must render an accounting of the 1,124 *reals* in vellon forwarded in the letter of Tomás de Santa Coloma and of 1,000 *reals* in silver for the above matter and 550 *reals* in silver, representing one third (two thirds being due from the seigniory and the town) of the costs of procuring the latest expedient in the suit over Commissioner Leguina. Zabala is owed only his salary for this year and 800 *reals* in vellon, representing the total expenses of a warrant from the Council on behalf of Juan de Barraycua in connection with the reduction of the *ballines*. He has not sent any other statement to the House of Trade. Joseph de Lacuesta has been instructed to secure the accounts from Zabala.

The *averia* duty of the House of Trade is collected with much difficulty, and since it is found by experience that the collections are slow, every work of the Consulado is delayed in execution. If possible, the *averia* of every ship should be levied as soon as it discharges its cargo; then it would be extremely advantageous to proceed with its collection before granting sailing papers. This could be done at the same time the captain collects the freight charges, with the assistance of the collector of the House of Trade. As a result, the Consulado would be able to avail itself of the funds promptly and would not have to accept the risk of promissory notes, many of which are defaulted, as is well known, because of absence, or bankruptcy, or the postponement of payment.

During recent years an effort has been made to secure from His Majesty an order or decree for the purpose of circumventing the injuries suffered by merchants in this town from the presence here of many executors seeking to collect wool duties on the basis of writs of assignment *(escrituras)*. In view of the failure to accomplish this, because of the laxity of the [Consulado's] agent, it seemed appropriate to renew the petition, especially since a firmer foundation for the complaint has been presented by virtue of a certain lawsuit litigated in the *audencia* of the *corregidor* between Francisco de Villegas, plaintiff, and Asencio de Jauregui, defendant, in which it is sought to collect 21,000 *maravedís* in costs from Jauregui on the basis of transcripts of certain writs whose principal sum amounted to 13,839 *maravedís*. The latter was condemned to pay the aforesaid costs, in spite of a precedent to the contrary which appears in the proceedings; so it is evident that an injustice has been done to Asencio de Jauregui. With this information in hand and having studied the case for this purpose, Dr. Ocariz was consulted as to whether it would be proper on these grounds to have the attorney of the House of Trade petition the *corregidor* for a copy of all the proceedings, so that it would be possible to apply at the proper place for redress, which would serve the common good of all business. As it seemed to him that the occasion and the objective were justifiable, he drew up the petition and it was presented, and an order was issued for the delivery of a copy of the proceedings. Therefore, it would seem desirable to dispatch the proceedings and the petition to the [Consulado's] agent, to the end that in the Royal Council of Castile he may request an appropriate remedy for such an inordinate influx of vagabonds seeking to maintain themselves at the expense of the merchants—of men who in Madrid manage to have suppressed the notices of assignment so that the merchant who wishes to make payment cannot locate the assignees: then the time limit expires and the bills are remitted to these individuals whose malicious conduct is witnessed every day.

After inspecting the estuary and the bar it has been realized that in the section of Uduondo near the river it is necessary to make a jetty of brushwood weighted down with stone, so that the channel will be preserved and the river will not spread out so much in that area.

In Portugalete a dry mole has been commenced, in the neighborhood of Santurce where the rock-pit is located, in order that such rock as can be broken up may be placed along the edge of the water. Contracts have been made with several residents of Somorrostro for the construction of ten *estados* [*ca.* 70 feet] of breakwater at 30 ducats per *estado;* 21 feet wide at the base, 6 feet high, and 16 feet wide at the top, the structure has to be completed during September this year. One hundred ducats have been advanced to the contractors, bond having been furnished by Sebastián de Herrera. If it appears possible to continue this work, it would be extremely desirable for the breakwater to extend to the *solar* of Portugalete; and from that point forward out to the bar it will be necessary to continue dumping stone from barges so that the channel will be deep enough for anchorage. Instructions have been given for dumping one hundred loads this year, and for this purpose agreements have been made with different bargemen of Lejona and Uduondo. They are to be paid 30 *reals* for every load dumped in under the supervision of Sebastián de Herrera, and the stone must be loaded under the direction of the pilot-major, whose work also has to be paid for.

The masonry work in Isleta has been satisfactorily completed, following the destruction of part of the pier by the overflowing of the river last winter, a thick wall with a floor of flagging at the shoulder of the pier having been added as a reinforcement. The bills of the master masons and others who worked on this project have been verified and paid.

It has been noticed that the river adjoining this work has begun to make a channel in the direction of Albia, and whenever it seems proper, the breakwater should be continued to within a few fathoms of Isleta, especially near Abando; and in order to do it at least cost, it may be built upon one or two large rocks, with a foundation of good royal rubble of the type used in the Deusto highway, so that a channel will always be preserved in this section.

The various shoals which are known to exist in the estuary of Olaveaga furnish evidence that some ships which arrive in ballast in order to take on cargoes of wool unload their sand ballast through the port-holes into the roadstead, at the wrong time and at night, thus filling up the estuary. Much harm arises from this practice as well as from other knavish acts which occur out there, such as cutting cables and choosing improper sites on shore to throw out the ballast which is unloaded by lighters. For the correction of all these things, it would be wise to name a thoroughly reliable individual as overseer of the river bank to keep watch along the bank of the river and to inspect all the ballast carried by ships coming in to anchor; and the ships that have to cast off ballast should do so in places pointed out to them by the overseer. The Consulado would give him his instructions and pay him an adequate salary for the work so that, if possible, the overseer would be relieved of the necessity of working as a bargeman.

Since it was realized that lighters and other vessels could not reach the Plaza quay, either to load or to unload, on account of the growing pile of gravel on the embankment, agreements were made with several bargemen of the town to clear away a section of the bank at a cost of 150 ducats in vellon, payable in thirds. It was specified how much they have to remove, that is, down to the point marked by a piece of wood buried in the bank, even with the stake and down until the bank remains level with the river at low water during springtide. And they have to finish the job by August 24 and must dump the gravel on the works at Isleta; and at the expense of the House of Trade the work of removing the gravel away from the quay should be continued, furnishing material for the Isleta embankment.

Martin de Orbe, constable of the House of Trade, has been ordered to look after the quays adjoining the Plaza and other quays used by ships discharging cargo and not to let anyone throw refuse on them which will impede the transfer of goods and, in regard to the unloading of ballast, stone, and lumber, to make the owners take away their property promptly and not to allow them to leave their goods to obstruct the quays. It would be a good idea to repeat these instructions.

From the bad practice of bargemen in unloading sand, which they throw upon the jetties and quays, it is observed that they cause damage to the estuary by letting much of the sand fall into the water while unloading at the edge of the quay, as a result of which ships cannot get to the quay to load and unload, and all concerned are injured. To put a stop to this, it would be wise to issue a proclamation advising everyone against employing this method of unloading sand, unless they put up some barrier on the side so that the sand will not fall overboard.

Some muleteers who carry goods from this town into Castile have made repeated complaints of the extortions which they suffer in the customhouses when paying duties on the goods they transport. The administrators refuse to accept payment of duties in gold, claiming that it must be made in silver, which is contrary to law. And to obviate this barrier to the transit of goods, it will be necessary to request a decree from His Majesty, in the name of the Consulado as protector of commerce.

VI. Revenues of the Barcelona and Seville Guilds

A

INCOME FROM THE *periatge* DUTY IN BARCELONA*

Years	Income, in Barcelona pounds	Rate
1432-33	3,835	1 *malla* (.2%)
1433-34	5,435	
1448-49	920	
1449-50	635	
1450-51	1,545	
1452-53	1,545	1 *diner* (.4%)
1454-55	1,695	
1455-56	2,095	
1473-74	2,200	3 *diners* (1.2%)
1474-75	1,590	2 *diners* (.8%)
1476-77	1,405	
1484-85	1,175	
1502-03	1,355	2½ *diners* (1%)
1521-22	1,405	
1522-23	1,365	
1523-24	1,350	
1524-25	1,430	
1525-26	1,930	
1526-27	1,990	
1529-30	1,925	
1530-31	1,385	
1548-49	2,815	
1549-50	2,730	
1551-52	1,710	2½ *diners* (1%)
1553-54	2,405	
1557-58	1,305	
1559-60	2,570	
1572-73	3,850	
1573-74	3,020	

* Sources: IEC, B[a] 161-75; BAB, Nos. 32-34, 37, 41. So far as I know, there are no account books available for years not listed.

1575-76............	2,940	
1576-77............	3,040	
1577-78............	3,195	
1579-80............	3,915	
1581-82............	3,040	2 *diners* (.8%)
1582-83............	5,040	
1583-84............	5,160	
1585-86............	4,315	
1605-06............	3,875	1 ½ *diners* (.6%)
1644-47............	6,110 per annum	Not known†
1647-50............	6,610 " "	
1650-54............	5,500 " "	
1654-57............	4,610 " "	
1657-63............	6,000 " "	
1663-64............	5,000 " "	
1664-75............	4,000 " "	
1679-80............	5,871	
1680-81............	5,957	
1681-82............	6,000	
1685-87............	3,300 per annum	
1693-94............	6,825	2 *diners* (.8%)
1694-95............	6,260	
1695-96............	7,080	
1696-97............	8,905	
1697-98............	6,805	
1698-99............	9,785	

B

INCOME FROM THE CONSULAR DUTY *(blanca al millar)*
AND SALES OF *escrivanias* IN SEVILLE*

	Income in thousands of *maravedís*	
Years	*Blanca al millar*	*Escrivanías*
1556-60.....................	1319	
1561-65.....................	2112	

† The income for the years 1644-87 represents the sum which tax farmers contracted to pay to the Consulado for the years specified.

* Sources: AGI, Contaduría, leg. 587-593.

1566-70†	1039	
1571-75‡	498	
1576-80	2012	1858
1581-85	2429	2560
1586-90§	1823	2236
1591-95	1926	2181
1596-1600	1613	2729
1601-05	3408	2292
1606-10	2859	2293
1611-15	2366	2741
1616-21	2381	3814
1622-25	1089	2373
1626-30	2517	2201
1631-35	1282	5750
1636-40	1349	6372
1641-45	951	5185
1646-50	923	5583
1651-56	571	5922
1657-61	630	4330
1662-65	458	3391
1666-70	472	3959
1671-75	553	2179‖
1676-81	744	2432¶
1682-85	318	1632**
1686-89	379	920††
1690-95	943	1197
1696-1700	344	1446

† Accounts for 1570 are missing.
‡ Accounts for 1571, 1572, and 1573 are missing.
§ The *blanca al millar* was not collected in 1589.
‖ 1671-76.   ¶ 1677-81.
** 1682-86.   †† 1687-89.

BIBLIOGRAPHY

BIBLIOGRAPHY

I. MANUSCRIPT SOURCES

A. CONSULAR ARCHIVES

Although every Consulado maintained its particular archives, fire, flood, and war have contributed to their dispersion and destruction, so that no consular archives have been preserved intact and some have disappeared completely. A reasonably diligent search has not brought to light any remnant of the archives of the Consulados of Gerona, Saragossa, and Valencia; in other cases, the existing documentation is doubtless but a shadow of the original store of papers.[1]

Barcelona

The Institut d'Estudis Catalans, Barcelona, is in possession of the major portion of the extant documents of the Consulado. The 288 *Expedientes*, or bundles of papers, deal primarily with the eighteenth-century *Junta de Comercio*; the 148 *Libros*, which are bound volumes, belong chiefly to the period of the early Consulado. The MS B^a 30, *Expedientes*, contains an inventory of the consular archives in 1796, revealing how small in comparison is the existing store of records.

Among the collection of *Libros*, the following are noteworthy:

B^a 194, *Libre dels privilegis e altres actes fahents per los honorables Consols de la mar de Barchinona.*

This is a repertory of privileges and legislation of interest to the Consulado, begun in the fourteenth century and continued to 1430.

B^a 191, 192, and 193 are copies of B^a 194, carried to a later date.

B^a 161-175: receipts and disbursements of the consular duty (the *periatge*).

B^a 189, *Libre de la matricula dels mercaders.*

B^a 253, *Llibre intitulat de anima dels insiculats.*

B^a 145 and B^a 200 are *Acorts* and *Deliberacions* of the guild council of twenty for several years in the fifteenth and sixteenth centuries.

[1] The writer has not visited the Spanish archives, except those of Barcelona, since 1931. It is obviously impossible, in view of the events of 1936-39, to offer any assurance of the present state, or even location, of all the documents used for this study.

Two volumes of *Deliberacions,* together with other records from the consular archives, are deposited in the Library of the Ateneu Barcelonés.[2]

Bilbao

A large part of the consular archives is preserved in the Museo Provincial of Bilbao. The series consulted include:

Libro de decretos, 1512-1593.

Many volumes of *Registros,* classified as: *Registros de Cédulas reales; Consultas; Cuentas de Averías; Dictámenes; Executorias; Memoriales y representaciones; Ordenanzas; Pragmáticas reales; Privilegios reales; Provisiones reales; Títulos de pilotos.*[3]

Burgos

Although most of the archives were destroyed in the sack of Burgos by the French in 1808,[4] about 150 *libros* and *legajos* (bundles of unbound documents) are preserved in the Archivo de la Diputación Provincial of Burgos. Mainly a miscellany, the documentation includes one important series:

Registros donde se asientan pólizas de seguridad, leg. 37-44, 60-61, and 66 (1566-1619).

Majorca

The Archivo Histórico Regional de Mallorca (Palma) has a considerable portion of the archives of the consular court and guild. The following series represent a total of 104 volumes:

Calculs, inventaris, testimonials, sequestres (1603-1763).
Extraordinaria de la curia del Consulat (1500-1763).
Llibre del diner del moll (1594-1715).
Provisions de la curia del Consolat (1576-1763).
Sentencies de la Cort del Consolat (1477-1763).

Medieval privileges of the Consulado, as well as one of the seven extant codices of the *Llibre del Consolat de Mar,* are found in the

---

[2] Nos. 29-50 in the *Catáleg dels manuscrits de la Biblioteca del Ateneu Barcelonés* (Barcelona, 1902).

[3] For a fuller description of these archives, see A. Mousset, *Les Archives du Consulat de la Mar à Bilbao* (Paris, n.d.).

[4] E. García de Quevedo y Concellón, *Ordenanzas del Consulado de Burgos de 1538* (Burgos, 1905), p. 14.

Libre de Sant Pere.[5] The MSS *Rosselló vell* and *Rosselló nou* are also important collections of Majorcan privileges.

Perpignan

The Archives Départementales, Pyrénées-Orientales, possess the only extant records from the early consular archives. They are catalogued as:

Series B, Nos. 206, 250, 254, 255, 292, 374, 377.
Series C, Nos. 1533, 1534, 1543, 1544, 1546.[6]

San Felíu de Guíxols

The charter of the Consulado, in parchment, and a MS, *Liber Consulatus Maris,* a record of court proceedings in the seventeenth century, are found in the Municipal Archives of this town.

Seville

The Archivo General de Indias was once the home of the Consulado of Seville. Although the vast treasure of documents now preserved in the Archives of the Indies are mainly papers of the House of Trade and Council of the Indies, more than one hundred *legajos* contain the originals or duplicates of correspondence, accounts, and instructions drawn up by the Consulado or prepared for that institution. The modern (1931) *signaturas* are employed in the following list of *legajos* consulted:

Sección de Contaduría: leg. 120, 420-421, 587-634, 636-643.
Sección de Contratación: leg. 61, 120-122, 181, 192, 628-629, 643, 710, 798, 814, 816, 858, 870, 1077, 4553, 4882, 5014, 5100, 5750, 5800.
Sección de Indiferente General: leg. 1660, 1971, 2039, 2326-2344, 2350-2357, 2359-2364, 2366, 2688, 2730, 2741, 2829, 2839-2840.

The following MSS are deposited in the Biblioteca y Museo Provincial of Cádiz:

Inbentario protocolo del archivo del Consulado y Comercio de Indias.
Libro de cartas de Consulado . . . 1559-1562.
Libro de escrivanías de todas las flotas y armadas, 1570-1586.
Papeles escriptas del Comercio de Cádiz y Sevilla.

[5] See J. M. Quadrado, *Privilegios y franquicias de Mallorca* (Palma, 1894), pp. 47-56.
[6] See *Inventaire-sommaire des archives départementales antérieures à 1790: Pyrénées-Orientales: Archives civiles,* Vol. I (Paris, 1886), Vol. II (Paris, 1877).

A large number of *legajos* pertaining to the Consulado of Seville before 1717 and to the Consulado of Cádiz from 1717 to 1829 were transferred from the Biblioteca y Museo Provincial to the Archives of the Indies, but as late as 1931 they were not available for examination.[7]

Tortosa

A privilege. of 1449, on parchment, and a MS *Dietarium curiae Consulatus Civitatis, 1638-53,* deposited in the Municipal Archives of Tortosa, appear to be the only surviving records from this Consulado.

B. OTHER MANUSCRIPT SOURCES

Municipal archives (in addition to references above) are frequently sources for correspondence concerning the Consulado and for municipal ordinances and other acts affecting the guilds. The following is a selected list of important unpublished papers:

Archives Communales, Perpignan

A few early privileges and regulations are found in the *Llibre vert majeur,* the *Llibre vert mineur,* and the *Llibre de provisions.*[8]

Arxiu Històrich Municipal, Barcelona

> *Libre del Consell, 1395-98.*
> *Registre de crides, ordinacions, e bans.*
> *Registre d'ordinacions.*

Many series of documents from these archives have been published and are referred to elsewhere in the Bibliography.

Archivo Municipal, Bilbao

> *Cajón* 1, *registro* 2; ca. 2, reg. 1; ca. 4, regs. 4-5; ca. 12, regs. 8-10; ca. 14, reg. 15; ca. 15, reg. 25; ca. 37, reg. 17.

Archivo Municipal, Burgos

> *Histórica: Reales cédulas,* No. 41; *Reales provisiones,* No. 3104.

Archivo Municipal, Cádiz

> *Reales órdenes i papeles sobre la conservación del comercio en Cádiz.*

---

[7] A partial inventory of this collection will be found in J. Humbert, " 'L'Archivo' du Consulat de Cádiz et le commerce de l'Amérique," *Journal de la Société des Americanistes de Paris,* I (Paris, 1904), 231-236.

[8] See *Ville de Perpignan: Inventaire-sommaire des archives communales antérieures à 1790* (Perpignan, n.d.).

Archivo Municipal, Gerona

> *Libre vermell*, f. 100 (charter of the Consulado).

Archivo Municipal, Valencia

The MS *Llibre del Consolat de Mar* contains, in addition to the procedural code of the consular court of Valencia, an appendix of fourteenth- and fifteenth-century documents devoted primarily to the court. The *Manuals de Consells*, or journals of the city government, are fairly complete from 1306 to 1700, but they rarely deal with affairs of the Consulado.

Additional documentation is found in the following libraries and state and regional archives.

Academia de Historia, Madrid

> *Colección de Muñoz*, t. 34, No. 2, f. 4-75, "Discurso é informe que en 13 de abril de 1669 hizo D. Eugenio Carnero al Excmo. Sr. D. Cristobal Crespi, sobre . . . establecimiento de Compañías."
> Scattered papers are in:
> *Colección de Muñoz*, tomos 76, 85, and 87.
> *Colección de Mata Linares*, tomos 6, 12, 22, 67-68.

Archivo General de la Corona de Aragón, Barcelona

The principal material in these archives, one of the most important sources for the study of all phases of Aragonese history, consists of copies of royal privileges and decrees in the *Registros de la Cancellería*. Numerous citations in the text indicate the specific use of documents concerning the Consulados of Barcelona, Gerona, Perpignan, Majorca, Tortosa, and Valencia.[9]

Archivo General Central de Alcalá de Henares

The *Sección de Fomento* contains about one hundred *legajos* on various Consulados, but the material deals almost exclusively with the eighteenth and nineteenth centuries.

Archivo General de Simancas

Secretaría de Hacienda, leg. 901, and a few scattered papers in other *legajos*.

---

[9] The *Colección de documentos inéditos del Archivo General de la Corona de Aragón* (40 vols.; Madrid, 1847-76) is practically barren with respect to the history of the Consulado. A large number of documents from these archives have been published in Capmany's *Colección diplomática* (see below, p. 155).

Archivo Histórico Nacional, Madrid

The *Cedulario índico* is an important collection of *cédulas* on American trade and the Consulado of Seville.

The *Pleitos del Consejo* in the section *Escribanía de Cámara del Consejo de Indias* comprise several large *legajos* relating to disputes over the financial administration of the Seville guild. Although mainly concerned with suits instituted after 1700, the documentation frequently reaches back into the two preceding centuries.

Archivo Provincial de Guipúzcoa, Tolosa

A dozen *legajos* in *Sección* 2, *Negociado* 22, and a few *legajos* in *Sección* 2, *Negociado* 12, deal with the Consulado of San Sebastián. Most of the papers fall in the period after 1700, since the Consulado was not established until 1682.

Archivo General del Reino de Valencia, Valencia

Bailía General, Letrès e privilegis, ts. 1, 5, 60, and 69.

Real Audiencia, Procesos, Part I, letre d, Nos. 1735 and 1737.

Biblioteca del Ministerio de Hacienda, Madrid

In *Sala* 1, estante 1, t. 4, is the MS *Historia de la Real y General Junta de Comercio, Moneda, y Minas, y Dependencias de Estrangeros, y Colección íntegra de los reales decretos, pracmáticas, resoluciones, órdenes, y reglamentos . . . para el gobierno de los comercios y manufacturas del Reyno*, composed by Eugenio Larruga y Boneta. This is an exceedingly valuable source, especially for the eighteenth century. The first four volumes contain Larruga's history, based upon documents reproduced in the remaining eight volumes, the whole work running into several thousand pages.

Biblioteca Nacional, Madrid

Sección de manuscritos, MS 13,256.

British Museum, London

Additional MS 28,368, Nos. 10, 13, 18, 27-28, 66, 70-75, 83, and 88.

Asientos of the Consulado of Seville.

II. PRINTED DOCUMENTS

A. ORDINANCES AND PRIVILEGES

An important prerogative of the Consulado was its ordinancemaking power. Rules of procedure in the court, election rules and regulations, and general ordinances governing such matters as maritime insurance, charterage, sea-loans, exchange, and other aspects of commerce and navigation were drafted by committees of the guild and submitted to the crown for approval. Royal confirmation gave them the force of law.

Barcelona

Several copies of the privileges and regulations of the early Consulado were deposited in the secretariat of the guild, but no general compilation was published before the eighteenth century.

In addition to the so-called "Customs of the Sea" and the procedural code of the Valencian court of the consuls, Barcelona editions of the *Llibre del Consolat de Mar* contain a considerable amount of statutory law applicable to the Consulado of that city. The latest edition of the *Consolat de Mar* (3 vols.; Barcelona, 1930-33), edited by Ferran Valls i Taverner, includes:

Aragonese Maritime Statutes of 1340.

Procedural Code of the Barcelona Consulado.

Ordinances of the City of Barcelona on Sea Loans (1435) and Maritime Insurance (1435, 1458, and 1484).

Bilbao

The first ordinances consisted of the charter of 1511 and certain regulations which governed the Consulado of Burgos from 1494 to 1511. They were not printed until 1552.

Las prematicas: ordenanças: ley: y facultad dada por sus Magestades por privilegio especial, a la Vniversidad de la Contratación de los fiel, y cónsules de la muy noble villa de Bilbao. Alcalá de Henares, 1552.[10]

An ordinance dealing with consular duties was approved in 1518.[11] General ordinances ratified by the guild in 1531[12] appear not to have secured royal confirmation nor to have been published. The ordinances drafted in 1554 and confirmed in 1560 represent a revision of the ordinances of 1531.

Ordenanzas de la Casa de Contratación de la mvy noble, y leal villa de Bilbao. Bilbao, 1691.[13]

[10] Copy in the Archivo Consular, Bilbao, *Reg. 1 de ordenanzas,* No. 6; reprinted in T. Guiard y Larrauri, *Historia del Consulado y Casa de Contratación de Bilbao,* I, 563-571.

[11] Reprinted in Guiard, *op. cit.,* I, 575-579.

[12] Reprinted in *ibid.,* I, 582-598.

[13] The MS of the ordinances as approved in 1560 is in the Archivo Consular, Bilbao, *Reg. 1 de ordenanzas,* No. 6. They are reproduced in Guiard, *op. cit.,* I, 598-

The 1691 edition contains supplementary ordinances on bills of exchange (adopted in 1672 and 1677)[14] and on elections in the guild (1675 and 1688). A partial revision of the ordinances occurred in 1725, and they were approved in 1731.

Ordenanzas nuevas de la Universidad, y Casa de la Contratación de esta noble villa de Bilbao. Bilbao, 1732.[15]

Probably the most complete set of consular ordinances ever compiled were those made by the Bilbao guild in 1737.

Ordenanzas de la ilustre Universidad y Casa de Contratación de la M.N. y M.L. villa de Bilbao. Bilbao, 1738.[16]

The Ordinances of 1737 were an integral part of subsequent commercial law in Spain and in America. They remained in force in Mexico until 1884.[17]

Burgos

Important regulations form a part of the charter granted in 1494. The general ordinances, approved in 1538 and published in 1553, include the charter and most of the laws in force up to 1538.

Ordenanças hechas por el prior y cónsules de la Universidad de la Contratación desta ciudad de Burgos por sus Magestades confirmadas para en los negocios y cosas tocantes a su juredeción y juzgado. Burgos, 1553.[18]

The ordinances were revised and reprinted in 1572.

Reales ordenanzas del Consulado y Casa de Contratación de esta M.N. y M.M.L. ciudad de Burgos. Burgos, 1752.[19]

No further revision took place until 1766.

---

621. J. G. T. Graesse, in *Trésor de livres rares et précieux* (Berlin, 1922), V, 36, refers to an edition of 1669.

[14] Both reprinted in Guiard, *op. cit.*, I, 621-625. The 1672 law was published separately: *Cédula real de su Magestad, obtenida por la Casa de la Contratación . . . en la qual se declara con toda distinción, la forma que se ha de guardar en los protestos y pagamentos de letras . . .* (Bilbao, 1675).

[15] MS and printed copies in the Archivo Consular, Bilbao, *Reg. 2 de ordenanzas*, No. 14.

[16] MS copy in the Archivo Municipal, Bilbao, reg. 3°, No. 15. There were many editions in the eighteenth and nineteenth centuries.

[17] T. W. Palmer, *Guide to the Law and Legal Literature of Spain* (Washington, 1915), p. 63.

[18] MS in the Archivo Consular, Burgos; printed copy in the Archivo Consular, Bilbao, *Reg. 1 de ordenanzas*, No. 4; reprinted in García de Quevedo, *op. cit.*, pp. 145-292.

[19] Copy in the British Museum, 503.h.19; reprinted in Larruga, *Memorias*, XXVIII, 216-297, and XXIX, 1-84.

Real cédula de confirmación, y nuevas ordenanzas del Consulado, Universidad, y Casa de Contratación de la M.N. y M.M.L. ciudad de Burgos. Madrid, 1766.[20]

Majorca

Most of the privileges and rules of the early consular court exist only in MS. Various ordinances of the guild were codified and published in 1656.

Privilegis, y capitols concedits per los serenissims Reys, en favor del Collegi de la Mercaderia. Mallorca, 1656.[21]

They were reprinted in substantially the same form: Mallorca, 1733.

Perpignan.

A collection of the privileges and ordinances of the guild and court was published in 1651.

Llibre de privilegis, vsos, stils, y ordinacions de consvlat de mar de la fidelissima vila de Perpinya. Perpignan, 1651.[22]

San Sebastián

The first general ordinances were approved in 1682, but appeared not to have been published before 1714.[23] The ordinances were revised and approved in 1766.

Ordenanzas de la ilustre Universidad, Casa de Contratación, y Consulado de la m. noble, y m. leal ciudad de San Sebastián. San Sebastián, 1768.[24]

Seville

The *real cédula* founding the Consulado forms a part of the general ordinances approved in 1556.

Ordenanzas para el prior y cónsules de la Vniversidad de los Mercaderes de la ciudad de Sevilla.[25]

[20] Copy in the British Museum, T.16 (B5); reprinted, in part, in Larruga, *op. cit.,* XXIX, 91-184.

[21] Copy in the British Museum, 503.f.13.

[22] Copy in the British Museum, 5384.bbb.10 (1). Bound with this copy is: *Crides, y edictes, fets per lo excelentissim . . . bisbe de Barcelona . . . sobre la erectio de fires, y cambis, en la vila de Perpinya,* apparently printed in Perpignan, *ca.* 1624.

[23] A MS copy of the ordinances as approved in 1682 is in the Archivo Consular, Bilbao, *Reg. 2 de ordenanzas,* No. 13. Although described in booksellers' manuals, no copy of the 1714 impression has come to light during the progress of this study.

[24] Copy in the British Museum, 8247.g.35.

[25] Published in 1556 and in 1585, according to Haring, *op. cit.,* p. xvii. I have used the text found in the 1647 edition of the *Ordenanzas reales, para la Casa de la Contratación de Seville,* f. 69-86 (British Museum, 1323.k.14). The ordinances of

Most of the chapters of the Ordinances of 1556, along with later laws governing the Consulado, are found in the *Recopilación de leyes de los Reynos de las Indias* (4 vols.; Madrid, 1681). The sixty-four laws of *título* vi, *libro* ix, and miscellaneous laws in several other titles, are pertinent to the guild.

Valencia

Excepting the procedural code of the consular court, the privileges and ordinances of the Valencian Consulado were not published prior to the eighteenth century. Several privileges and early laws are found in Capmany's *Colección diplomática* (see below, p. 155).

B. OTHER DOCUMENTS*

Allegación en drecho, en favor del Magistrado de la Lonja de la Mar . . . de que no deve dar cuenta en el oficio de Maestre Racional . . . del drecho de periatje. Barcelona, 1634. Reprinted in *Manual de novells ardits* (see below, p. 155, *Colecció de documents inédits*), XI, 723-748.

Assiento y capitulación que los Señores Presidente y del Consejo Real de las Indias tomaron con Adriano de Legaso, por si y en nombre del Prior y Cónsules de la Universidad de los cargadores a las Indias de la ciudad de Sevilla . . . sobre la cobrança y administración del derecho de la Avería, y despacho de las armadas y flotas de las Indias, por tiempo de seis años. . . . Madrid, 1627. In BM, 8245, f. 2.

Assiento y capitulación . . . con el Prior y cónsules, y Comercio de Sevilla, sobre la cobrança y administracion del derecho de la Avería . . . por tiempo de tres años. . . . Madrid, 1640. In BM, 8223.d.33.

Aureum opus: privilegia civitatis et regni Valentiae. Valencia, 1515.

Breve resúmen de la información, y fondeo que se ha hecho del estado de lo antiguo, y presente del Puerto y entrada de la ciudad de San-Lúcar, y su gran seguridad, y abrigo, assi para los Reales derechos, como para las invasiones de enemigos, hecho en 5 de agosto de 1701. . . . n.d. In BM, 1323.k.14 (31).

the Consulado were published separately in Seville, 1678 (copy in the Archivo Consular, Bilbao, *Reg. 1 de ordenanzas*, No. 5).

* In the case of several rather obscure memorials and pamphlets, information is given on the location of copies at the present time. Abbreviations used are: AHB, Arxiu Histórich Municipal, Barcelona; BN, Biblioteca Nacional, Madrid; BM, British Museum, London.

Brocá, G. M. de. "Creació del Consolat mercantivol a Girona," *Revista Jurídica de Cataluña,* XXII (Barcelona, 1916), 567-574. Charter of the Gerona Consulado.

Capmany y de Montpalau, Antonio de. *Código de las Costumbres Marítimas de Barcelona, hasta aquí vulgarmente llamado Libro del Consulado.* Madrid, 1791.

――――. *Memorias históricas sobre la marina, comercio y artes de la antigua ciudad de Barcelona.* Madrid, 1779-1792. 4 vols. The valuable *Colección diplomática* forms Vols. II and IV of the *Memorias.*

Carta escripta por el Tribunal de el Consulado, y Comercio de Lima, al de la ciudad de Sevilla, su fecha de 25 de julio de 1706 ... *en que les remite testimonio de lo acordado por aquel Comercio sobre la baxada a la Feria de Puerto-velo.* . . . n.d. In BM, 1323.k.15 (32).

Colecció de documents histórichs inédits del Arxiu Municipal de la ciutat de Barcelona. Barcelona, 1892-1922. 22 vols. Seventeen volumes comprise the *Manual de novells ardits, vulgarment appellat Dietari del antich consell Barceloni,* and the *Rubriques de Bruniquer: Ceremonial dels magnífichs consellers y regiment de la ciutat de Barcelona* are in five volumes.

Compendi de lus prerrogativas, ordinacions, oficis, beneficis, y utilitats, que lo Magistrat del Consolat de la Casa de la Llotja del Mar, y estament mercantivol, reben de la Excelentísima Ciutat de Barcelona, y dels prejudicis que aquells han donat, y donan a la dita Excelentissima Ciutat. Barcelona, 1703. In AHB.

Constitvtions y altres drets de Cathalvnya. Barcelona, 1909. Facsimile of a three-volume work published in 1704.

Discurso informativo por el Consulado de la ciudad de Sevilla. n.d. In BN, *varios,* ca. 1-59-36.

Explicación de la vltima determinación del Real y Supremo Consejo de las Indias, en el Pleyto entre el Comercio de España, y los hijos de estrangeros, nacidos en estos dominios. n.d. In BM, 1323.k.15 (32).

Gilliodts-van Severen, L. *Cartulaire de l'ancien Consulat d'Espagne à Bruges.* 2 vols. Bruges, 1901-1902.

Hall, J. E. "The Judicial Order of Proceedings before the Consular Court," *American Law Journal,* II (Baltimore, 1809), 385-391; III (Philadelphia, 1810), 1-13.

Índice de documentos referentes a la historia vasca que se contienen en los archivos de Brujas. San Sebastián, 1929.

Iuris responsum ad dubia tradita in causa vertenti in Regia Audientia, inter Petrum Paulum Vives . . . et syndicum Logiae Maris. Barcelona, 1638. In AHB.

Iuris responsum pro Consulatu Logiae Maris . . . contra R. Roure et C. Thalavera, mercatores. Barcelona, 1637. In AHB.

Iuris responsum pro syndico Logiae Maris Barcinonis contra evocationem causae executionis literarum cambii. Barcelona, 1659. In AHB.

Moliné y Brasés, E. "L'antich orde judiciari observat en la cort dels consols de la mar de Barcelona," *Revista Jurídica de Cataluña,* XXIII (Barcelona, 1917), 223-258.

———. *Les Costums Maritimes de Barcelona, universalment conegudes per Llibre del Consolat de Mar.* Barcelona, 1914. Catalan text of "The Sea Consulate," together with documents from archives of the Barcelona Consulado.

Novísima recopilación de las leyes de España. Madrid, 1805.

Nueva recopilación de las leyes destos reynos. Madrid, 1640.

Ordenanças para remedio de los daños e inconvenientes, que se siguen de los descaminos, y arribadas maliciosas de los navios que navegan a las Indias Occidentales. Madrid, 1619. In BM, 710.1.21 (5).

Ordinacions, y svmari dels privilegis, consuetuts, y bons usos del Regne de Mallorca. Mallorca, 1663.

Paz y Mélia, A. *Series de los más importantes documentos del archivo y biblioteca del Excmo. Señor Duque de Medinaceli* (Madrid, 1922), pp. 435-807. Statutes of the Catalan Consulate in Bruges.

Perels, L. "Orden judicial del Consulado de Mar de Barcelona," *Revista Jurídica de Cataluña,* XXV (1919), 289-307.

Pons, A. *Constitvcions e ordinacions del Regne de Mallorca.* Palma, 1932.

Por el Magistrado de la Lonja del Mar . . . contra los magníficos y nobles Dotores . . . del Consejo de su Magestad en el de la Baylia General de Cathaluña. Barcelona, 1679. In AHB.

Pro syndico Logiae Maris Barcinonis contra I. Palleia, et caeteros arrendatarios iuris pariatici. Barcelona, 1675. In AHB.

Recopilación de diferentes resoluciones y órdenes de su Magestad, consultas, informes y dictámenes . . . sobre si la Casa de Contratación, el Consulado y la Tabla y Juzgado de Indias, debe residir en Sevilla, Cádiz o en otra parte. Madrid, 1722. In BM, 1323.k.14 (29).

Representación al Rey . . . que haze . . . la muy noble ciudad de San Lúcar de Barrameda, sobre desvanecer los obices que vulgarmente suponen para la entrada de las armadas, galeones, y flotas de la carrera de Indias, por la barra de su puerto. n.d. In BM, 1323. k.14 (30).

Representación que el Consulado, y Comercio de Sevilla acordó poner en las Reales manos de su Magestad en los días 18 de julio y 5 de agosto de 1707, sobre el restablecimiento de los comercios de España, y de las Indias, como tambien sobre que para su manutención se prohiba el tráfico de todos los navios estrangeros . . . por todos los puertos de los mares del Norte, Sur, y Buenos-Ayres. n.d. In BM, 1323.k.14 (19).

Representación que los priores y cónsules que han sido del Consulado de la Universidad de Cargadores a Indias de la ciudad de Sevilla desde el año passado de 1689 hasta el de 1705 hazen a su Magestad, en vista de los cargos, notas y resultas del pedimento fiscal. n.d. In BM, 1323.k.14 (14).

Traslados de quatro cédulas reales de su Magestad tocantes a la contribución y repartimiento de averías, para la dotación y caudal fixo de los despachos de las reales armadas, y flotas de la carrera de las Indias, y assiento sobre ello. Sevilla, 1668. In BM, 1323. k.14 (5).

Twiss, Travers. "The Judicial Order of the Court of the Consuls of the Sea," *Black Book of the Admiralty* (London, 1876), Appendix, Pt. IV, pp. 449-495. Text and English translation of the Valencian procedural code.

Verdad sólida, que manifesta una mal fundada quexa del Magistrado de la Lonja del Mar de Barcelona. Barcelona, 1710.

Voto de D. Gerónymo de Uztáriz, Secretario de la Junta, mandada formar para el examen de la restitución de tribunales y otros puntos a la ciudad de Sevilla. n.d. In BM, 1323.k.15 (3).

III. OTHER SOURCES*

†Antúnez y Acevedo, R. *Memorias históricas sobre la legislación y gobierno del comercio de los españoles con sus colonias en las Indias occidentales.* Madrid, 1797.

Artíñano y de Galdácano, G. de. *Historia del comercio con las Indias durante el dominio de los Austrias.* Madrid, 1917.

* Titles marked with a † contain significant documentary material.

Asso, Ignacio de. *Historia de la economía política de Aragón.* Zaragoza, 1798.

Blancard, L. "Du consul de mer et du consul sur mer," *Bibliothèque de l'École des Chartes,* XVIII (Paris, 1857), 427-438.

Boletín de la Sociedad Arqueológica Luliana, Vols. I-XXII. Palma, 1885-1929. Sometimes published as *Boletí de la Societat Arqueológica Luliana: Revista d'Estudis Histórics.*

Bordas, L. *Memoria acerca de la erección y progresos de la Junta de Comercio de Cataluña y de su Casa Lonja.* Barcelona, 1837.

Bosch, A. *Svmmari, index o epitome dels . . . titols de honor de Cathalunya, Rosselló, y Cerdanya. . . .* Perpignan, 1628.

Bové, M. Salvador. *Institucions de Catalunya: Les Corts, la Diputació, lo Concell de Cent, los gremis y 'l Consolat de Mar.* Barcelona, 1894.

Campaner y Fuertes, A. *Cronicón mayoricense.* Palma, 1881.

Capmany y de Montpalau, A. de. *Memorias históricas,* Vols. I and III. History based on the *Colección diplomática* (see above, p. 155).

Domínguez Vicente, J. M. *Ilustración, y continuación a la Curia Philípica* (2 vols.; Madrid, 1736-1739), cap. xv, lib. ii.

Elías y Suarez, A. "Una excursión a través de las instituciones jurídicas contenidas en las Ordenanzas del Consulado de Bilbao," *Las Ordenanzas del Consulado de Bilbao* (Bilbao, 1931), pp. 75-104.

Finot, J. *Étude historique sur les relations commerciales entre la Flandre et l'Espagne au moyen-âge.* Paris, 1899.

Girard, A. *Le commerce français à Séville et Cádix au temps des Habsbourgs.* Paris and Bordeaux, 1932.

———. *La rivalité commerciale et maritime entre Séville et Cádix jusqu'à la fin du xviiie siècle.* Paris and Bordeaux, 1932.

†Guiard y Larrauri, T. *Historia del Consulado y Casa de Contratación de Bilbao.* 2 vols. Bilbao, 1913-14.

———. "Noticia de la fundación, desenvolvimiento y extinción del Consulado de Bilbao," *Las Ordenanzas del Consulado de Bilbao* (Bilbao, 1931), pp. 7-44.

Hamilton, Earl J. *American Treasure and the Price Revolution in Spain, 1501-1650.* Cambridge, Mass., 1934.

———. "Wages and Subsistence on Spanish Treasure Ships," *The Journal of Political Economy,* XXXVII (Chicago, 1929), 430-450.

†Haring, C. H. *Trade and Navigation between Spain and the Indies in the Time of the Hapsburgs.* Cambridge, Mass., 1918.

Hevia Bolaños, J. *Laberinto de comercio terrestre y naval,* lib. ii, cap. xv. First published in Lima, 1617 (British Museum: 1029, d. 15), the *Laberinto* forms the second volume of the author's *Curia Filípica* in a later edition (Madrid, 1825).

Hussey, R. D. "Antecedents of the Spanish Monopolistic Overseas Trading Companies, 1624-1728," *The Hispanic American Historical Review,* IX (Durham, N. C., 1929), 1-30.

Klein, Julius. *The Mesta: A Study in Spanish Economic History, 1273-1836.* Cambridge, Mass., 1920.

Larruga y Boncta, E. *Memorias políticas y económicas sobre los frutos, comercio, fábricas y minas de España.* 45 vols. Madrid, 1787-1800. Volumes XXVII-XXX on the Consulado of Burgos.

Pardessus, J. M. *Collection de lois maritimes antérieures au xviiie siècle.* 6 vols. Paris, 1828-1845. Volumes II, 1-48; V, 321-332; and VI, 492-495 deal with the court and laws of the Consulado.

Perels, L. "Die Handelsgerichtsordnung von Barcelona aus dem fünfzehnten Jahrhundert," *Zeitschrift für das gesamte Handels- und Konkursrecht,* LXXXV (Stuttgart, 1921), 48-92.[26]

Piernas Hurtado, J. *La Casa de la Contratación de las Indias.* Madrid, 1907.

Reparaz, G. de. *Catalunya a les mars.* Barcelona, 1930.

Riera y Soler, L. *La Casa Llotja del Mar de Barcelona.* Barcelona, 1909.

Ripoll, Acacio de. *De magistratvs logiae maris antiqvitate, praeheminentia, ivrisdictione . . . tractatus.* Barcelona, 1655.

Scelle, Georges. *La traite négrière aux Indes de Castille: contrats et traités d'assiento.* 2 vols. Paris, 1906.

———. "The Slave-trade in the Spanish Colonies of America: the Assiento," *American Journal of International Law,* IV (Washington, 1910), 612-661.

†Smith, R. S. "Documentos del Consulado de Mar en Gerona y en San Felíu de Guíxols," *Revista Jurídica de Cataluña,* XXXIX (Barcelona, 1933), 128-132.

[26] Translated into Catalan in the *Revista Jurídica de Cataluña,* XXXVII (Barcelona, 1931), 1-35.

―――. "The Early History of the Spanish Sea Consulate," *Politica*, No. 3 (London, 1935), 312-324.

―――. "Legal Foundations of the Spanish Consulado," *The Juridical Review*, XLVIII (Edinburgh, 1936), 147-160.

Solórzano Pereyra, Juan de. *Política indiana*. 3d edition. 2 vols. Madrid, 1736-39.

Torres y López, M. "El proceso de formación de las Ordenanzas de Bilbao de 1737," *Las Ordenanzas del Consulado de Bilbao* (Bilbao, 1931), pp. 47-72.

Usher, A. P. "Deposit Banking in Barcelona, 1300-1700," *The Journal of Economic and Business History*, IV (Cambridge, Mass., 1932), 121-155.

Valroger, L. de. "Étude sur l'institution des consuls de la mer au moyen-âge," *Nouvelle revue historique de droit français et étranger*, XV (Paris, 1891), 36-75, 193-216.

Veitia Linage, José de. *Norte de la contratación de las Indias occidentales*. Sevilla, 1672.

† Zabala y Allende, F. de. *El Consulado y las ordenanzas de comercio de Bilbao*. Bilbao, 1907.

INDEX

INDEX

Acapulco, 101
Admiralty courts, 22 n., 24 n., 30
Africa, 79
Agriculture, 117
Alava, 69
Alexandria, 46, 50 n., 51, 57, 64 n.
Alicante, 13
Almadén, 103
Almería, 15
America, 3, 14, 15, 20, 79, 91 ff.,
    120. *See also* Trade, American
Andalusia, 67, 91 ff.
Appellate judges. *See* Consular courts,
    appeals
Aragon, 3, 10, 11, 14, 20, 22, 24,
    34, 35, 36, 46, 49, 51, 53, 56, 66,
    116
Archives, 45, 46
Archives of the Indies, 106
Armadas, 47, 85, 95, 96, 97, 99, 100.
    See also Navy; Trade
Artisans, 28, 35, 42 n., 119
Asia, 94
Asiento, 97-100
    Negro, 103-104
Asso, I. de, 12, 37, 38
Athens, 46
Audiencias, 31 and n.
Averías, 69 n., 78, 87, 96-100, 108
Avisos, 98

Badajoz, 15
Balearics. *See* Majorca
Bankruptcy, 25, 27, 58
Banks, 27, 46, 58
Barcelona, 6, 10, 12, 13, 19, 20, 21,
    22, 24, 26, 28, 30, 32, 34, 36, 38,
    39, 40, 46 ff., 115, 116, 125-128,
    129-130, 139-140
Beirut, 57
Bilbao, 14, 16, 20, 23, 24, 44, 67 ff.,
    91, 116, 117, 128-129, 133-138
Bills of exchange, 27, 33, 57, 58, 60,
    72, 80, 86
Biscaya, 49, 67, 68, 69, 71, 72, 74,
    82, 85, 90
Blanes, 10 n.
Bodin, J., 7

Bonaparte, J., 116
Bougie, 46
Bourse des marchands, 12 n.
Brokers, 60
Bruges, 57, 64, 68, 69, 81
Buenos Aires, 16, 82, 94
Burgesses, 5, 19, 34, 35, 39, 40, 119.
    See also Municipal councils
Burgos, 6, 14, 16, 20, 21 n., 23, 24,
    31, 41, 44, 67 ff., 91

Cádiz, 14, 56, 92, 99, 109, 115
Cagliari, 33 n.
Calatayud, 11
Canary Islands, 94
Caracas, 16
Caracas Company, 82
Cardona, T. de, 102
Carranza, A. de, 102
Cartagena, 16, 100
Casa de Contratación. See House of
    Trade
Castile, 3, 13, 20, 22, 24, 26, 41, 49,
    56, 57, 67, 69, 75, 116
Castro Urdiales, 74
Catalan law, 7
Catalonia, 3, 11, 12 n., 38, 46, 47,
    54, 57, 61, 108
    Generality, 47, 54, 59, 64
    Parliament, 47
Catholic Kings. *See* Ferdinand and
    Isabella
Centani, F., 73
Cerdagne, 3 n.
Ceuta, 51
Chamber of Commerce, 17, 121
    Marseilles, 12 n.
Charity, 65, 85, 88, 105 n.
Charles II, 108
Charles III, 15, 117
Charles V, 64, 67 n., 85, 95
China, 101
Citizens. *See* Burgesses; Merchant
    class
City councils. *See* Municipal councils
Ciutadans. See Burgesses
Clergy, 30, 57, 58, 113, 120, 121
Cloth trade, 54, 55, 57, 94

[163]